SIGILL : COLL : CARLETON
DECLARATIO SERMONUM TUORUM ILUMINAT
NORTHFIELD, MINN. A.D. 1866

## LIBRARY

*Gift of*

**The Bush
Foundation**

D1297368

# Software Development Failures

# Software Development Failures
## Anatomy of Abandoned Projects

Kweku Ewusi-Mensah

The MIT Press
Cambridge, Massachusetts
London, England

©2003 Massachusetts Institute of Technology

All rights reserved. No part of this book may be reproduced in any form by any electronic or mechanical means (including photocopying, recording, or information storage and retrieval) without permission in writing from the publisher.

This book was set in Sabon by SNP Best-set Typesetter Ltd., Hong Kong.

Printed and bound in the United States of America.

Library of Congress Cataloging-in-Publication Data

Ewusi-Mensah, Kweku.
  Software development failures : anatomy of abandoned projects / Kweku Ewusi-Mensah.
    p. cm.
  Includes bibliographical references and index.
  ISBN 0-262-05072-2 (hc. : alk. paper)
  1. Computer software—Development. 2. Software failures. 3. Risk management. I. Title.
QA76.76.D47E88   2003
005.1—dc21
                                                          2002045504

10   9   8   7   6   5   4   3   2   1

QA
76.76
.D47
E88
2003

050404-3080 m8

To Maame and Paapa,
in loving memory.

# Contents

# Preface

Software development failure is a persistent problem in software development practice that has consistently defied solution. This is so primarily because, despite the enormous expenditure of resources in the area of software development, organizations have been reluctant to devote resources to studying the root causes of software development failure and even more reluctant to share their experiences for the benefit of the software industry. Second, the study of the problem is relatively recent because researchers, like organizations, have also failed to show the requisite interest. Thus the problem has persisted, often with devastating consequences to organizations and individual professional careers. Given the billions of dollars of public and private funds that are spent annually on software development projects that end up as failures, it is surprising that little effort is directed toward studying the problem in order to recoup some of the investments made and to minimize recurrence of the problem.

We characterize *software development failure* as the "perceived inability of the development project to meet the requirements or expectations of various combinations of organizational stakeholders." A *stakeholder* is any "claimant within the project development organization with a vested interest in the project and its successful completion or termination if necessary" (Ewusi-Mensah and Przasnyski 1994). Software development failure is likely to occur whenever any group of stakeholders perceives major potential problems in the project's development that may prevent the project from being successfully completed and implemented. A software development project is a collection of "interrelated activities undertaken in sequence and/or in parallel by some members of the stakeholder groups with the objective of producing a software system to satisfy some organizational requirements." The book's focus is entirely on *project development failures*; thus no attention is paid to the issue of *implementation failure* after software has been deployed within the organization. There is an important distinction between software development failure and implementation failure. Although the latter problem has received and continues to receive widespread attention in the Information Systems literature, software development failure has not been adequately researched due to the reluctance of management to acknowledge the existence of the problem within their organizations and also to the difficulties faced by researchers in gaining access to the relevant data from these organizations.

This book is intended to help improve the science and practice of software development by making conspicuous the problem of software development project failures in both public and private organizations of all types. In spite of the remarkable progress made in software engineering in the last thirty years, we still face intractable problems in software development because we have not devoted adequate resources and attention to research the factors that may be at the root of the software crisis. Software development as a labor-intensive creative endeavor requiring collaboration among disparate stakeholder groups in an organization presents special challenges. Although these challenges are unlike those faced by engineering teams in the design of physical structures, we in the software development profession could well benefit from adopting the engineers' practice of studying and publishing their failures in an effort to understand what has gone wrong on a project and why, and, even more significant, how they could prevent its recurrence in the future.

Software developers and their managers have devoted little attention or resources to study software development failures, and they have shied away from making public the results of any such inquiries. This status quo has persisted in part because, in our increasingly litigious societies, parties involved in failed software development projects look to the courts to settle their disputes instead of turning to the software engineering profession for an understanding of the root causes of the failure. Available in the public domain are only those few spectacular cases that attract the attention of investigative journalists whose interests, understandably, are not ours: to engage in a scientific inquiry sufficient to produce a cumulative body of knowledge to improve our understanding of software development theory and practice. I believe all organizations that engage in software development should, as a matter of professional practice, also have formal structures and procedures in place for studying and publicizing problems and difficulties encountered in the course of any software development that might have contributed to the project's failure. It is not enough that such inquiries into software development failures are carried out internally; the results of the inquiries should also be made available in order that others in society and within the profession may learn from them. I advocate openness as an essential concomitant in dealing with problems of software development failures. Learning from organizational software development project failures must be institutionalized within organizations to the extent that maintenance of implemented software in which corrections and enhancements are made to the operating software is considered standard practice in organizations.

## Outline of the Book

This book offers empirically grounded explanations of the variety of organizational, managerial, and other relevant factors that have contributed to project failures, based on survey data and validated by analyses of different cases of failed software projects reported in the public domain. The book is made up of three parts. The first part lays out the concepts, issues, and methods at the core of the software development process. I discuss the conceptual explanatory factors underlying software development that make it a process vulnerable to problems, including failure from requirements analysis and determination to design and implementation.

The second part examines the multiplicity of cofactors—organizational and managerial—that make software development a risky undertaking whose outcome often cannot be predetermined. The discussion covers the organizational, managerial, economic, and technical and technological problems that lie at the root of the failed projects and presents empirical data obtained through surveys of organizations.

Part III discusses lessons that organizations can learn from the analyses of failed projects and how those lessons can be used to improve software development practices. I offer a learning paradigm intended to encourage widespread learning and sharing of experiential knowledge about failed projects and improve collectively the practice of software development throughout the industry. I also outline some of the critical issues organizations must pay attention to during the course of project development in order to maximize the chances of successful project outcomes. I highlight the promise provided by the evolutionary approach to software development; this approach emphasizes modularization and intensive collaboration between developers and users who provide constant feedback on early versions of the software. Finally, I examine the aftermath of project failures and elucidate the empirical factors that critically affect project outcomes, and I suggest ways that project termination decisions could be made that would minimize damage to employees' and project teams' morale and to safeguard organizational resources for future project developments. I end by enumerating the telltale signs of "problem projects," which should be aggressively scrutinized by project developers and organizational executives.

**Who Should Read This Book?**

The book is primarily addressed to software developers in industry and academia. I believe software practitioners will benefit from the discussion and analysis of the root causes of software project failures that I cover in this book. For students of software engineering at all levels, I believe this book offers a picture of the plurality and diversity of factors involved in software development outside of the technical "prescriptive and deterministic" view of software development typically covered in the software engineering and computer science curricula. I hope this will provide students with a broader perspective and appreciation of the complexity of the cofactors that are the bane of software development projects. I trust such exposure early in their professional training will better prepare such students for tackling software development projects in their careers. I believe that a comprehensive analysis of the variety of factors that contribute to successful software projects will permit professional software developers to appreciate more deeply the complexities of the task of software development and learn better how to handle these factors at different stages of the development process.

The secondary audience of the book comprises senior management and executives responsible for software development projects. Senior managers need to be aware of the nontechnical issues involved in managing software development and to recognize the role management can play in minimizing the risk of software development failures in their organizations.

## Acknowledgments

Many people have contributed in a myriad of ways to the writing of this book. When I began researching the problem of software development failure over a decade ago, I had not anticipated the enormity of the problem and the difficulties I would encounter in acquiring data to analyze and study in order that I might uncover the root causes of the software crisis. Over the years I have received assistance from various sources, and it is with a deep sense of gratitude and obligation that I acknowledge this help. I am especially grateful to my friend and colleague Ish Przasnyski who has been engaged with the research ever since I first broached the subject with him. The papers we coauthored that are cited in this book demonstrate his important contribution. In addition, he found the time to read through an early version of the manuscript and provided helpful comments. My friend Seev Neumann of Tel Aviv University and Claremont Graduate University found time to review an early version of the manuscript and provided critical comments and suggestions. His interest, encouragement, and support of my research over the years have been invaluable. In this regard I would also like to acknowledge the extremely helpful comments and suggestions provided by the anonymous reviewers, which have contributed significantly to the final version of the manuscript. I would also like to thank Ferry Kusnowo and Michael Macauley for their assistance in tracking down several published articles on failed software projects. Over the years I have received intermittently financial assistance from the University Research Committee at Loyola Marymount; this assistance has helped me to pursue the research that culminated in this book, and for that I am most grateful.

When I embarked on this journey I had no prior experience in dealing with publishers and was quite unsure of what to expect, but the people at MIT Press, especially my editor Doug Sery and his colleagues Sandra Minkkinen, Susan Clark, and Elizabeth Judd, provided the considerable guidance, encouragement, and assistance I needed at every turn; they made the experience both enjoyable and worthwhile. Doug was particularly helpful in getting me to focus on the main issues I needed to address in the book and guided me along cleverly to achieve our goal. My secretary Cissy Easter was invaluable in typing several versions of the manuscript despite her busy schedule, especially during the academic year. I am especially appreciative of her unfailing professionalism and cheerfulness even under tight deadlines.

Finally, it is with a special sense of joy, pride, and gratitude that I acknowledge the enormous help and support of my family throughout this long process. My daughters Maame and Ewurama were both extremely generous with their time, despite their very busy schedules, and carefully read through several versions of the manuscript. They made copious and meticulous editorial suggestions that have greatly improved the quality of the manuscript, making what I was trying to convey lucid and readable. It is profoundly gratifying to me to see their editorial handiwork throughout the book and to share in the delight of seeing our hard work come to fruition. And finally, it is indeed with great pleasure that I pay special respect to my wife, Araba, for providing the support and encouragement I needed throughout the arduous process, and for tolerating my seizure of the kitchen table for its warm environment and inspiring garden view during most of the early writing.

# I
## Conceptual Issues

# 1

## Software Development Project Failures

The use of information technology (IT) has become pervasive in the management of organizations in the public and private sectors in today's information economy; it is impossible to imagine any organization, however small, not using computers in some manner to stay competitive. One of the main elements of the all-consuming influence of IT is software. *Software* is the collective term used to describe the set of program instructions that have turned the computer into such a formidable extension of the human capacity to store and process vast quantities of data. The increasing pressures of the information economy to make organizations more efficient and productive in the marketplace have driven executives in almost all organizations to look for that competitive and strategic advantage through the judicious use of software. Software has thus come to be viewed as a vital component of any organization's efforts to remain competitive in the information economy. New software projects are constantly being proposed for development in organizations to meet their computing and information needs. Despite the best efforts of these organizations, their well-thought-out plans for various software projects may end up as failures—sometimes monumental failures with unforeseen consequences, and with blame and recriminations throughout the organization. In some rare instances the software failures have even been known to endanger the very survival of the organization (the case of FoxMeyer Drug Company, reported in the *Wall Street Journal*, provides an example (Wysocki 1998)).

Organizations in both the public and private sectors have often been forced to cancel software projects that have far exceeded their original cost estimates and schedule or time-of-completion estimates, or that have failed to achieve the desired minimal functionalities. The costs of such project cancellations have been staggering in recent years, owing in part to the increased size and complexity of new software technology. Most of the software failures, especially in private-sector organizations, remain unreported and are written off as part of the cost of doing business. However, in some cases the costs involved and the circumstances surrounding the failure are so spectacular that the details are reported in the news media, as happened for example in the cases of AMR Inc.'s CONFIRM (Oz 1994); FoxMeyer's Delta project, which contributed to its bankruptcy (Jesitus 1997; Wysocki 1998); Hershey Foods' ERP project (Collet 1999; Stedman 1999; Osterland 2000); IRS's Tax System Modernization (TSM) (GAO, 1995, 1996); Denver International Airport's Baggage Handling System (BHS) (Rifkin 1994); Bank of America's Masternet System (Szilagyi 1998); Pacific Gas & Electric's Customer Information System ("PG&E Dumps CIS Project," 1997); and the Medicare Transaction System of the Department of Health and Human Services (GAO, 1997). A number of studies have estimated the dollar drain on the U.S. economy to be in excess of several billion dollars a year. For example, in 1995 a study by the Standish Group of U.S. companies and government agencies found that 32 percent of corporate IT projects were *abandoned* before completion at a staggering cost of $81 billion. A later study by the Standish Group, reported on by Rick Whiting (1998, 20) in *Software Magazine*, showed similar figures for 1998. The failure record overall is not very encouraging, as they state: "In the United States, we spend more than $250 billion each year on IT application development of approximately 175,000 projects. . . . A great many of these projects will fail." They go on to describe the chaotic state of software development, warning that we can no longer ignore the problem of software failures (also see Standish Group, 1995; Johnson 1995; Wysocki 1998).

Other studies have confirmed that the problem of software failures is not unique to the United States. In the United Kingdom, a study by the KPMG Consulting Company titled *Runaway Projects* found that "runaway projects have become the bane of organizations' attempts to transform their business" (Cole 1995, 3). The study goes on to provide more detailed statistics to support this claim, which we will discuss in a later section. Another UK study by a special interest group (OASIG) concerned with the organizational aspects of IT concluded that most investments in computer-based systems fail to achieve the objectives of the organizations using them (OASIG, 1996). Again, we examine the details of the study in a later section. A study of Canadian federal government IT projects reported on in *Infosystems Executive* by Erik Heinrich (1998) found similar disturbing news of several billion Canadian dollars spent on projects with questionable results. In some cases outright cancellation occurred, as with the Canadian Automated Air Traffic Control System (CAATS), which ended up costing more than one billion Canadian dollars over a ten-year period. Software failures are not limited to any geographic region, industry, or market group, nor are they restricted to specific organizational size. The Standish Group study reports failures in organizations of all sizes.

**Outline**

This book offers empirically grounded explanations of the variety of organizational, managerial, and other relevant factors that have contributed to project failures, based on survey data and validated by analyses of different cases of failed software projects reported in the public domain. The book is made up of three parts. The first part lays out the concepts, issues, and methods at the core of the software development process. It discusses the conceptual explanatory factors underlying software development that make them vulnerable to problems, including failure from requirements analysis and determination, to design, and failure in implementation. Chapter 1 broadly explains why issues of management and organization are still at the heart of software development. Chapter 2 expands on this analysis by examining the inherent characteristics of software that produce software development crises, despite the remarkable progress made in software development methods over the last several decades. Chapter 3 analyzes the traditional life-cycle method of software development, the challenges it poses in the development process, and its critical influence on project outcomes. To provide a perspective on the multidimensional nature of software project abandonment, the book presents a framework of factors that contribute to the abandonment decision. It draws attention to the risks and uncertainties present in each phase of the systems development process that may contribute to project failure. Throughout, it emphasizes the significance of the organizational and managerial issues at the root of many software project failures. These issues, and the project failures they cause, have persisted since the birth of software development as an engineering science at the NATO conference of 1968, in spite of major developments in the field.

The second part of the book examines the multiplicity of cofactors—organizational and managerial—that make software development a risky undertaking whose outcome often cannot be predetermined. The discussion covers the organizational, managerial, economic, and technical and technological problems at the root of the failed projects, and presents empirical data obtained through surveys of organizations. Chapter 4 deals with the set of empirically derived socioorganizational factors and problems arising in the development organization, which have the potential to derail software development projects. This is followed in chapter 5 by an enumeration of the technical and technological factors that may be at the core of abandoned software projects. Finally, chapter 6 explores the significance of economic issues that contribute to decisions to abandon projects. In each chapter, the empirical data are validated with analyses of actual reported cases of abandoned software projects in organizations. Chapter 7, the final chapter of this part, reveals the views of users—in a case study of an abandoned software development project in an electronics distribution company. Particular emphasis is placed on the role of users in the development process and on the organizational politics associated with the project development. Each chapter of this part of the book ends with an assessment of the significance of each factor to the different states of the software development process.

The third part of the book puts forward lessons that project organizations can learn from the analyses of failed projects and shows how those lessons can be used to improve software development practices. Chapter 8 offers a learning paradigm. This paradigm is intended to encourage widespread learning and sharing of experiential knowledge about failed projects and to collectively improve the practice of software development industrywide. Chapter 9 provides a paradigm of software development that outlines some of the critical issues organizations must pay attention to during project development in order to maximize the chances of successful project outcomes. The discussion highlights the promise of the evolutionary approach to software development, which emphasizes modularization and intensive collaboration between developers and users, who provide constant feedback on early versions of the software. Published studies by MacCormack and colleagues (MacCormack 2001; MacCormack, Verganti, and Iansiti 2001) suggest that the evolutionary development methodology is particularly appropriate in development environments where the technology and the requirements for systems development are dynamic and unstable. Finally, chapter 10 examines the aftermath of project failures. It both elucidates the empirical factors that critically affect project outcomes and suggests ways decisions on project terminations should be handled to minimize damage to employees' and project teams' morale and to safeguard organizational resources for future projects. The book ends by focusing attention on telltale signs of problematic projects that need to be aggressively scrutinized by project developers and organizational executives.

**What Is Software Development Failure?**

The problem of software development failure has been with us since the early days of the computing revolution and will likely persist in the future. The hope is that with time, as software developers become more informed and understanding of the intricacies of the technology, the incidence of software failures will subside substantially until they are relatively rare. Until that time arrives, we need to do more to understand the problem and ways to tackle it.

Software failure can be classified into two broad categories, the first dealing with the inability of the implemented software to perform to the expectations of the users and the second dealing with the inability of the software developers to produce a working or functioning system for the users. These categories are two sides of the same problems, but our main focus in this book is on the latter issue—that is, on the developers' failure to deliver a working or functioning system to the users. Thus software failure can be formally described as a development failure. It can be further characterized in a number of more specific ways. The failure may be with respect to meeting the original cost or schedule estimates, or it may lie in an inability to achieve the functional objectives of the project. Software development failure can be described as the occurrence of one or more of the above types of failure, and such failures can occur at any stage of the development life cycle.

Software product development is a labor-intensive, intellectually demanding creative activity. The challenge is to be able to manipulate symbols and words to construct a logical flow of the sequence of activities or tasks to be performed to achieve the desired goal or objective for the software product. The difficulty stems in part from determining what information or data requirements will enable the specified objectives to be achieved. A further difficulty arises from the need to determine what resources—that is, technical and technological, financial capital, and others—are needed to be able to attain the desired software product objectives within some previously estimated time frame.

Underlying the above difficulties are the risks and uncertainties associated with the entire software development effort. When the software development fails to attain any of the targeted goals of the project—that is, the cost and schedule estimates for completion, or the satisfaction of the project's functional objectives—the development effort can be described as a failure. It is important to point out that whether the original cost and schedule estimates were inaccurate or indefensible is not relevant because once the project is begun, under whatever agreed-on conditions, the inability of the project team to achieve the targeted goals makes the project development effort a failure.

Others characterize the types of development failure described above in a variety of ways. For example, the KPMG study used the term *software runaways* to describe instances of development failure in which the cost overruns exceeded the original estimates by at least 30 percent and/or the project failed to significantly achieve its objectives (Cole 1995). Robert Glass (1998, 3) found the 30 percent figure too restrictive, instead offering a more expansive definition of what constitutes "software runaway" as "a project that goes out of control primarily because of the difficulty of building the software needed by the system."

The Standish Group (1995), on the other hand, categorized software failure in two ways: as projects that are "challenged"—that is, where even if the projects are completed, they are invariably "over-budget, over the time estimate, and offer fewer features and functions than originally specified"—and as projects that are "impaired," in other words, "where the projects are canceled at some point during the development cycle."

Still another conception of software development failure is offered by Lyytinen and Hirschheim (1987), who focus on the expectations of the stakeholder groups. If the software development effort or process fails to meet the stakeholders' expectations as to the systems objectives and/or cost and time-of-completion estimates vis-à-vis the benefits to be derived from the system, and if the project is allowed to continue, it is considered a failure. I will use this concept of software failure in my discussion because it seems to capture the essence of the problem more closely than the concepts mentioned earlier, for the following reasons. First, it involves the interaction of the relevant stakeholders engaged in the project development effort. Second, it is more encompassing of the various descriptions of software failure described above, because it appropriately captures the interacting relationships existing in the software development process among the underlying entities of systems objectives, development costs, and other resources needed to produce a functioning system within the estimated time frame to the satisfaction of the stakeholder groups. Indeed, software failure has been aptly described, in Lyytinen and Hirschheim's (1987, 274) analysis of IS failure, as "an extremely complex web of social and technical phenomena."

In summary, it can be said that software development failure is characterized by several factors; it is multifaceted and multidimensional, and any one of the various contributing factors may be sufficient to bring down the entire edifice of the software structure. However, the software development enterprise is a purely abstract and conceptual endeavor, and as such places an undue burden on all the stakeholders to collaborate with a clear vision of what is to be achieved, how it is to be achieved, and at what cost and in what time frame. When that vision falters or is somehow impaired, failure of the project becomes a distinct possibility. When the software development process becomes so imperiled that continuation is pointless, abandonment of the project becomes a necessary option. It is this class of software project failures or abandoned software development projects that this book explores.

**Software Engineering and Software Development Failures**

Software development as an engineering science was born at the 1968 NATO conference convened to address the problems encountered in the software crises of the 1960s (Wasserman 1980; Blum 1994; Robinson et al. 1998). The emergence of software engineering as a systems development discipline was based on the perception that the modern scientific method—with its emphasis on formalism, rationality, and objectivity—could provide the correct approach to solving the host of problems associated with software systems development. Some of the proponents of this approach, including Dijkstra (1968), Hoare (1984), and Lehman (1989), argued that the adoption of a formal logical or structured approach would provide the "silver bullet" that would aid the discipline in overcoming the crises of systems development. For example, they argued that applying the objective standards of the modern scientific method to computer programs would enable systems developers to "intersubjectively" test their programs for correctness. Over the years, considerable energy was devoted to formulating concepts and solutions involving proofs of program correctness, stepwise refinements, functional decomposition, structured analysis and design, modular structure, information hiding, and structured programming, in a concerted effort to reduce the inherent complexities associated with formulating and solving the right systems problems (Sommerville 1997; Blum 1994; Marciniak 1994). In time, several different process models were developed to improve the practice of software development. The common theme underlying the various process models is the abstraction of the sequence of activities needed to create a software product from the user's problem description. At present, as Sommerville (1997, 2260) has rightly observed, there are "no accepted standards for describing process models." The majority of software development models in use in organizations are based loosely on some generic process model for generating the documentation required to communicate with the project team, clients, and management. Robinson et al. (1998, 366), in a critique of this era in systems development, has characterized this approach as one based on the erroneous belief that "software engineering embodies a view of the world as being composed of unitary problems, each capable of rational solution via the application of technology." This analysis of the use of "formal conceptual schema" to model the complexities of the real-world problem domain is based on the premise that natural language—with its inherent ambiguities and varied ways of describing a problem—is somewhat unsuited to handling the rigor of the "deep semantic structure of a given" problem context. Although considerable progress has been made over the last several decades in tackling systems development problems, the software crises are still with us.

The view of software as a purely objective artifact or product that is created devoid of context is somewhat misleading. Context—be it organizational, cultural, managerial, or technological—shapes the software development process and the final product created. The weakness of the modernist approach to software development, with its emphasis on rationality, highlights the need to pay adequate attention to all the issues that legitimately direct the development process. The significant evolution of the tools and techniques of software development has tended to emphasize the rational or formal problem-solving perspective. However, the complexities of the cofactors that shape the "solution space" of the software development process have not diminished over the years. Hence the persistence of software crises and the continual search for ways to reduce their incidence in software development practice.

In Brooks's (1987) view, no "silver bullets" exist capable of coping with the inherent difficulties associated with the nature of software and the manifestations of those difficulties in the systems development process. Brooks's realism leads him to opine that as far into the future as he can see, there exists "no simple development in either technology or in management technique, that by itself promises even one order-of-magnitude improvement in productivity, in reliability, in simplicity" in software development (p. 10). In essence, the software crises will always be with us. Thus the best we can do is to find ways to reduce their impact on the software development process. Harel (1992, 10), commenting on Brooks's pragmatic but somewhat pessimistic verdict, offers a more encouraging recitation of developments in software engineering that may provide "a vanilla framework for system modeling" and that indicate good prospects for the improvement of systems development. Robinson et al. (1998), however, see a breakdown in the "modern" scientific or formal approach as employed to tackle systems development. They argue that the formal systems derived by this rational/logical approach must eventually be "connected" to the real world they purport to represent in order to be validated. "It is at these points of connection that problems may occur," they suggest, "for this is where the implications of the epistemologies of the system and the world connect. The system's success depends on whether these epistemologies collide or co-operate" (p. 368). These are precisely the problems inherent in the nature of software that Brooks describes as the "essence" and "accidents" of software development. Adding to these problems are the inherent difficulties users have of communicating their tacit knowledge of the problem domain in the form of systems requirements to the systems developers. Moreover, as Eischen (2002, 39) observes, the users' tacit problem-domain knowledge is often "undefined, uncodified and developed over time" and is "constantly evolving," especially in a dynamic organizational environment.

Software development from a postmodern perspective as described by Robinson et al. (1998, 368) is "an amalgam of various analytical, design, implementation, predictive and managerial activities, embedded in dynamic social systems, replete with already developed sites of cooperation and conflict." This view of software development explicitly recognizes that a "multiplicity of cofactors" are always at work in the software development process, any combination of which may be problematic and may be at the root of software failures, whether during development or after implementation. Thus in software development the complexity of the systems problem and its real-world organizational context must all be accounted for—from the requirements-determination phase through to the implementation. This view of software development pays the requisite attention to the management, the organizational, and the nontechnical dimensions of the software development process, areas that the modernist approach tends to ignore.

In the remainder of this chapter we briefly review the extent of software development project failures, then pursue the nature of the problem. We end with a detailed description and analysis of abandoned software projects. *Abandonment* refers to the cancellation of the projects prior to their complete implementation in the organization, and thus can occur at any juncture in the systems development process.

## Motivation for the Book and Readership

The motivation for this book was a desire to understand the causes of the software crises. Many authors have pointed to the existence of these crises. McFarlan (1981), in an article outlining a portfolio approach to IS development in organizations published in the *Harvard Business Review*, provided anecdotal evidence of the extent of the problem. He documented the cost overruns and schedule delays of even well-structured and routine systems development projects such as payroll projects in established companies. Glaser (1984, 45) offered further support for McFarlan's claims, when he reported in an article dealing with the management of computer projects that "in the computer industry . . . [project] objectives are missed and schedule and cost targets overrun with distressing regularity and, at times with equally distressing results." But a search for published empirical studies on the problem yielded no results. Consequently, in the late 1980s I undertook a comprehensive research effort to empirically examine the nature and extent of the problem in both public and private organizations. Since then a number of books have been published on the subject, but they have all dealt with specific cases of project failures (Glass 1998; Flowers 1997; Yourdon 1997; Sauer 1993). In the 1990s various studies of an empirical nature were published that shed more light on the widespread nature of the problem and showed the extent of organizational resources consumed by failed projects (Ewusi-Mensah and Przasnyski 1991, 1994, 1995; Ewusi-Mensah 1997; Johnson 1995; OASIG 1996; Cole 1995; Standish Group 1995, 1998). But more attention to the root causes of the project failures is needed.

By focusing on the underlying causes of the software crises, this book tries to fill this gap. I attempt to convey in one volume what I have learned thus far from the published empirical literature, and what that literature says about management and organizational issues in particular. The book does not address issues of systems failure after their implementation in organizations. Lucas's book *Why Information Systems Fail* (1975) provides an early window into the problem of implementation, which he determined from his analysis of a "large amount of data" to be primarily "organizational behavior patterns" (p. 2). I believe that an understanding of the socioorganizational and managerial cofactors that cause abandonment may provide additional insights into the process of software development and may help minimize the future incidence of software project development failures.

The book is primarily addressed to software developers in industry and academia. I believe software practitioners will benefit from the discussion and analysis of the root causes of software project failures covered in this book. For students of software engineering at all levels, the book offers a picture of the plurality and diversity of factors involved in software development, outside of the technical "prescriptive and deterministic" view of software development typically covered in the software engineering and computer science curriculums. This will hopefully provide students with a broader perspective and appreciation of the complexity of the cofactors that are the real bane of software development projects. Such exposure early in their professional training will better prepare students to tackle software development projects in their careers. I believe that the comprehensive analysis the book provides of the factors that make for successful software projects will give professional software developers a deeper appreciation of the complexities of software development as well as insight into improved ways of handling these factors at different stages of the development process. Over time, as software developers learn from the failure factors discussed in this book, the art and practice of software development may be improved industrywide. The secondary audience for the book consists of senior management and executives responsible for software development projects. Senior managers need to be aware of the nontechnical issues associated with management matters in software development and of the role they can play in minimizing the risk of software development failures in their organizations.

## Abandoned Software Projects

Abandoned software projects are failed projects because organizations do not routinely invest substantial organizational resources in a project unless certain criteria are met. First, an organization has to have identified a need for the system within the framework of its operational and strategic goals; second, it has to have determined that it has the requisite capabilities to get the system developed and implemented. Under such a scenario, when the organization decides to cancel the project later in the software development process, it can reasonably be surmised that the project was a failure because the organization did not achieve its original objectives with respect to the project. An enumeration of the factors that may contribute to the decision to cancel a project, the intensity of each factor, and the extent of their contributions to the cancellation decision is the focus of this book. The extent to which the factors are or may be repeated in other projects in different organizational settings or environments is equally significant in helping to shed light on the totality of the circumstances at the heart of abandoned projects.

In its description of software failures, the Standish Group (1995) differentiates what it considers "challenged" software projects from "impaired" ones. The "impaired" software project is eventually "*canceled* at some point during the development life cycle" (emphasis added). The "challenged" project is not canceled; rather, it may eventually be completed, albeit over budget, over schedule, and possibly with limited functionality. Thus the distinction between the two types of software projects has to do with whether a project is canceled or not. There are, in fact, many similarities between software failures in general and abandoned software projects. The abandoned software project may be a consequence of a perceived failure of the project prior to its full implementation. Thus in anticipation of that fact, the stakeholder group—that is, senior executives with the responsibility for safeguarding organizational resources, sometimes in consultation with the other stakeholder groups—decides to "pull the plug" on the project. In this sense, we can characterize software project abandonment as an endemic part of the much broader organizational problem of software failures described above (Ewusi-Mensah and Przasnyski 1991).

Boehm (2000), however, challenges the Chaos report's (Standish Group, 1995) conclusions by arguing that some project terminations are justified and, in fact, even necessary to safeguard organizational resources. He arrives at this conclusion on the basis of personal experience, knowledge, and "review of about 20 term papers per year on failed industry projects," among other sources of information. He lists the sources of project termination in the Chaos report and provides explanations as to why termination was desirable in each case. His basic concern is that project termination should not be used as a scapegoat to damage the careers of project managers who might in the future be more likely, as a result, to continue with projects whose strategic and competitive value to a company may have diminished as a result of changes in the project's original assumptions. Consequently, Boehm argues that not all project terminations should be equated with project failures, especially in rapidly changing technological, organizational, and market environments. Project terminations of 31 percent, in his view, should not be considered too high in dynamic development environments, as opposed to stable environments.

While I share Boehm's basic concerns, I feel that project terminations of 31 percent are, in fact, indicative of fundamental problems that require thorough investigation. It is not satisfactory to suggest that such high termination rates are the risk-acceptance rate for undertaking software development projects, even in a rapidly changing development environment. I believe that proper understanding of the multiplicity of cofactors at work in software development projects, as well as knowledge of the risk-acceptance rate of particular organizations, will give software developers, project managers, and their senior management and end users a deeper appreciation of the uncertainties of software development and provide for better decision making in project selection and management.

Subsequent chapters shed light on this looming problem of abandoned software projects in organizations. In particular, they discuss the variety of factors contributing to decisions to abandon software projects and show how abandonment decisions are made in practice. What characteristics do abandoned software projects have in common? What benefits, if any, do organizations derive from past decisions to abandon projects? And finally, what guidelines and lessons can be offered to management to aid in software project selection and project management to minimize the frequency of abandonment decisions in organizations?

## Types of Abandonment

What, in essence, constitutes software project abandonment? Software project abandonment occurs whenever senior management decides, for whatever reason, to discontinue temporarily or retire permanently a software project under development. Three types of software project abandonment are identified by Ewusi-Mensah and Przasnyski (1991) and will form the basis of the classification in this discussion.

### Total Abandonment

The first and most frequent case of software project abandonment is total abandonment. *Total abandonment* describes the instances where there is complete termination of all activity on the software project prior to full implementation. This classification is analogous to the "impaired" project category of the Standish Group's three-resolution categorization, consisting of completed, challenged, and impaired projects. The incidence of this type of abandonment reported in published studies ranges from a low of 10 percent (Cole 1995) to a median of 31 percent (Standish Group, 1995) to a high of 40 to 44 percent (OASIG, 1996; Ewusi-Mensah and Przasnyski 1994). It is also one of the most costly expenditures organizations incur in their software project portfolio, with estimates ranging in the area of several billion dollars for both public- and private-sector organizations (Standish Group, 1995; Wysocki 1998; Heinrich 1998).

### Substantial Abandonment

The second category of abandoned software projects is described by Ewusi-Mensah and Przasnyski (1991) as substantial abandonment. *Substantial abandonment* refers to instances in the software development process where a major truncation or simplification of the project occurs prior to full implementation to make it radically different from the original specifications. This category is approximately analogous to the

Standish Group's "challenged" project classification, because the "truncation or simplification of the project" may result in "fewer features and functions than originally specified," as the Standish Group study suggests. Substantial abandonment may also be similar to the "software runaway" description offered by the KPMG study, and may even come under the rubric of Glass's (1998) more expansive definition of what constitutes "software runaway." The KPMG study found that 62 percent of the respondents had experienced a "runaway project" and that the number had not changed from a previous study five years earlier. In Glass's view, abandonment is not much of a solution to the problem of software failure or runaway. Judging by his somewhat dismissive remark of "some remedy" in commenting on abandonment of the project as discussed in the KPMG study, total abandonment should only occur if "it stops or rapidly slows project bloodletting, such as money and resources" (Glass 1998, 242). Still, Glass grudgingly concedes that "most of our case studies in Part 2 [i.e., of his book] resulted in some form of project cancellation." Thus, by Glass's own description of what constitutes a "software runaway," the abandoned project can belong to either of the above categories—that is, total or substantial abandonment.

In substantial abandonment, projects may still be continued or carried to completion even if cost overruns and schedule delays occur, so long as the reduction in systems functionality will enable the organization to salvage some of its investment in the project. This is perhaps the most significant distinction that can be made between substantial and total abandonment. However, in the case of total abandonment, reduction in systems functionality may not achieve the desired goals even if management allows for the cost and schedule overruns, thus making complete termination of the project the only viable option.

**Partial Abandonment**
The third category of abandonment is identified by Ewusi-Mensah and Przasnyski (1991) as partial abandonment. *Partial abandonment* describes the case in which a reduction of the original scope of the project is made without entailing major changes to the project's original specifications prior to its full implementation. This classification provides a

limited, indeed a restrictive view of abandonment to reflect in essence some reduction in systems functionality but nothing so significant as to drastically affect the original project specifications. Such cases seem to occur frequently in practice, albeit with some cost overruns and schedule delays. In fact, the KPMG study (Cole 1995, 4) provides data to indicate that about 30 percent of "software runaways" can be attributed to "reduction in scope of [the] project." In addition, this class of abandoned projects is probably in general to be expected, because organizations would rather make changes to the scope of their projects than risk total abandonment or even substantial abandonment if they believe such changes would enable them to achieve their original project's specifications. This would be a more rational use of organizational resources in the development of software projects than the other two alternatives would be.

All three types of abandonment occur in organizations in both the public and private sectors. However, of the three types of abandonment, the most costly and at times the most disastrous is the total-abandonment category, as many reports bear out (see, for example, Cole 1995; Capers Jones 1995; Glass 1998; Standish Group, 1995; Wysocki 1998; Gibbs 1994; OASIG, 1996; Heinrich 1998; "PG&E Dumps CIS Project," 1997; Ewusi-Mensah and Przasnyski 1991, 1994).

Table 1.1 provides a summary of the data on abandoned software projects from four published studies, and figure 1.1 summarizes the same

**Table 1.1**
Summary data on software project–abandonment

| | Type of abandonment | | |
| | Total (%) | Substantial (%) | Partial (%) |
| Published study | | | |
|---|---|---|---|
| Standish Group (1995, 1998)* | 31 (28)* | 52.7 (46)* | Not available |
| KPMG (Cole 1995) | 10 | 28 | 24 |
| OASIG (1996) | 40 | 25 | 80 |
| Ewusi-Mensah and Przasnyski (1994) | 44 | 16 | 9 |

*Reported in Whiting 1998

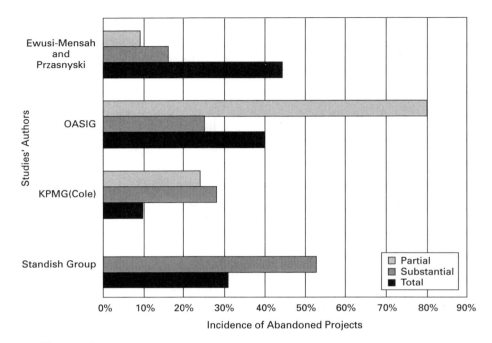

**Figure 1.1**
Summary data: Abandoned software project studies

data in graphic form. The totals do not add up to 100 percent because the incidence of abandonment reflects different projects in different organizations.

The data deal only with abandoned or "runaway" projects; successfully completed projects are not included in the data analysis reported. The total-abandonment figure from the Standish Group, with a total sample size of 365 respondents in the United States, breaks down as follows according to the size of the organization: 37.1 percent of most projects in medium-sized companies (i.e., companies with annual revenues of between $200 and $500 million); 29.5 percent in large companies (i.e., companies with annual revenues of more than $500 million); and 21.6 percent of projects in small companies (i.e., companies with less than $200 million in annual revenues) (Standish Group, 1995). No comparable figures are provided for the substantial-abandonment projects.

The KPMG study, based on a sample size of 120 organizations responding in the United Kingdom, does not provide any equivalent statistics other than to indicate that 62 percent of the respondents experienced runaway projects as defined in the study. The 10 percent total-abandonment figure was the "remedy" applied to the runaway projects by some respondents, as was the 28 percent given for substantial abandonment, defined as "reduction in scope of project." Some other remedies applied to the runaway projects were "more money" (45%), "more people" (55%), and "more time" allotted to the projects (80%). Among other measures, more than 55 percent also instituted "better project management procedures." (See Cole 1995, 4, for further details.)

The OASIG (1996, 12) study was also based in the United Kingdom and "drew on the expertise of leading management and organizational consultants and researchers" covering about 14,000 organizations in all major sectors of the economy. There is no detailed statistical breakdown along the lines of those provided by the Standish Group and the KPMG study. The OASIG study states that around 40 percent of developments fail or are abandoned; "less than 25% properly integrate business and technology objectives" (presumably this deals with the scope of the project); and "about 80% of systems are delivered late and over budget."

Finally, the Ewusi-Mensah and Przasnyski (1994) study was based on 82 responses from Fortune 500 companies in the United States that had experienced abandoned software development projects. In this study, the three categories of abandonment were defined and respondents were asked to indicate which of the categories appropriately fit the description of the abandoned project in the organization. The figure that provided for each category of abandonment in table 1.1 was based on the total number of respondents who indicated that they had experienced a specific type of abandonment. Of the 78 usable responses received, 34 respondents indicated that they had experienced total abandonment, about 44 percent; another 13 respondents indicated they had experienced substantial abandonment, about 16 percent; and yet another 7 respondents indicated they had experienced partial abandonment, about 9 percent. Finally, 24 respondents indicated they had experienced no abandonment—about 31 percent. Further discussion of the results of this study is provided in later chapters, notably in chapters 4 through 6.

The data from the above studies confirm that abandonment is not confined to any particular market segment or type of organization, nor is it "associated with any particular business sector or size of organization," as the KPMG study (Cole 1995, 3) concludes. In general, software abandonment occurs "when problems arise in perceiving, analyzing, designing, or configuring the system objectives; when the technological basis for the system and its behavioral, political or organizational (including economic) issues directly or indirectly affect ways that could bring the project to a successful completion, within the estimated budget and/or schedule constraints; and/or when the organizational environment factors combine to reduce the project's expected benefits or increase its expected costs" (Ewusi-Mensah and Przasnyski 1991, 68).

**Failed Software Projects: Two Cases**

I briefly describe and analyze two reported cases of failed software development projects—Highmark's HighBAR project and Hershey Foods' ERP project—to illustrate the complexities of the underlying managerial and organizational issues that contribute to project failures.

*Highmark's HighBAR Project*    Highmark, a $5 billion health insurance company based in Pittsburgh, Pennsylvania, contracted with the KPMG consulting group in May 1999 to develop an electronic billing and accounts receivable system for the company at an estimated cost of $15 million. The project was to be completed by the end of the first quarter in 2002.

The project, named HighBAR, was divided into four phases, and work on the first phase was begun in July 1999. In April 2001, KPMG requested $8 million to complete the first phase in addition to the $12 million already paid by Highmark for what was only 20 percent of the project. When Highmark refused payment, KPMG ceased work in June 2001. Highmark sued KPMG on charges of fraud, malpractice, misrepresentation, and breach of contract (Mearian 2001a, 2001b).

The allegations Highmark made in its suit dealt with the failure of KPMG to properly inform Highmark of progress on the project. Specifically, Highmark alleged that KPMG "failed to 'satisfactorily' complete several aspects of the project, including database design, software design specifications and a detailed application architecture "(Mearian 2001a, 2). Coding was allowed to proceed on the project even though the design was still undergoing revisions, which resulted in several thousand hours of coding having to be redone due to changes in the design. The net result was that the project was more than a year behind schedule and several million dollars over budget. The project, according to Highmark, never progressed beyond the second stage. KPMG responded that the project was a collaborative effort between itself and Highmark and that the latter failed to carry out its part of the collaboration "to ensure a successful implementation of the payment system on time and on budget" (Mearian 2001a, 2).

HighBAR illustrates several of the managerial and organizational factors identified as contributors to abandoned projects. In particular, although there was a consensus on the overall project goals and objectives, the failure of Highmark senior management to stay engaged with the project development may have contributed to KPMG's alleged failure to keep Highmark informed of progress with respect to project costs, labor hours, and deadlines. A full 80 percent of the estimated cost of the project—that is, $12 million—was paid to KPMG for what was less than 20 percent of the project, which was alleged to have been completed in an unsatisfactory manner (Mearian 2001a). The changes in the design, probably due to changes in requirements, may have played a role in this scenario, because several thousand hours of coding had to be jettisoned. Cost overruns and schedule delays are generally symptomatic of more fundamental problems in the project life cycle. For example, Highmark alleged that KPMG fraudulently claimed it had the requisite knowledge and experience in object-oriented analysis and design to enable it to successfully complete the project. KPMG's alleged misrepresentation of its experience may have led to the frequent changes in the design, which in turn resulted in substantial recoding. Highmark senior management must also share the blame for failing to thoroughly investigate the technical experience and expertise of KPMG. In addition, had management remained engaged and asked persistent questions early in the life of the project, some of the problems might have been uncovered earlier and dealt with before they mushroomed into the reported fiasco.

***Hershey Foods' ERP Project*** Enterprise Resource Planning (ERP) systems is a comprehensive applications systems package that organizations use to automate their back-office operations. For example, it permits order processing and distribution functions to be fully integrated for smooth operation of the business. It is with these ambitious goals in mind that Hershey Foods embarked on its ERP project in 1996: to integrate the disparate legacy applications systems for handling order processing, inventory, and human resource operations at Hershey into one computing platform. Hershey engaged the services of four different consulting firms to work with its IT department to install SAP AG R/3 software in conjunction with software from two other vendors—Manugistics Group for its planning applications software, and Siebel Systems for its pricing-promotion-package software. The project was estimated to cost between $112 and $115 million (Osterland 2000; Stedman 1999).

In July 1999, with implementation already three months behind schedule, Hershey went live with the conversion from the old legacy system to the new SAP AG R/3 system. Two months after the implementation was supposed to be completed, Hershey was still finding fixes to the system. The company's sales dropped in its third quarter—its busiest sales season of the year—by more than 12 percent. With it, there was a corresponding drop of more than 18 percent in revenues compared to the previous year; Hershey experienced a 29 percent increase in project inventory; and its mean delivery time for orders increased from five to twelve days, as reported in several publications. (See, for example, Osterland 2000; Collett 1999; Stedman 1999; 2000; Songini 2000; "ERP Stumbles," 2000; Wheatley 2000; Nicholson 1999.)

The implementation period was originally estimated at four years but was later shortened to thirty months—for unspecified reasons—despite the fact that the R/3 software modules were to be integrated with software from two other vendors. The consequence of the compressed implementation time frame was that insufficient time was devoted to test runs of the modules and training of the users. The implementation problems often associated with ERP systems reported in the media are more often than not attributed to these overly ambitious time frames and inadequate user training, which combine to create havoc in the organization when the system is fully activated. Because of the complexity of the R/3 software, any implementation that involves customization with other vendors' software frequently has unintended and/or unanticipated consequences that are difficult and time consuming to find and correct. It took about a year for Hershey to fix all the related implementation bugs and to get the company back to normal operating conditions and profitability (Songini 2000).

In the Hershey ERP R/3 project problems, we see echoes of FoxMeyer's Delta project, analyzed in detail in chapters 4 through 6. For example, the drastic reduction of the implementation time from four years to thirty months is generally identified as a major contributor to the problems the project experienced when it went live. FoxMeyer experienced similar problems, which contributed to its bankruptcy. However, Hershey was able to avoid a similar fate because of its size and the superior resources it could summon to deal with the emergencies resulting from the implementation failure.

**Internet- and Web-Based Software Projects (and Project Failures)**

With the collapse of a significant number of e-commerce Internet- and Web-based companies in 2000 and 2001, there has been a general perception, often erroneous, that the failure of the companies can perhaps be blamed on the technology. This misperception is unjustified because, as growing evidence reveals, the failure of the companies was due more to the failure of the underlying business models on which the entire future and competitive strategies of the companies rested. Indeed, as Berghel (2001, 17) has argued, "The problem that caused the Y2K e-commerce meltdown is . . . an over-reliance on technology to overcome the weakness of a bad business model." Clearly, the often-irrational foundation on which the companies derived their wealth based on capitalization of their stock-market shares even when they were frequently operating in debt was not a failure of the technology. In fact, it was the

promise and capabilities of the Internet- and Web-based technologies that
tended to sustain what in a normal business environment would have
been untenable business practices. The lure of the Internet and the Web,
fueled by speculations in the financial markets, gave free reign to the rise
of the companies' stock value until investors realized that the trend of
ever-increasing share prices could not be sustained forever. For example,
a company like Amazon.com had a share price of $427.12 at its peak
market valuation on April 27, 1999, and three years later a share price
of $13.96 on April 23, 2002 (<Yahoo.finance.com>), even though it had
never turned a profit, because investors were led to believe that the rev-
olutionary nature of the underlying Internet- and Web-based technologies was the wave of the future. And so despite evidence to the contrary,
investors continued to invest heavily in the company's future. Amazon's
operating business paradigm was widely replicated in other e-commerce
companies; these eventually collapsed because the business models were
not sustainable, notwithstanding the capabilities of the Internet- and
Web-based technologies.

The Internet- and Web-based technologies that formed the core of the
companies' business strategies are therefore not the culprits in the failures of those companies. The flawed business models and the companies
that staked their existence and survival on them produced the failures of
the software development projects, which were intended to exploit the
e-commerce phenomena. There is nothing innate in the Internet- and
Web-based technologies that poses special problems for the software
development process. For example, Internet- and Web-based software
projects are invariably based on client-server architecture often implemented or deployed in a network environment. A number of the failed
software project cases discussed in the book, including Confirm,
FoxMeyer's Delta, DIA's BHS, and the Hershey Foods' ERP project, are
all based on such an architectural framework. Hence we do not focus
on Internet- and Web-based software projects in our discussion, because
such an approach would not provide any additional insights into the
causes or contributors to the failure of those projects beyond what is
applicable to complex software development projects. In addition, as discussed in Ewusi-Mensah and Przasnyski 1991, 1994, some software projects may fail as a result of changes in the organization's structure or

competitive business environment; these changes may require a reexamination of the basis for the continued funding of the projects in question. For instance, some projects may fail as a result of mergers and acquisitions; these may call for a reexamination of organizational priorities involving those projects, among others, and for a reassignment of organizational resources to satisfy different priorities. We can therefore surmise that some of the e-commerce software project failures can be classified as similar to the aforementioned types of projects with respect to their complexity, innovativeness, and dynamic development environments, among other factors.

## Conclusion

This chapter has examined the nature and extent of software development failures. We have discussed the role software engineering as a science has played in helping to provide solutions to the software crises. We have also described the problem of software abandonment and provided three classifications of abandonment. In addition, we have pointed out the inherent characteristics of software projects that make them susceptible to failure in general and abandonment in particular, and explained why the main focus of the book would be on management and organizational issues in software development projects. The main audience for the book, we suggested, consists of students of software engineering and professional software developers as well as their corporate managers, who should be aware of the organizational and managerial issues that play a significant role in decisions affecting successful project development outcomes. We have briefly described and analyzed two reported cases of failed software development projects in organizations to illustrate the organizational and managerial issues at the heart of most failed projects. We ended with an explanation of why software project failures in Internet- and Web-based companies cannot be blamed on the technologies, but rather must be blamed on flaws in the underlying business models.

# 2

## Software Project Characteristics

Software is so crucial to the operations and management of organizations worldwide that it is inconceivable that any organization could compete successfully in the information economy without substantial investments in software projects. Investments in software, however, come with significant risks of failure. Indeed, it is common knowledge in the information technology (IT) industry that software projects are over budget and behind schedule and often have less functionality in far more cases than IT professionals and management find acceptable. The questions that need to be answered include the following: What factors intrinsic to software development projects make them particularly susceptible to such fiascoes? How do such factors combine to make software projects vulnerable to cancellation and other problems, such as cost overruns and schedule delays? This chapter looks closely at some of the characteristics of software development that can affect software project outcomes. In addition, it reviews a number of studies examining the assessment and management of the risks and uncertainties in software development. It compares the results of the risk-assessment studies with factors that have been identified as contributing to the failure of software projects and points out underlying similarities between the two sets of results.

Software production is a complex and exceedingly difficult creative process. It involves the sustained collaboration of disparate groups of stakeholders to achieve performance objectives intended to satisfy organizational requirements. The intrinsic properties of software projects include, for example, project size and complexity, problem formulation and abstraction, project-team composition, and project risks and uncertainties. This list is not meant to be exhaustive, and some items overlap. For instance, unwieldy project size and complexity contributes substantially to the risks associated with the development effort. Also, technical and technological issues involved in software development are not specifically mentioned but can be subsumed under project size and complexity and project-team composition. These characteristics of software projects play a significant role in the software crises that form the subject of this book. Let us examine each of these characteristics to determine the nature of their contributions to the software development problem.

**Project Size and Complexity**

The difficulty of software design is heightened as the size of the project increases, and with increasing project size comes a level of complexity that is orders-of-magnitude higher. Software design is concerned with the creation of artifacts or products that are robust and reliable and meet the functional specifications of the user in the problem-solving context (Winograd 1996). Computer programs are the implementation or realization of the design objects. The processes of creating the design and of implementing the design in a programming-language context add to the complexity of the endeavor. The complexity stems partly from the difficulties in comprehending the various facets of the design problem in order to come up with a robust and reliable design. Complexity also stems from the difficulty in coordinating the activities of various professionals engaged in the enterprise. The orders-of-magnitude increase in the level of complexity of a software project often overwhelms our capacity to fully comprehend all the possible states of the designed system. This failure to comprehend all the states of the design invariably has consequences for the implementation of the system, as is often revealed by testing of the system. Thus, as Fred Brooks ([1975] 1995) has said, the complexity of software is an essential property of the entity that cannot be stripped away or minimized through abstraction.

The size of the project invariably increases the complexity dimension of the problem. Large software projects are orders-of-magnitude more complex than small projects, in part because they often require more personnel. The coordination and communication required for the collaboration of the various groups add another level of complexity to an already-complex creative process. It is common knowledge in the computer industry that small software projects are often quite successful in meeting schedule and cost estimates but that the "risks and hazards" of cancellation and/or major delays and cost overruns tend to rise significantly as the size of the project goes up (Capers Jones 1995). This is not to suggest that project complexity is a function of or that it correlates with project size. Small projects can also be rather complex, depending on the types of problems they address. But in general, large projects are especially complex and difficult.

A number of design techniques in use are intended to reduce the complexity of software projects. Notable among these approaches are concepts such as top-down hierarchic design. This structured technique uses top-down design in an attempt to reduce the intrinsic complexity of systems problems by imposing a hierarchic structure. The architectural schemes available to the software designer include the ability to derive these hierarchic structures from complexity. The interactions that take place in hierarchic structures can be distinguished to reflect *intersubsystems* interactions as separate from *intrasubsystems* interactions (Simon 1984). This ability to create subsystems out of complex systems makes it possible to focus attention on each individual subsystem in order to understand it. But we are still faced with the need to understand the interactions among subsystems in order to fully comprehend the entire complex system. Thus the hierarchic systems demand a great deal of learning and comprehension on the part of the software designer in terms of the designer's ability to visualize the whole picture posed by the design problem. David Parnas (1985, 16) has written ably about this problem, stating that "even in highly structured systems, surprises and unreliability occur because the human mind is not able to fully comprehend the many conditions that can arise because of the interactions of these components."

Finally, the complexity that is a permanent feature of software projects is unlike the complexity in natural systems, because it is not redundant; no aspect of its structure can be inferred from any other. Indeed it is what Brooks (1987, 1996) insightfully labels *arbitrary complexity*. It is the kind of complexity that is most difficult to deal with because its various interactive states and levels are hidden and must be painstakingly uncovered one layer and type of interaction at a time. This is the ultimate challenge software developers face, and as projects tackle more and more intricate and demanding problems, we can expect the size and level of complexity of the projects as well as the difficulties associated with them to increase. Parnas (1985, 18) explains why this is the case: "All of our experience indicates that the difficulties in building software increase with the size of the system, with the number of independently modifiable subsystems, and with the number of interfaces that must be defined. Problems worsen when interfaces may change. The consequent modifications increase the complexity of the software and the difficulty of making a change correctly."

Experience thus far seems to show a failure of the modernist approach to software development to "deliver the promises of high rationality" (Robinson et al. 1998, 367). Indeed Brooks (1987, 1996), Parnas (1985), and others—including Robinson et al. (1998), Barwise (1989), Fetzer (1988, 1989), and Leith (1986)—have forcefully cautioned against such utopian ideals of rationality in software development, because of our limited ability to fathom, much less describe or model, all the subtleties of a problem in a software product. Hence the persistent need to revisit even the "successfully" implemented and operational software to "correct" the errors or problems and omissions in the "finished" product. The formal methods and tools may prove inadequate to the complexities of the task. At other times the software problems may result from the inability of developers to fully and accurately grasp the essence of the problems from the beginning; this inability lays the foundation for the problems that will later manifest themselves—even in software projects that do make it to completion. Furthermore, the inappropriate or inaccurate use of the most suitable formal methods and tools applied to the right software task may generate its own set of development problems, even in the absence of any difficulties in describing the requirements for the software. The human and organizational aspects of software development are perhaps the most compelling yet stubborn dimension of the entire process and provide the most convincing explanations as to why software development as a process cannot be completely rationalized to overcome the problems outlined above.

## Problem Formulation and Abstraction

Software problems in general defy definitive descriptions. The abstracted version of a software problem that designers start with may at some later stage in the development process be found to be structurally deficient— sometimes in some fundamental way that may render the rest of the development problematic. Abstracting away the complexity of the problem in an attempt to get at the problem's essence may thus carry with it risks and uncertainties that could eventually spell disaster for the project.

Software projects invariably address problems that are conceptual in nature. Unlike engineering or architectural problems, where tangible products are the expected end of the development, software "solutions" are abstractions of symbols and words, put together under specific guidelines and methodologies to satisfy some functional requirements that constitute the software problem. There are, at the core, real and fundamental differences between the development of software as an abstract or conceptual artifact and other physical artifacts such as buildings or bridges. Fred Brooks's (1987, 12) description of software as "pure thought-stuff, infinitely malleable" and as "invisible and unvisualizable" underscores the difficulty of problem formulation in software development. Although the software may be "invisible and unvisualizable" inasmuch as the human eyes are concerned, the behavior of the software must be visualizable in the mind's eye of its creator or designer. Part of the problem-formulation difficulty arises from the designer's inability to fully conceive of all the possible behavioral states of the working software prior to its implementation (Parnas 1985).

In discussing the dilemmas that planners face in tackling real-world problems with several stakeholders, Rittel and Webber (1973) have coined the term *wicked problems* to convey not only the difficulties but to some extent the sense of frustration planners experience in dealing with planning problems in a pluralistic society. The term *wicked problems* is defined not from a moralistic or ethical perspective but rather from the standpoint that these problems are representative of an amorphous class of complex problems that defy comprehensive descriptions. Such problems are usually characterized as one of a kind. Software problems (at least of the type discussed here) belong to this class of problems. Like planning problems, software projects tend to deal substantially with problems that are unique.

Every software project is bound to have peculiarities that override any apparent commonalities that the project may appear to have with previously implemented systems in the organization. It must be recognized that every new software project is intended to satisfy an identified need in the organization's systems portfolio. Also, like Rittel and Webber's planning problems, software projects handle problems that have no set stopping rule or criteria for arriving at the desired "solutions" or implementation. Consequently, the entire design effort is geared to coming up with a satisfactory implementation of a software problem that does not have a "right or wrong solution." The implementation can rather be characterized as good or bad in terms of whether it addresses the functional requirements of the systems problem. The implementation arrived at has broad consequences for the organization and, wickedly, offers practically little chance to learn by trial and error. So the systems developers may not be able to come up with alternative satisfactory implementations due to the enormous costs of time and money involved in the process.

Fundamentally, software projects tend not to have a definitive formulation of the information requirements at the core of the development effort. Any number of groups of stakeholders, in particular the users, may have their own perspective on the nature and significance of the problem and what the software must be able to accomplish. The need for consensus among the stakeholder groups becomes crucial to bridging the gap among the differing interpretations of the information needs of the organization. Arriving at a satisfactory formulation of the software problem is not a trivial task and may often be the hidden source of problems uncovered at later stages of the development process. In addition, there is a need to prioritize the requirements problems and introduce some element of flexibility into the development process. This will allow for later incorporation of some deferred requirements problems into an implemented system. It will also help to control for the complexity and size of the project in the initial stages of development.

The tools and procedures of software development vary as widely as the problems the projects tackle. There is something unsettling about the variety of approaches to software projects. The intrinsic conceptual nature of the problems the projects are intended to address is probably partly to blame for this disturbing state of affairs. As noted earlier, software projects are often abstracted from real-world problems, which are difficult to model conceptually without losing some inherent attributes of the problems in question. In the final analysis, software developers are left with no option but to come up with a variety of attempts to get at the essence of the problem, to counter the fundamental difficulty of dealing with the "invisible and unvisualizable" characteristics of the projects. In addition, the learning that takes place on a project is for the most part not transferable wholesale to new projects. Each new software project carries within its structure some intrinsic properties that make it unique and thus not easily amenable, adaptable, or applicable to information transfer from other successfully completed and implemented projects.

The problem-solving processes of software development projects are in general not repeatable, nor do they have parts that can be grafted onto new projects without major reworking or modifications. The software developer is thus forced into a selective trial-and-error approach to building software as each new project takes on a new software problem. The experience gained from earlier projects may help inform us about some feasible options, but nothing in the form of concrete "solutions" can be assumed as applicable to new software development problems in the organization. The selective trial-and-error approach does contribute to the proliferation of tools and procedures, as each new software development problem forces the developers to come up with novel and often untried and untested means of accomplishing the desired functional requirements. The tools and procedures that aid in the successful implementation of the software problem then become part of the collection of promising toolkits to be consulted as appropriate in future software development projects.

**Project-Team Composition**

Software project size and complexity make a given project virtually incomprehensible to any one individual developer. Software projects are, therefore, virtually unique in that they are among perhaps a handful of projects undertaken in organizations where three groups of employees with sometimes vastly different backgrounds are required to work together. First, there are the technical personnel or developers, who usually have highly technical training and experience but may have limited knowledge in the problem domain. Second, there are the end users, who, in most instances, have limited technical background or experience in information technology but are knowledgeable in the relevant application problem domain. And finally, there is management, which may be the "sponsor" or "champion" of the project. In instances where management may lack the requisite technical background and/or the necessary knowledge of the problem domain to oversee the detailed direction of the project, they may delegate that responsibility to other senior technical members of the team.

Software projects are thus group-oriented activities organized and executed in teams. As such, work on any software project is subject to all the vagaries of group dynamics, interactions, coordination, and communication. The diverse backgrounds of the team's constituent members make the ability to communicate a crucial prerequisite if the team is to work successfully on the project's development. How the team is put together from the various stakeholder groups, together with the individual and collective capabilities of the team, are issues of great consequence to the project development effort. To the extent that the work of the project team involves acquisition and sharing of the problem-domain knowledge among the team members, how the team is put together becomes a crucial factor in its success. In addition, effective coordination of the activities of the stakeholders and subgroups involved in the project is critical in ensuring the success of the project (Krault and Streeter 1995; Constantine 1993).

The various roles expected to be performed collectively by the members of the project teams are usually complemented by the specific roles and responsibilities of individual members of the teams. For example, it is important that for each task of the project a leader is assigned with specific responsibility for organizing how the task is to be carried out and what the deliverables should be when it is completed. The critical role played by the overall project leader is necessary to facilitate the coordination and communication essential to the collaborative work of the teams. Software projects are inherently characterized by the dimensions of teamwork and communication, without which failure is eminently possible.

The postmodernist view of software development explicitly recognizes the need for a plurality and diversity of shared responsibilities of all the stakeholder groups involved in the development, so that all legitimate and relevant views will be heard and incorporated into the problem formulation (Robinson et al. 1998; Klein, Jiang, and Tesch 2002). From the postmodernist perspective, no superior or inferior status is conferred on any class of people involved in the project development, be they technical developers, user groups, or management. All the members of the project team play complementary roles and work on the basis of mutual interdependence because of the unique qualifications and experiences each brings to the project team. The changing dynamics of such a team in the life of a project may itself be a source of potential risk. For example, the attrition that occurs when people leave and perhaps are replaced by new people in the course of the life of the project may affect the resources consumed and may further add to the uncertainties of the project development environment.

## Project Risks and Uncertainties

Software development projects are inherently risky. Apart from the conceptual nature of the projects, there are often intrinsic risks and uncertainties that are difficult to assess with any degree of reliability prior to the start of the projects. In discussing cost-benefit evaluations of projects, Corti (1973, 75) defined risk as involving "situations in which the outcome is not certain but where the range of possible outcomes is known and the probabilities associated with these outcomes are known or can be estimated with some accuracy." Uncertainty, on the other hand, is described as related to "those situations where either the range of outcomes is known, but where probabilities cannot be estimated accurately, or where even the range of possible outcomes is not known." Thus, in risky situations, according to Fisher (1971, 202), "The outcome is subject to an uncontrollable random event stemming from a known probability distribution." But in uncertain situations, though the outcome may still be subject to random events, it is distinctly characterized by an unknown probability distribution (Ewusi-Mensah 1989).

We do not currently have accurate estimation methods for assessing the probabilities of the various risk factors associated with projects outcomes (Boehm 1991). We do, however, know for a fact that there is an ever present uncertainty as to whether a project may be completed or abandoned for a variety of factors: whether a project may or may not exceed the budgeted costs; whether the schedule for completion will be delayed; and whether the functional specifications will be fully or even partially implemented. In essence, the uncertainty inherent in the outcome of the software development process is a consequence which can be partly attributed to:

• The nature of the real world problem domain and the need to abstract from that domain in formulating the software product to be created

• The imprecision and incompleteness of the requirements definition and the functional specifications on which the software design alternative solutions are based

• The nature, type and magnitude of the errors which may be inherent in the coding, testing and systems integration during the implementation phase of the software development

• The changing organizational and/or developmental environments as, for example, when changes are made to the original specifications, and/or as some current team members leave the project and are replaced by new ones.

For large and complex projects there is an order-of-magnitude increase in the risk and uncertainty factors associated with the project's outcomes. Some of the risks and uncertainties that may be unique to software projects include, for instance, large project size. The size of the project may add to the amount of communication and coordination necessary to a successful project outcome by introducing additional layers of interactions among the team members. The complexity of the problem domain may contribute its own risks and uncertainties. This applies to both the design and implementation phases, as bugs introduced in the design phase due to faulty comprehension of the problem domain persist in the implementation phase, adding to outcome uncertainties in the testing of the source code.

Large and complex projects invariably require team-oriented approaches. This introduces yet another dimension of risk and uncertainty into the development equation, because large and complex projects are invariably more difficult to comprehend and manage and are even more prone to problems with communication and coordination of the work of the various subteams than smaller projects are. Typically, large and complex projects are often prone to changes in requirements, which become necessary as new learning and insights gained in later stages of the development necessitate corrections to earlier phases of the development. This forced iterative approach to the development introduces yet another dimension to the risks and uncertainties factors, which if not carefully controlled may create additional hazards for the project.

Technology and technical know-how or experience on the part of the project team may be another factor in a list of risks and uncertainties associated with the project outcome, in particular if the project team has minimal or insufficient experience with the technology needed to undertake the project. The learning capabilities of the team to master the technology to be used in the project may add to the risks and uncertainties associated with the project outcome. The difficulties associated with being able to integrate, in large and complex projects, the different component systems into a composite system create still another layer of underlying risk and uncertainty with respect to the project's outcome. Other potentially problematic factors include the level of commitment of the other members of the stakeholder groups—that is, the users and management—to the successful completion of the project (Keil et al. 1998; Ewusi-Mensah 1997; Barki, Rivard, and Talbot 1993).

In addition to the factors just discussed, there are concerns that may not be unique to software projects but that nonetheless pose their own difficulties. Software projects, in particular applications software, are sociotechnical in nature. They possess a technical or technological dimension, which must be properly understood and managed, as well as a social or organizational dimension, which must also be well understood and properly factored into the dynamics of the development process. The interaction effects of the two critical dimensions introduce yet another layer of risk and uncertainty into the project's outcome. Finally, software projects are capital intensive, requiring the investment of substantial capital and other resources in the development effort. Being able to manage the optimum use of all the resources entails further risk, because projects may be canceled or terminated for lack of funds.

**Managing Software Development Project Risks**

The inherent risks and uncertainties associated with software development projects have often been cited to explain software project failures. A number of studies have suggested that the best approach to the problem of software failure is to gain a better understanding of the risk factors associated with project development and to manage the impact of these factors. Boehm's (1991) early work, identifying ten software risk factors based on an analysis of several hundred projects, was a pivotal contribution. The factors included providing unrealistic schedules and budgets, changing requirements, and shortfalls in personnel, furnished components, and technology (i.e., "computer science capabilities").

Barki, Rivard, and Talbot (1993), citing but criticizing the pioneering work of Boehm, attempted to extend our understanding of the risk factors plaguing software projects by developing an empirically based set of five risk-factor categories that can be used to assess the risks and uncertainties associated with software development projects. The five categories they identified include the newness of the technology needed for the project, the project size, the level of expertise of the team engaged in the development effort, the technical complexity of the project, and the nature of the organizational environment supporting the project team. The factors were derived from an analysis of survey data obtained from 120 software projects, covering organizations in both the public and private sectors in the Canadian province of Quebec in the early

1990s. A later study by Barki, Rivard, and Talbot (2001) acknowledged how unrealistic it was to apply the same set of risk-assessment factors to all varieties of software projects in different organizational settings. A contingency model based on the information processing capacity of the organization's project team was therefore proposed to attempt to make the risk assessment fit the project-profile characteristics. This study was based on an analysis of seventy-five projects in Quebec from both public and private organizations. The central result of the study was that to increase project performance, a project's risk management profile needs to vary according to the project's risk exposure. Barki and colleagues found evidence to support the proposition that high-risk projects had high information processing capacity, as evidenced by the extensive formal planning undertaken, the intensity of internal integration, and the high levels of user participation in development decision-making situations. They used the ability to meet project budgets and the system quality after implementation as criteria for assessing project performance.

Ropponen and Lyytinen (2000) studied risk-management practices of project managers in Finland using a survey of eighty-three software projects in a variety of organizations. The risk items they developed were mostly based on or derived from Boehm's (1991) original list, mentioned earlier. The list of six risk components the study produced included scheduling and timing, the functionality of the software, the requirements-management concerns of the software, subcontracting, resource usage and performance, and the management of the personnel associated with the project. Ropponen and Lyytinen found that project managers who had extensive prior experience using software risk-management methods did better than their counterparts with less experience. Similarly, technically well-educated project managers were able to manage their projects' risks better than their not so well-educated counterparts. Finally, project managers who used formal analysis and design procedures were able to control and manage their project development risks better. In addition, software projects were influenced by a variety of organizational environmental factors having to do with the individual characteristics of the project, the specific circumstances of the organization, and technology-related issues underlying the project. The results of the study by Ropponen and Lyytinen thus broadly coincide with the findings of Barki, Rivard, and Talbot (2001), on the need to adopt a contingency approach to software development project risk management. It is the prudent strategy for project managers to adopt in order that their project risk-management decisions fit the specifics of the project within its organizational context.

The studies reported on in the preceding paragraphs deal specifically with project risk factors and how they can be managed to minimize their adverse effects on project outcomes. Table 2.1 summarizes the risk components identified by Boehm (1991), Barki and colleagues (1993, 2001), and Ropponen and Lyytinen (2000). The table also lists, in the fourth column, the main factors identified as contributing to the abandonment of software projects. A review of the information contained in the table shows significant similarities between the results of the software project risks identified by Boehm and others, and the factors identified by Ewusi-Mensah (1997) and other researchers (e.g., Cole 1995; Johnson 1995; OASIG 1996; Standish Group 1995; Whiting 1998) as contributing to the abandonment or failure of software projects. (Chapter 3 provides more detail on each of the abandonment factors.) The cogent explanation for the apparent similarities is that while the focus of the two sets of studies may be different, both deal with software development projects. The similarities probably stem from the fact that the underlying causes of the projects' outcomes reflect the risks and uncertainties inherent in software development projects.

For example, Boehm (1991) and Ropponen and Lyytinen (2000) cite problems associated with requirements as project risk factors. Barki, Rivard, and Talbot (1993) list application complexity as a risk factor, which is just a different way of describing essentially the same underlying problem. That problem is that difficulties in comprehending the complexities of the application often lead to revisions in the requirements, as developers and users alike gain a better understanding of the problem domain. The problem of changing requirements is also identified as contributing to abandonment of software projects. Barki, Rivard, and Talbot (1993) cite the expertise of the development team or organization as a project risk factor. Boehm (1991) and Ropponen and Lyytinen (2000),

**Table 2.1**
A comparison of software project risk factors vs. abandoned-project risk factors

| Boehm 1991 | Barki, Rivard, and Talbot 1993, 2001 | Ropponen and Lyytinen 2000 | Abandonment factors |
| --- | --- | --- | --- |
| Personnel shortfall | Newness of the technology | Scheduling and timing risks | Unrealistic project goals and objectives |
| Unrealistic schedules and budgets | Application size | System functionality risks | Inappropriate project-team composition |
| Developing the wrong functions and properties | Lack of expertise | Subcontracting risks | Project management and control problems |
| Developing the wrong user interface | Application complexity | Requirement management risks | Inadequate technical know-how |
| Gold plating | Organizational environment | Resource usage and performance risks | Changing requirements |
| Continuing stream of requirements changes | | Personnel management risks | Problematic technology base/ infrastructure |
| Shortfalls in externally furnished components | | | Lack of executive support and commitment |
| Shortfalls in externally performed tasks | | | Insufficient user commitment and involvement |
| Real-time performance shortfalls | | | Cost overruns and schedule delays |
| Straining computer science capabilities | | | |

however, cite risks associated with subcontracting or externally furnished components or performed tasks. Again the two risk factors may appear to be different, but both refer to the risk caused by inadequate expertise within the team. A development team that recognizes its lack of expertise and seeks outside consulting help has merely succeeded in shifting the risk exposure from itself to the outside agents. The project still faces the risk, because the outside agents may not have the requisite expertise to complete the parts of the project contracted for either. Another risk factor that Barki and colleagues (1993) mention is the underlying technology and its newness to the development team. Ropponen and Lyytinen (2000, 98), on the other hand, cite "resource usage and performance risks," which probably refers broadly to the technological infrastructure in place in the organization to support the project. Similarly, Boehm (1991, 35) uses the phrase "straining computer-science capabilities," which again can presumably refer to technological capabilities. The abandonment factors include technology base or infrastructure as a potential contributor to project failure, especially if deemed inadequate to the requirements of the project (Ewusi-Mensal 1997). The issue of schedule and budgets or project costs is listed by Boehm (1991) and Ropponen and Lyytinen (2000) but not explicitly by Barki and associates (1993) as a risk factor in project management. The abandonment factors also include escalating project costs and missed deadlines as a cause. However, as I will argue later, particularly in chapter 6, I believe that that factor is only symptomatic of deeper underlying problems— such as changing requirements and lack of expertise. These underlying problems may add to the problems of the project, thus extending the completion time and potentially increasing the cost. Finally, on the issue of the size and composition of the project team, both Boehm (1991) and Ropponen and Lyytinen (2000) list risks involving project personnel, while the abandonment factors suggest that project-team composition in addition to project management and control are potential contributors to project failures. The above specific instances give us some indication of the underlying commonalities between the two sets of studies—one dealing with broad risk factors that software projects generally face, and the other dealing with the specific risk factors that are at the root of abandoned software projects. Thus it can be observed that all software projects face risks; the severity of these risks and the manner in which they combine ultimately decide the fate of the project.

## Conclusion

We can therefore surmise that software projects possess the intrinsic characteristics described above, which collectively make them susceptible to the problems of failure—in terms of cost overruns, schedule delays, incomplete functional specifications, and, at times, even outright termination or abandonment. The risks and uncertainties just discussed are always present in a software project. Thus, in essence, the outcome of the software development process is intrinsically risky and uncertain owing to a multiplicity of factors, not all of which may be known with any degree of reliability or consistency from project to project.

In the preceding pages, we have discussed the main factors intrinsic to software development projects. We have focused on four significant issues: project size and complexity, problem formulation and abstraction, project-team composition, and project risks and uncertainties (including the project risk factors that need to be managed to minimize the possibility of failure). In this regard, we have reviewed the highlights of some studies on assessing and managing project risks and compared some of the factors identified as major contributors to abandoned software projects. As indicated earlier, the list is not exhaustive, because readers may come up with additional characteristics that make software projects unique and their development fraught with pitfalls. However, we have laid a foundation for dealing with the persistent issue of software project failures or runaways, some of which eventually lead to termination. The next chapter discusses the factors critical to abandonment decisions on software projects and their varying impacts on different phases of the software development process.

# 3
# Factors Critical to Abandoned Software Projects

The failure of software development projects defies straightforward explanation. These projects fail due to a combination of interacting factors. The failure may result in less functionality for some completed projects; it may result in cost overruns; it may also result in schedule delays; and in some instances, it may result in the cancellation of the projects. Consequently, like the failure of software projects in general, the abandonment of software projects may be the result of a "multiplicity of cofactors"—that is, technical, organizational, political, managerial, sociological, and economic factors, among others. The abandonment of software projects can occur at any stage of the software development process. In this chapter, we briefly discuss the various stages of the systems development process and examine the factors identified by researchers as contributing to the abandonment of software projects. We subsequently build on these analyses of the software development process and of the factors contributing to abandoned software projects by constructing a framework to help us understand the critical impact these factors have on abandonment decisions at different stages of the process. In subsequent chapters we discuss in detail the various groupings or classifications of the factors that are particularly crucial in a project's cancellation.

## Software Development Models

Chapter 1 offered a theoretically based explanation for the persistence of the problem of software development failure based on a view of software development grounded in the modern scientific method of rationality. As Robinson et al. (1998), Brooks (1987), Parnas (1985), and others have argued, the modernist approach seems to break down because software projects are not completely amenable to the modern scientific method. As a result, in spite of the enormous progress made in software engineering methods and procedures, the practice of software development will continue to be plagued by socioorganizational problems—from problem formulation in ascertaining the requirements for the software to the full implementation of the completed software artifact in the organization. The scientific or modernist approach thus far has not succeeded in providing a reliable, valid, and verifiable way to develop software that gets at the core of the problem of software project failures.

In a review of software technology, Glass (1999) examines the productivity- and quality-improvement claims that heralded the introduction of six development technologies, ranging from structured techniques to process models and object orientation. He concludes that the claims are not substantiated by the empirical data—at least in the cases where data are available. Software project failures are still a recurring problem for projects of all sizes and levels of complexity, including both structured and unstructured application problems. Several process models for developing software are in use, perhaps the most widely known being the iterative version of the conventional life-cycle or waterfall model. The term *software process model* describes the sequence of activities that the developers need to undertake to produce a software product. In addition to the conventional life-cycle model and its various derivatives, there are the prototyping model, the clean-room model, the capability-maturity model, and the evolutionary model, among others. Software development in an organization will typically proceed with a variant of the process model it deems appropriate to the project based on the organization's own knowledge, past experience, and expertise regarding the use of the model in question. As Sommerville (1997, 2260) suggests, "There are currently no accepted standards for describing process models. The vast majority of models are expressed informally, using diagrams and descriptive texts." In addition, the work of the development team will be shaped by the existing organizational culture—that is, the "beliefs, commitments, styles and power relations" of the project team, as Tellioglu and Wagner (1999, 76) have found in their analysis of five software development projects.

The focus of the discussion here will be on the problems encountered in software development—regardless of the process or method used—that may be at the root of software failures, of runaways, and in extreme cases of complete abandonment. I do not intend to discuss the strengths or weaknesses of the various software process models used in software development. Interested readers may wish to review the analysis by others, such as Sommerville (1997) and Ramamoorthy et al. (1984). To the extent that software failures are not tied to any process model, my failure to discuss the software problems as they relate to the software process models does not diminish or detract from the validity of the analysis. I know of no empirical studies showing a correlation between software project and the development process model used. Perhaps future studies may be able to demonstrate a link or correlation between software failures and the type of process models used in the development. I agree with Sommerville (1997) that software systems failures are the result primarily of human errors in design, and are not a consequence of, for example, material failure.

**The Life-Cycle Model**
The widespread use of the conventional life-cycle model in organizations, which have adapted the model to fit their technology environment, is a testament to its enduring value. It will therefore be helpful to draw on the elements of this model as a basis for our discussion. When used in the various process models, none of the productivity- and quality-improvement techniques reviewed by Glass (1999) seems to have had any noticeable impact on the problem of software project failures and runaways. However, regardless of the particular process model an organization may use, four basic elements are common to the project development process. Every software project will feature: (1) the requirements-definition and functional-specification phase; (2) the design phase, during which the functional specifications are fashioned into various systems design "solution" alternatives conceptualizing how the requirements will be achieved; (3) the implementation or the coding and testing phase, in which the selected design "solution" is developed into

source code, tested, and integrated to determine if the original requirements for the system are satisfied; and (4) the installation, operation, and maintenance phase, during which the completed system is put into operation for use by the organization.

Over the years, several critiques of the conventional life-cycle sequential approach to software development have been offered. The most compelling focuses on the delay between the specification of the functional requirements and the coding, testing, systems integration, and final installation of the working system. This delay, it is argued, hides from early discovery some potential problems that may only be uncovered after much time and effort have already been expended on the development. The second major criticism is concerned with the changes brought about by the critical learning that takes place as the development proceeds from one phase to the next. This need for iteration and recursion induced by the organizational learning and validation of the previous phase also introduces additional costs and delays in an already-stretched system for software development. (See, for example, Sommerville 1997; DeGrace and Stahl 1990; Lyytinen 1987; Ramamoorthy et al. 1984; Gladden 1982.) The above criticism of the conventional life-cycle model notwithstanding, I believe the problem of software failures and runaways leading to abandonment is not limited to what methodology or technique was used to tackle the development effort. Software failures, including abandonment, have a complex parentage, and for each case of an abandoned or failed project, one can find several candidate factors to blame for the fiasco.

Software project failures, runaways, or abandonment can occur at any one of the four life-cycle stages when the expectations of any of the stakeholder groups are unrealized, creating a situation that, in some instances, compels management to terminate the project prior to its installation and operation. The failed expectations of the stakeholder group leading to project abandonment may be traced to any combination of factors. The requirements specifications spell out the expectations for the software project development to the management of the project or the stakeholder group responsible for the project's budget, and the expectation-failure concept described here refers to the failure of the software developers to satisfy the terms of the project contract they proposed based on the requirements specifications. This view of expectation failure is different from what Sauer (1993) finds objectionable in his critique of Lyytinen and Hirschheim's (1987) definition, because it is based on the expectations for the development and completion of the project reflected in the contractual terms agreed on in initiating the project. It encompasses completion failure as well as failure to meet budgetary and scheduling estimates. We will examine these abandonment factors and group them into broad categories for further analysis. This further classification will point out the common characteristics of the various factors and help to focus attention on specific problems in the development process that may be harmful to the project's outcome if left uncorrected. Furthermore, we will show the relevance of each factor to each of the three stages of project development prior to the final installation and operation of the system. However, our analysis of the factors contributing to failure will not extend to including operational failure. Interested readers, however, can consult Lucas 1975, Kumar 1990, Markus 1983, and other sources in the information systems failure literature.

## Abandonment Factors

We have seen in earlier chapters that abandonment of software development projects is caused by a multiplicity of cofactors. The studies by the Standish Group (1995, 1998), Johnson (1995), Ewusi-Mensah (1997), OASIG (1996), KPMG (Cole 1995), and Ewusi-Mensah and Przasnyski (1994, 1991) confirm that fact. The data compiled through surveys of canceled projects (mainly in the United States and United Kingdom) in the studies cited above provide the list of factors briefly described in this section. We defer detailed analysis and discussion of the factors and their relevance to the different stages of the development process of the conventional life cycle to the next section, in which we develop a framework to aid in the analysis.

### Unrealistic Project Goals and Objectives

This factor deals with the "lack of general agreement on a well-articulated set of project goals and objectives" as a major issue (Ewusi-Mensah 1997, 75). The KPMG study (Cole 1995) describes this factor as the failure to fully specify the project's objectives, and it was the most significant of the factors that study uncovered. The Standish Group lists "incomplete requirements" as the culprit with regard to this factor as well as "unrealistic expectations," presumably stemming from overly ambitious and perhaps ambiguous project objectives.

**Inappropriate Project-Team Composition**

The critical issue here is concern regarding the depth and diversity of talent from all the stakeholder groups on the team charged with the responsibility for developing the project. "A weak or problematic project team" is a concern raised by Ewusi-Mensah (1997, 75). The KPMG study lists "insufficient senior staff on the team" as an important factor, in addition to "inappropriate project staffing" (Cole 1995, 4). The roles and responsibilities of the team members are issues of major significance to the overall project outcome.

**Project Management and Control Problems**

The main concern here is the "lack of a measurement system to measure progress and identify potential risks in time to mitigate them." The lack of experienced and knowledgeable project "leadership responsible for making critical decisions at different phases of the project," as indicated by Ewusi-Mensah (1997, 75), provides an additional source of uneasiness. The KPMG study (Cole 1995, 4) also confirms this factor and describes it as "inadequate or no project management methodology," while the Standish Group simply calls it a "lack of IT management."

**Inadequate Technical Know-How**

Here the concern is with the "level of expertise and experience together with the relevant application domain knowledge" of the project team; lack of adequate expertise in quantity and quality will have a potentially fatal impact on the project (Ewusi-Mensah 1997, 75). The Standish Group (1995) lists "technology illiteracy" as being a major issue, while the KPMG study (Cole 1995, 4) expresses concern about the "poor performance by suppliers of hardware and software" as a possible contributory factor. In the KPMG study, the concern is presumably about the work of the suppliers of technology to the project, hence its inclusion here.

## Changing Requirements

This factor deals with unstable requirements and the functional specifications emanating from them. The Standish Group (1995) presumably lists this as a concern because of its potential impact on the design and other phases of the project development. Changing requirements have the tendency to increase project costs, delay schedules, and frustrate the work of the project team as continuous revisions have to be made to previously completed work. The ripple effects of changing requirements may at times cause even the project goals and objectives to be revised, especially if the original objectives were based on an incorrect and/or incomplete understanding of the software program. This development is extreme, because such revisions will likely have a drastic effect on the project's outcome. Thus changing requirements can introduce a whole new level of complexity in the design of the project, generally complicating the development process.

## Problematic Technology Base/Infrastructure

This factor speaks to the adequacy of the technology infrastructure available in the organization and whether it is satisfactory to support the project development work (Ewusi-Mensah 1997). An unsatisfactory technology base is always problematic, because the accompanying level of technological illiteracy that may exist in the organization will most likely be incompatible with a satisfactory project outcome. Alternatively, if the technology is "new to the organization," the learning curve of the project team will add another layer of uncertainty to the project's schedule and outcome (Cole 1995, 4).

## Lack of Executive Support and Commitment

The lack of active participation of corporate management in monitoring progress on the project and in making decisions at critical junctures is a major concern (Ewusi-Mensah 1997). The Standish Group (1995) also confirms this factor as a major contributor, because of the varied negative influences "lack of executive support" may have on the overall project outcome. The KPMG study (Cole 1995, 4) lists this factor as "insufficient senior staff on the team," which can be broadly interpreted to include lack of executive commitment to monitor progress on the project and to stay engaged to handle the various decisions that must be made over time.

**Insufficient User Involvement and Commitment**
The Standish Group (1995) lists this factor separately as "lack of user involvement" in the project development. The significance of this factor is well documented in the literature on software development within specific application domains or contexts, as is generally the case in organizational information systems projects (see, for example, Ewusi-Mensah 1998; Newman and Noble 1990). Inadequate and/or unsatisfactory user commitment and involvement are bound to seriously hamper the project team's ability to come up with requirements that are complete, consistent, and capable of satisfactorily meeting the expectations of the users.

**Cost Overruns and Schedule Delays**
This factor is generally symptomatic of the occurrence of any combination of the factors discussed above, because those factors have the potential to add to the cost of the project and push the delivery date further back. For example, the constant changing of requirements will cause designs to be revised each time, and this will affect all subsequent work based on the earlier designs. In most instances, this adds to the cost of the project and delays the schedule as well. Over time, the project may be faced with a critical shortage of resources, as the Standish Group (1995) revealed. The KPMG study (Cole 1995, 4) found a major contributor to this factor to be "bad planning and estimating," which renders the original cost and schedule estimates inaccurate and thus presents a false impression of project cost escalation and/or schedule delays.

The factors cited above are not intended to be exhaustive or mutually exclusive. Future studies may find other factors that should be added to the list. In addition, the colinearity of the factors conveys the essential fact that an abandoned project can result from the occurrence of any combination of factors. In the next section we examine which of the factors are critical in which stage of the systems development process. We are interested in developing a framework of abandonment factors that will aid in discussions of particularly vulnerable issues in the different phases of the systems development process.

## Framework of Abandonment Factors

This section builds on the analysis of the previous discussion to present a framework for organizing the factors that contribute to the abandonment of software projects. The framework developed here is primarily intended to focus attention on factors that are critical, either singularly or in conjunction with others, to the different phases of the project development life cycle. It affords project management, in particular, with a way of looking at decisions and activities associated with the project development and how they may impact the project's outcome. The factors are characterized in terms of their significant influence or impact on identifiable activities in the systems development process.

• *Critical* factors are those scoring 6 or 7 on a seven-point scale. These are the factors considered to be of major significance in influencing the performance and outcome of an activity.

• *Mildly critical* factors are those in the midrange—that is, 3, 4, or 5 on the above scale. These factors are judged to be of moderate significance in influencing the performance and outcome of any activity.

• *Less critical* factors are those scoring 1 or 2 on the scale. These factors are considered to be less significant but still have some influence on an activity's performance and outcome.

The classification scheme is intended to convey a general sense of the impact a factor may have on an activity in order to motivate project management and others to pay the requisite attention to it in the course of project development. Of course, depending on the specifics of the project, a particular factor's impact may vary. For example, for a well-structured problem in a moderate-sized project, the project's goals and objectives may be unambiguous and precise such that no major disagreements can be expected. Consequently, the project's goals and objectives may not be as critical as they might otherwise be in determining the system's requirements. However, as a general proposition a project's goals and objectives should be perceived as being critical to a complete, consistent, and even realistic assessment of the requirements of the project.

Previously, we have briefly described the three major phases of the systems development process. In attempting to understand the role each abandonment factor plays in each phase of this process, we have summarized in table 3.1 the general observations (or propositions) about each factor's impact on each of the three phases. Table 3.1 shows the link between the various stages of the systems development process and

**Table 3.1**
Impact of abandonment factors on software development stages

| Abandonment factors | Software development stages | | |
| --- | --- | --- | --- |
| | Requirements | Design | Implementation |
| Unrealistic project goals and objectives | Critical | Critical | Critical |
| Inappropriate project-team composition | Less critical | Critical | Mildly critical |
| Project management and control problems | Less critical | Critical | Critical |
| Inadequate technical know-how | Less critical | Critical | Critical |
| Problematic technology base/infrastructure | Less critical | Critical | Critical |
| Changing requirements | Critical | Critical | Critical |
| Lack of executive support and commitment | Critical | Mildly critical | Mildly critical |
| Insufficient user commitment and involvement | Critical | Mildly critical | Less critical |
| Cost overruns and schedule delays | Less critical | Mildly critical | Critical |

the various factors identified as contributing to decisions to abandon software projects. This table illustrates the relative significance of each factor for each stage of systems development and the extent to which each may contribute to decisions to abandon a software project.

### Impact of Each Abandonment Factor on Software Development Stages

A review of the impact of each of the abandonment factors on the three stages of software development presented in table 3.1 shows how the entire systems development effort is fraught with risks and uncertainties. Below, we discuss the significance of each factor's impact on the stages of systems development.

*Project goals and objectives* must be precise, unambiguous, and not overly ambitious in order to be able to derive complete, consistent, and realistic requirements on which the rest of the development will depend. Fred Brooks (1987, 17) suggests that "the hardest single part of building a software system is deciding precisely what to build." Laura De Young (1996, 255) comes to a similar conclusion from her consulting experience when she writes: "Most managers will tell you that it is *critical* [emphasis added] to have clear, realistic goals, and yet software projects fail everyday because of problems with goals." She describes the importance of maintaining effective goals as follows: First, reaching consensus on goals is a fundamental prerequisite to determining, without dispute, whether success has been attained. Second, when the goals change, as they often do, it becomes important to communicate the changes to all stakeholder groups. In the context of a complex project with several interacting subcomponents, it is especially difficult to keep all the interested stakeholder groups, sometimes with hidden competing agendas, focused on the same set of project goals and objectives.

The difficulty stems, in part, from attempting to specify conceptually valid functional requirements of the system that the design phase could satisfactorily work with. The burden is thus on the analysts and designers to come up with the right set of functional specifications— specifications that capture the essence of the project goals and objectives, that have "limited ambiguity," and that all the stakeholder groups consider achievable. Failure to meet this objective will have potentially disastrous consequences for both the design and the implementation phases—that is, the coding/testing and systems integration phases. Changing requirements necessitated by unclear and ambiguous goals and objectives will have to be fed back into the design phase and later into the coding/testing and systems integration phases, thus creating a ripple effect with repercussions for the other phases. Project goals and objectives are therefore judged to be particularly critical in the requirements phase of the software development process, because the requirements will in turn drive the design and the subsequent implementation of the software product.

The impact of *project-team composition* is not particularly significant in the requirements phase because determining what the system must do depends more on the project goals and objectives and less on the project team as a whole. Obviously, the team members involved in the requirements should understand the problem domain sufficiently to be able to specify what the requirements for the system ought to be. The design phase is, however, critically dependent on the team composition as alternative approaches to satisfying the functional specifications are considered and trade-off decisions are made that will still satisfy the requirements. Not having the right group of stakeholders involved in the design may lead to problems of omission, and misunderstandings not properly resolved may lead to further problems at the coding/testing stage. The work of the implementation phase—that is, the coding/testing and systems integraton stage—is a mildly critical issue to the project team; because of its technical nature only a select group of the project team members will be involved. However, those team members must be judged technically competent and capable of the tasks they are assigned; otherwise the project may still experience major problems with cost overruns and schedule delays. Technical competence on the part of the project team thus represents a significant risk factor at the design stage of the software development process and must be recognized and managed to ensure the project's successful outcome.

*Project management and control* is very important to both the design and implementation (i.e., coding/testing and systems integration) stages. The deliverables produced at each stage make it possible to assess the progress of the project against budget and schedule estimates. Whenever changes are necessitated by changing requirements, these will affect the performance and deliverables of the design and coding/testing and systems integration stages. Hence, project management and control will be constrained to monitor and limit, or otherwise control for, these changes to minimize their impact on the rest of the development. In terms of the requirements, project management and control is not seen to be overtly critical at this stage except, perhaps, in the planning of the development. It plays a very limited role in terms of determining the requirements on which the rest of the development will be based. When managing any software project, but in particular complex ones, the management and control activities will have a significant impact on the project's performance and outcome. The monitoring of the various activities at the design and implementation stages of the development process is of critical importance in identifying or spotting potential problems early so they can be satisfactorily resolved before they become major obstacles to a successful outcome.

*Technical know-how* plays an important role in the project team's ability to come up with the right design and to code and test the source program. The significance of this factor is based on the fact that without sufficient expertise and experience, the project team may be hard pressed to come up with the appropriate design and to follow through with its successful implementation. However, in terms of determining the requirements of the system, the technical know-how may not be that critical in conceptualizing the needs of the system and deciding what should be the basis for the systems design. Other factors, such as the involvement of end users, may be far more crucial to the requirements phase than the technical expertise of the team members. Lack of expertise has been identified in risk-assessment studies as a major risk factor contributing to software project performance and outcome problems (see, for example, Barki, Rivard, and Talbot 1993, 2001; Boehm 1991; Ropponen and Lyytinen 2000). The project team will largely be responsible for translating the requirements specifications into an appropriate design solution and subsequent implementation. Their expertise is such a major risk factor because concretizing the abstractions embodied in the requirements document is fraught with potential pitfalls—from misunderstanding of the requirements to outright failure to solve the design puzzle and its subsequent implementation.

*Changing requirements* exert the same pervasive influence as project goals and objectives on the three phases of the systems development process. Changing requirements play a significant role in determining the final set of requirements on which the functional specifications as well as the design and coding/testing and systems integration phases of the development will essentially depend. Thus failure to control for the changes in the requirements is bound to have a deleterious effect on the other phases of the development and will significantly contribute to budget overruns and schedule delays as the design and coding/testing and systems integration activities are continually revised to reflect the new changes in the requirements. The enormous impact of this factor is attributable to the role it plays in shaping the final requirements document, which in turn drives the final design and implementation decisions. Changes in requirements can have untold consequences for the project's outcome, especially if the starting premise of the project's goals and objectives was open to varied interpretations among the stakeholder groups. Even in cases where no such disagreements exist regarding the project's goals and objectives, changes in requirements brought about by changes in technology or the like can have a significant impact on design and implementation. The further along in the development process the changes occur, the greater their impact will be on the project's final outcome and the more costly they are likely to be, both financially and in terms of schedule delays. The risks posed by this factor to project outcome have been well documented in the risk-assessment literature (Barki, Rivard, and Talbot 1993, 2001; Ropponen and Lyytinen 2000; Boehm 1991).

The influence of the *technology base/infrastructure* on the requirements phase is not so significant because it does not shape what the needs of the organization should be. However, like the technical know-how, the technology base is crucial in determining how the requirements needs of the organization will be achieved through the activities of the design and coding/testing and systems integration phases. Thus, if the technology base is judged inadequate to the design and coding/testing and systems integration activities, major problems will ensue that can spell disaster for the project. This factor is intrinsically linked with the technical know-how of the project team; any technically competent project team should first and foremost be able to assess the adequacy of the available technology infrastructure to tackle the project. Failure to solve this problem prior to the start of the project may derail the project. At the design and implementation phases of the software development process, the project's outcome is significantly influenced by the adequacy of the technology base and the competence of the technical team responsible for addressing the design and implementation challenges posed by the requirements.

The *commitment and support exhibited by senior management* are of particular importance, especially in the early stages of development as requirements decisions are being discussed. The influence of senior management in shaping the direction and focus of decisions on the needs of the organization bodes well for the rest of the project. For example, executive commitment and support are critical in helping to set and clarify project goals and objectives that will subsequently influence what the requirements of the system should be. The continued commitment and support of senior management, though still important in the design and coding/testing and systems integration phases, is not as crucial as it was previously. The major contribution of this factor to the design and coding/testing and systems integration phases is to make the rest of the project team aware of the continued interest of senior management in the project's outcome and, by extension, in the project's significance to the organization. Thus the engagement of senior management throughout the life of the project will yield important advantages for the project team and the organization, as the former works to realize the latter's technology vision embodied in the software product's requirements.

The influence of the *user commitment and involvement* factor is strongest in the early phase of the development and then decreases as the development moves from the requirements phase through design to coding/testing and systems integration. As the level of technical expertise required becomes pronounced, the level of user' commitment and involvement becomes less of a factor in the deliverables of those stages.

Consequently, user commitment and involvement are critically important in helping to determine what the requirements of the system should be. End users' active involvement in the requirements phase is crucial for providing the software developers with the requisite information to enable the analysis and design to reflect fully the needs and circumstances of the user community. This level of user involvement reflects the general view in software development that the developer is often not sufficiently informed about the "situations and circumstances" under which the user groups carry out the activities for which the software is being designed.

This view is reflected in the tenets of human-centered design of computer systems. Denning and Dargan (1996, 111), for example, argue that "understanding the domain of work or play in which people are engaged and in which they interact with computers, and programming computers to facilitate human action" are essential for project success. The three premises on which project success depends, they suggest, are as follows: first, the design must satisfy user needs; second, there must be collaboration between users and designers at all times during the development; third, there must be constant communication between the designers and users to ensure prompt resolution of conflicts and misunderstandings. Thus the overall role of the end users is vitally critical for the successful development of any software project. Still, we make the distinction between the level of user involvement and the significance of their contribution to the project development process as essential in helping to frame the discussion on how crucial their role may or may not be to each phase of the software development process.

At the design stage of the software development process, the influence of end users is mildly crucial as alternative design solutions to satisfy the requirements are discussed. The core issue at the design stage of the development becomes one of determining the technical feasibility of the functional specifications decided on at the requirements phase. The role of the end users is therefore mildly critical at this stage, because their involvement may perhaps best be characterized as that of providing clarifications of some as-yet-unresolved design problems stemming from, for example, incomplete requirements. Finally, at the implementation stage, the end users are even less influential because when the coding/testing and systems integration phase is tackled, their role will be more limited to determining if the tests satisfy the functional specifications of the requirements of the varied "situations and circumstances" that the software is intended to satisfy. We do not seek to diminish the users' role in providing critical feedback to the project team during the testing and integration phase of the emerging software product. This role is critical to determining if the product faithfully captures the functional specifications of the requirements, but as the project progresses through the latter stages of the development process, the role the users play as part of the development team diminishes.

It is a canon of the literature on software failures, runaways, and abandonment that the projects concerned often have *cost overruns and schedule delays*. However, budget overruns and schedule delays may only be symptomatic of more fundamental problems in other areas of the project development process. By definition, cost overruns and schedule delays play an essentially minimal role, if any, in determining what the requirements of the system should be. However, the role of cost and schedule overruns becomes important in the design and coding/testing and systems integration phases. This is because the product deliverables at these stages can be measured against estimated costs and schedules, and any cost or schedule problems might raise alarm bells with project management as well as with senior management with regard to the project's progress. Abandonment of the project may be an option if the problems persist and no remedy is found.

The framework discussed above demonstrates the multiplicity of cofactors at the core of software failures, runaways, and indeed of abandonment. The evidence suggests that abandonment of software projects can occur at any of the three stages of the software development process if a multiplicity of cofactors exists that can create a powerful synergistic effect capable of derailing the project, especially if no equally powerful counteractive force is found to mitigate this effect. In the next section we discuss the link between the abandonment factors and their collective impact on the various phases of the software development process.

## Software Development Phases and Critical Abandonment Factors

In this section we group together the factors considered critical to each phase of the development process to highlight their collective impact on that phase of the software development. Table 3.2 provides a summary of the critical abandonment factors associated with each systems development phase. At the *requirements stage* the multiplicity of cofactors is predominantly nontechnical and is instead socioorganizational. The abandonment factors listed as critical to requirements include unrealistic project goals and objectives, changing requirements, lack of executive support and commitment, and insufficient user commitment and involvement. The rest of the abandonment factors have a less significant influence in abandonment decisions at the requirements stage.

The *design stage* presents a mixture of technical/technological and socioorganizational factors the multiple occurrence of which can derail the project. The factors that wield critical influence in this context are

**Table 3.2**
Software development stage and critical abandonment factors

| Software | Critical abandonment factors |
| --- | --- |
| Requirements | • Unrealistic project goals and objectives<br>• Changing requirements<br>• Lack of executive support and commitment<br>• Insufficient user commitment and involvement |
| Design | • Unrealistic project goals and objectives<br>• Inappropriate project-team composition<br>• Project management and control problems<br>• Inadequate technical know-how<br>• Problematic technology base/infrastructure<br>• Changing requirements |
| Implementation | • Unrealistic project goals and objectives<br>• Project management and control problems<br>• Inadequate technical know-how<br>• Problematic technology base/infrastructure<br>• Changing requirements<br>• Cost overruns and schedule delays |

unrealistic project goals and objectives, inappropriate project-team composition, project management and control problems, inadequate technical know-how, problematic technology base/infrastructure, and changing requirements. Nontechnical factors such as lack of executive support and commitment, insufficient user commitment and involvement, and cost overruns and schedule delays are moderately influential in determining the project's outcome. The design stage is perhaps the most vulnerable stage in the development process because of the number of cofactors of a technical and socioorganizational nature that exercise a dominant influence in abandonment decisions. This is to be expected, because the design phase is where the most challenging work of the entire software development process takes place. The project team attempts to create a product from the requirements specifications. Two-thirds of all the factors are considered critical to abandoned projects. The remaining one-third of the abandonment factors are regarded as mildly critical to the success of the design stage. No other phase in the development process exercises such a vital impact on the software project's outcome as the design phase does.

The *implementation* or coding/testing and systems integration stage also exhibits a mixture of technical/technological, socioorganizational, and economic factors whose occurrence can create major problems for the project, perhaps even causing the project to be abandoned. The main factors of crucial influence at this stage are unrealistic project goals and objectives, project management and control problems, inadequate technical know-how, problematic technology base/infrastructure, changing requirements, and cost overruns and schedule delays. Nontechnical factors such as inappropriate project-team composition, lack of executive support and commitment, and insufficient user commitment and involvement play less critical roles in decisions to abandon projects at this stage. Next to the design stage, the implementation or coding/testing and systems integration stage is the second most vulnerable stage of the development process life cycle.

Further analysis of the factors contributing to abandoned projects, however, shows that these factors can also be appropriately grouped into three main categories—socioorganizational, sociotechnical, and economic. Table 3.3 provides a summary of the factor groupings into the

**Table 3.3**
Dominant factors in abandonment-factor categories

| Abandonment-factor category | Dominant factors |
| --- | --- |
| Socioorganizational | • Unrealistic project goals and objectives<br>• Changing requirements<br>• Lack of executive support and commitment<br>• Insufficient user commitment and involvement |
| Sociotechnical | • Unrealistic project goals and objectives<br>• Inappropriate project-team composition<br>• Project management and control problems<br>• Inadequate technical know-how<br>• Problematic technology base/infrastructure<br>• Changing requirements |
| Economic | • Cost overruns and schedule delays<br>• Unrealistic project goals and objectives<br>• Changing requirements |

three categories. Software development is a social activity undertaken in an organizational context where three groups of stakeholders—management, end users, and systems developers—are required to work together to create the software artifact to meet organizational needs. Software development can therefore be characterized as having a socioorganizational dimension, where the organizational component describes or deals with the set of organizational interests the artifact must serve, and the social component encompasses the interactions among the stakeholders working on the project. On another dimension, software development can also be characterized as being sociotechnical. The technical/technological component is mainly concerned with addressing the technical requirements of the software as specified in the requirements document. However, failure of the technical developers to pay sufficient attention to the concerns or needs of the underlying social system in the course of the project development may expose the project to unacceptable risks, which can contribute to its failure. As noted in chapter 1, this is the central argument of the postmodernist approach to software development, which attributes the persistence of the software crises partly, if not wholly, to the failure of the modernist approach, with its preoccupation with seeking purely technical "solutions." The economic dimension of the software development activity derives from the expenditure of resources needed to create the software artifact. The risks of project failure can be associated with any of the factor groups or combinations of them. The classification is based on the contribution each factor in the group is expected to make to each category. For example, in the economic category the factors include cost overruns and schedule delays, unrealistic project goals and objectives, and changing requirements. The contribution of cost overruns and schedule delays to this group is apparent. Not so obvious is the contribution of unrealistic project goals and objectives, or of changing requirements. Overly ambitious as well as imprecise and ambiguous project goals and objectives will affect this category by contributing not insignificantly to the cost and time frame of the project. Changing requirements have the potential to also increase project costs and delay the schedule if the frequency and complexity of the changes are not properly managed and controlled. All the abandonment factors have some bearing on the economic category in the sense that each has the capacity to influence the project cost and schedule. Nonetheless, this discussion focuses only on explicit economic factors to the exclusion of all others in the analysis. Similar explanations can be advanced for the remaining two categories—socioorganizational and sociotechnical—and the dominant factors that comprise each.

A review of tables 3.2 and 3.3 reveals some commonalities between the factor groupings of the two tables that show how the factor categories impact each stage of the development process. The factors that constitute the socioorganizational category in table 3.3 are the same factors considered critical to the requirements stage of the development process in table 3.2. Half of the socioorganizational factors also appear in the factor grouping critical to the design activity. The socioorganizational-factor group can therefore be classified as mildly critical to the design phase of the development process. Similarly, the implementation phase of the development is also mildly critically impacted by the socioorganizational category. The sociotechnical-factor category appears to be mildly critical to the requirements because half of the dominant factors in the requirements phase also appear in the sociotechnical-factor

**Table 3.4**
Software development stage by abandonment-factor category

| Development stage | Abandonment-factor category | | |
|---|---|---|---|
| | Socioorganizational | Sociotechnical | Economic |
| Requirements | Critical | Mildly critical | Mildly critical |
| Design | Mildly critical | Critical | Mildly critical |
| Implementation or coding/testing | Mildly critical | Critical | Mildly critical |

category. However, the sociotechnical-factor category is considered critical to the design and implementation phases because the majority of the factors dominant in each of those two phases are also dominant in the sociotechnical-factor category. Finally, the economic-factor category is considered mildly critical to the requirements phase because even though two of the three dominant factors in the economic category are also dominant in the requirements phase, the most significant factor in the economic group—cost overruns and schedule delays (which directly measures resource expenditures)—is not part of the requirements category. However, the same two dominant factors in the economic-factor category also appear as part of the factors making up the dominant factor groups in the design and implementation phases of the systems development process. Hence the economic-factor group is considered mildly critical to the design and implementation stages of the development process. In table 3.4 we summarize the abandonment-factor categories and their influence on any of the three stages of the software development process.

**Conclusion**

We have analyzed the factors in software development identified by researchers as contributing to the abandonment of software projects, which can occur at any stage of the software development process. We have discussed the impact each of the factors has on the three major phases—requirements, design, and implementation—of the software development process. The factors are classified into three major categories, namely, socioorganizational, sociotechnical, and economic, based on the dominant or critical influence the majority of the factors in each category have on the software development process. We have constructed a framework of the abandonment factors to draw attention to the significance of their collective impact on the requirements, design, and implementation phases of the software development process. We have also pointed out the important role nontechnical factors—in particular, organizational and managerial factors, including economic issues—play in decisions to abandon problematic software development projects.

In the next three chapters we examine the details of the factors in each abandonment category and how they contribute to the decisions to abandon the projects. In chapter 4 we explore the contributions socioorganizational factors make to project abandonment. This is followed, in chapter 5, by a discussion of the details of the sociotechnical factors' role in project abandonment. Finally, chapter 6 completes our survey by focusing attention on the details of the economic factors in the project-abandonment decisions. In each of the categories, we use examples of abandoned projects in both the public and private sectors to analyze and illustrate the role played by the factors in the decisions made to cancel the project in question.

# II

## Empirical Factors

# 4

# Socioorganizational Factors and Abandoned Projects

Software development is a social activity that takes place in complex organizational environments with various interacting social entities making up the project teams. Coordination of the work of the different teams as well as communication both within each team and among the different teams is extremely important to ensure the success of the development process. There are two dimensions to the organizational environment in which the work of the project teams takes place. The first dimension is social and deals with the social interactions among the various organizational entities engaged in the development. The second dimension is organizational and deals with the responsibilities and authority of the organizational structure, in particular the management hierarchy involved in the project. The organizational issues, including behavioral and political authority and the influence of management, all come into focus in shaping the project goals and objectives and in guiding the project to successful completion. Hence almost all the influences of a nontechnical nature that are critical in helping determine the project outcome can be subsumed under the socioorganizational-factor category.

In this chapter we will examine the socioorganizational factors that contribute to abandoned projects, emphasizing the critical influence of this factor category on decisions to abandon development projects. The discussion will proceed on two levels. On the first level I will show the mutual influence of the organizational and social dimensions of the systems development effort with empirical data adapted from earlier studies of abandoned projects by Ewusi-Mensah and Przasnyski (1994, 1991). On the second level, analysis of the influence of both the social and organizational issues will be based on a qualitative analysis of reported cases of abandoned projects in the public domain. I will examine abandoned projects from both public and private organizations. There are, however, no significant differences between the projects that end up being abandoned in public versus private organizations. In general, abandoned software projects share basic characteristics irrespective of their organizational origins.

## Empirical Analysis of Abandoned Projects

In two studies of abandoned projects, Zbigniew Przasnyski and I examined the role played by social and organizational issues in decisions to abandon software development projects (see Ewusi-Mensah and Przasnyski 1991, 1994). In this analysis I will discuss software projects within the context of an organizational environment in which the information needs of the organization are expected to be satisfied through the successful implementation of the software. Such software is conventionally referred to as information systems (IS)—that is, software systems designed specifically to address some organizational information requirements for operational and decision-making purposes. In the first study (1991, 83), we found that "all types of IS projects are susceptible to being abandoned—not necessarily just high risk, complex or unstructured ones. The major characteristics of the practice are rooted in organizational behavioral/political issues and, to a lesser extent, in economic and technical issues." This study was followed by the second study (1994) of Fortune 500 companies in the United States. This later study attempted to measure how each of the identified factors—organizational, technical, and economic—contributes to project abandonment. The results discussed in this section are broadly adapted from the Fortune 500 study, which had a larger sample size than the 1991 study and also had the data factor analyzed. Interested readers should refer to the two studies for details of the research protocols and other relevant issues.

## Profile of Abandoned Projects

This analysis is derived from the Fortune 500 study (Ewusi-Mensah and Przasnyski 1994). The study questionnaire required the respondent to provide detailed information relating to one typical abandoned project (even if the organization may have experienced more than one abandoned project). Table 4.1 provides a summary of the number of software projects abandoned. Less than a third of the respondents had not experienced any abandoned projects, and about another third indicated that five or more projects were abandoned in the period under investigation, namely, 1982–1986. Table 4.2 describes the type of abandonment experienced, with about two-thirds of the organizations experiencing total abandonment (not including the missing responses). The life-cycle stage during which the project was abandoned is given in table 4.3, and tables 4.4 and 4.5 provide a summary of the abandoned-project expenditures and durations respectively.

**Table 4.1**
Number of projects abandoned (1982–1986)

| Number of projects abandoned | Number of responses | Percentage |
| --- | --- | --- |
| 0 | 24 | 30.8 |
| 1 | 8 | 10.3 |
| 2 | 7 | 9.0 |
| 3 | 10 | 12.8 |
| 4 | 3 | 3.8 |
| 5 | 9 | 11.5 |
| >5 | 17 | 21.8 |
| Missing | 4 | |

*Source*: Ewusi-Mensah and Przasnyski 1994; adapted with permission

**Table 4.2**
Type of project abandonment

| Abandonment type | Number of responses | Percentage |
| --- | --- | --- |
| Total abandonment | 34 | 63.0 |
| Substantial abandonment | 13 | 24.1 |
| Partial abandonment | 7 | 13.0 |
| Missing | 28 | |

*Source*: Ewusi-Mensah and Przasnyski 1994; adapted with permission

**Table 4.3**
Stages of project abandonment

| Life-cycle stage | Number of responses | Percentage |
|---|---|---|
| Planning | 5 | 10.0 |
| Analysis | 11 | 22.0 |
| Design | 19 | 38.0 |
| Coding/testing | 15 | 30.0 |
| Missing | 32 | |

*Source*: Ewusi-Mensah and Przasnyski 1994; adapted with permission

**Table 4.4**
Estimated total project budget

| Dollars (in millions) | Number of responses | Percentage |
|---|---|---|
| <=$2 | 38 | 71.7 |
| $2–$4 | 8 | 15.1 |
| $4–$6 | 3 | 5.7 |
| $10–$15 | 2 | 3.8 |
| $15–$20 | 1 | 1.9 |
| $20–$30 | 1 | 1.9 |
| Missing | 29 | |

*Source*: Ewusi-Mensah and Przasnyski 1994; adapted with permission

**Table 4.5**
Estimated total project duration

| Duration | Number of responses | Percentage |
|---|---|---|
| 1–6 months | 16 | 29.6 |
| 7–12 months | 7 | 13.0 |
| 13–18 months | 8 | 14.8 |
| 19–24 months | 5 | 9.3 |
| 25–30 months | 2 | 3.7 |
| 31–36 months | 8 | 14.8 |
| >3 years | 8 | 14.8 |
| Missing | 28 | |

*Source*: Ewusi-Mensah and Przasnyski 1994; adapted with permission

As shown in table 4.3, more than two-thirds of the projects were abandoned at the design and coding/testing stages of the development process. The design stage exhibited the most instances of abandonment (almost two-fifths), showing how critical this stage is to the successful outcome of a project. The least vulnerable stage in the development process is the planning stage, followed by the analysis stage. Projects abandoned at the design and coding/testing stages of development invariably incur heavy expenditures of resources. The costs tend to be higher because of all the time and effort already expended before the decision to terminate the project is finally made, a decision presumably reached because insufficient progress is being made to satisfy the management stakeholder group's expectations. Table 4.4 illustrates the costs incurred for the various abandoned projects; more than 70 percent of the projects incurred less than $2 million in project costs. The remaining 30 percent of the projects incurred costs ranging from $2–$4 million (i.e., 8%) to as much as $20–$30 million (i.e., about 2%). Table 4.5 depicts the estimated project duration; less than a third of the projects lasted a maximum of six months, and another 30 percent or so lasted from a minimum of thirty-one months to more than three years.

The total number of IS and user personnel involved in the projects is given in table 4.6, where the number of people involved in the projects—both IS personnel and end users—ranged from about one to five for 50 percent of the respondents. More than a quarter of the respondents indicated six to ten IS personnel were involved in the abandoned projects versus just over 16 percent of end users. At the other end of the scale, less than 8 percent of the respondents indicated that at the time of abandonment more than twenty-five IS personnel were engaged in the project. The corresponding number of end users who reported working on abandoned projects was just under 15 percent, or twice the number reported for IS personnel. Table 4.7 shows the total number of departments involved, with the incidence of abandonment increasing when two or more departments are involved in the project. Ewusi-Mensah and Przasnyski (1991, 74) noted this trend and suggested that perhaps the increase in the incidence of abandonment may be attributed to the "extra problems in communication," coordination, and management "produced by increasing the number of departmental stakeholders."

**Table 4.6**
Project participants

| Number of people | IS personnel | | End user | |
|---|---|---|---|---|
| | No. of responses | Percentage | No. of responses | Percentage |
| 0 | 0 | 0.0 | 1 | 1.9 |
| 1–5 | 26 | 48.1 | 29 | 53.7 |
| 6–10 | 15 | 27.8 | 9 | 16.7 |
| 11–15 | 4 | 7.4 | 5 | 9.3 |
| 16–20 | 3 | 5.6 | 2 | 3.7 |
| 21–25 | 2 | 3.7 | 0 | 0.0 |
| >25 | 4 | 7.4 | 8 | 14.8 |
| Missing | 28 | | 28 | |

*Source*: Ewusi-Mensah and Przasnyski 1994; adapted with permission

**Table 4.7**
Project departments

| Number of departments | Number of responses | Percentage |
|---|---|---|
| 1 | 5 | 9.3 |
| 2 | 13 | 24.1 |
| 3 | 11 | 20.4 |
| >3 | 25 | 46.3 |
| Missing | 28 | |

*Source*: Ewusi-Mensah and Przasnyski 1994; adapted with permission

Table 4.8 shows the number of project managers working on abandoned projects, with over 50 percent reporting two managers, presumably with each manager in charge of a distinct part of the project.

Finally, table 4.9 gives a classification of the abandoned projects based on the type of decision or task the project was intended to accomplish. It also utilizes the perceptions of senior management with respect to the risks/complexity and benefits the project was anticipated to experience, as well as their perceptions of the strategic significance of the project to the organization. The table indicates that about two-fifths of the projects were considered to be of strategic value to the organization; they were urgently needed (60%) and were also considered to be highly beneficial

**Table 4.8**
Project managers

| Number of managers | Number of responses | Percentage |
|---|---|---|
| 1 | 25 | 45.5 |
| 2 | 30 | 54.5 |
| Missing | 27 | |

*Source*: Ewusi-Mensah and Przasnyski 1994; adapted with permission

**Table 4.9**
Abandoned-project classification

| Type of decision or task | Transaction processing | | Operational control | | Tactical control | | Strategic planning | |
|---|---|---|---|---|---|---|---|---|
| | No. | % | No. | % | No. | % | No. | % |
| Structured | 32 | 59.3 | 39 | 72.2 | 14 | 25.9 | 6 | 11.1 |
| Unstructured | 2 | 3.7 | 9 | 16.7 | 12 | 22.2 | 12 | 22.2 |
| Missing | 28 | | 28 | | 28 | | 28 | |

Senior management perception of project at its start

| | High | | Medium | | Low | |
|---|---|---|---|---|---|---|
| | No. | % | No. | % | No. | % |
| Risk | 8 | 14.5 | 24 | 43.6 | 23 | 41.8 |
| Complexity | 16 | 29.1 | 27 | 49.1 | 12 | 21.8 |
| Benefit | 35 | 63.6 | 17 | 30.9 | 3 | 5.5 |
| Missing | 27 | | 27 | | 27 | |

Senior management perception of project at its start

| | Number of responses | Percentage |
|---|---|---|
| Strategic | 23 | 41.8 |
| Nonstrategic | 32 | 58.2 |
| Urgent | 33 | 60.0 |
| Nonurgent | 22 | 40.0 |
| Missing | 27 | |

*Source*: Ewusi-Mensah and Przasnyski 1994; adapted with permission

(64%) to the organization. Less than two-fifths of the projects were considered moderately to highly risky, and less than four-fifths were perceived to be moderately to highly complex. The majority of the projects were of a structured or programmable type, dealing with operational control (more than 70%) and transaction processing (about 60%). Only about a tenth to a quarter of the respondents indicated that their projects were of a tactical control or strategic planning nature. However, more projects of the unstructured, less programmable, and more complex variety were reported to be of a tactical control and strategic planning nature. Thus it can be deduced that the projects reported abandoned by the responding organizations covered the entire spectrum of the variety of tasks or decisions the software systems were expected to support in those organizations.

**Organizational Issues in Abandoned Projects**    The data from the Fortune 500 study (Ewusi-Mensah and Przasnyski 1994) were factor analyzed for evidence of organizational, technical, and economic factors plus any hidden underlying interactions among them. Factor analysis is a statistical procedure used to determine the existence of structure in a large array of responses or measured variables typically obtained through a survey instrument. The factor analysis creates a minimum number of new variables that are linear combinations of the original variables obtained from the information given by the respondents. The new variables contain most, if not all, of the information in the original variables, with each new variable showing the contribution of the factors made by each of the original variables. By using this technique, one is able to show the total variability of the responses in terms of the new variables or factors (Reyment and Jöreskog 1993). The details of the factor-analysis data are discussed in Ewusi-Mensah and Przasnyski 1994. In this chapter I will limit the discussion of the factor-analysis results to social and organizational issues pertaining to decisions to abandon the project. Issues dealing with technical and economic factors are deferred to chapters 5 and 6, respectively.

Table 4.10 provides a summary of all twelve factors that emerged from the analysis; six of these factors can be grouped into a class representing socioorganizational issues based on a review of the data, as shown

**Table 4.10**
Summary of twelve abandonment factors

| Factor no. | Factor description |
| --- | --- |
| F1 | Escalating project costs and completion schedules |
| F2 | Lack of appropriate technical infrastructure and expertise |
| F3 | Actual project expenditures and duration below estimates |
| F4 | Technological shortcomings |
| F5 | Loss of critical personnel and management changes |
| F6 | End-user acquiescence |
| F7 | Management commitment and perceptions |
| F8 | End-user conflicts and technical disagreements |
| F9 | Satisfy existing or emergent technology |
| F10 | Lack of funds |
| F11 | End-user participation discouraged |
| F12 | Consequence of merger/acquisition by another company |

*Source*: Ewusi-Mensah and Przasnyski 1994; adapted with permission

**Table 4.11**
Socioorganizational factors (extracted from table 4.10)

| Factor no. | Factor description |
| --- | --- |
| F5 | Loss of critical personnel and management changes |
| F7 | Management commitment and perceptions |
| F12 | Consequence of merger/acquisition by another company |
| F6 | End-user acquiescence |
| F8 | End-user conflicts and technical disagreements |
| F11 | End-user participation discouraged |

in table 4.11. These six socioorganizational factors can be placed in two categories representing senior management and organizational matters, and end-user-related issues. The first category deals with management commitment, perceptions, changes, and personnel-related issues in connection with the development process—that is, factors F5 and F7. The third factor in this group, F12, pertains to organizationwide matters such as merger/acquisition and its effect on an ongoing project in the merged or acquired organization. In factor F5 the issue was described as "loss of critical personnel and management changes." Indeed, as was pointed out in the study by Ewusi-Mensah and Przasnyski (1994, 194) "Loss of personnel and management changes are experiences that all IS [i.e., software] development projects deal with in varying degrees." The explanation given was that "once a project loses the support of key management there is a high likelihood that, *ceteris paribus*, the project may eventually be abandoned." This is because the "loss of key management supportive of the project may be associated with the loss of adequate funding and/or loss of interest on the part of top management to even continue with the project."

A corollary to this factor (i.e., F5) was provided by factor F7—that is, "management commitment and perceptions" with respect to the project. Here also, the obvious explanation is that once there is "a lack of commitment on the part of senior management to provide resources for the project and/or senior management do not perceive the project as important to the organization, then there is a high likelihood that the project may not be successfully completed." The argument one can make is that the loss of senior management support or commitment typically means that "the project is not viewed favorably," thus making it more difficult to obtain the requisite resources to continue with it, which may ultimately sabotage progress on the project (Ewusi-Mensah and Przasnyski 1994, 195).

The third factor in this first group, factor F12, was the "consequence of merger/acquisition by another company." The explanation offered for this factor is that whenever a company is acquired by or merged with another company, a review of current projects is usually initiated, which may result in the cancellation of projects not deemed favorable in the strategic plans of the new organizational setup. This factor is therefore reflective of management practices in organizations in general. The results of the above analysis are confirmed by other observers who describe senior management commitment as being one of the requisite factors essential to project development success. (See, for example, Standish Group, 1995; Johnson 1995; Cole 1995.)

End-user-related issues dealt with the involvement and participation of this stakeholder group in the development process. Factors F6, F8, and F11 speak directly to these issues. Factor F6, termed "end-user acquiescence," was interpreted to mean that the development team should not take for granted the participation of end users. Failure to actively seek end user participation in the development process may cause the team to forfeit any chance of resolving potential conflicts and disagreements with the users, which may contribute to abandonment. Factor F8—that is, "end-user conflicts and technical disagreements"— provided a confirmation of factor F6 because it demonstrated the need for both senior management and software personnel to act speedily to resolve any conflicts, including technical disagreements, associated with the project and thus forestall the chance that those conflicts and/or disagreements could play a role in the eventual termination of the project (Ewusi-Mensah and Przasnyski 1994, 194 and 195). Finally, factor F11—that is, "discouraged end-user participation"—confirmed the validity of the earlier explanation that "if end-user participation is discouraged, then the basis for conflict resolution and other end-user-related issues on the project may cease to exist" (Ewusi-Mensah and Przasnyski 1994, 196). That is, if end users are discouraged from participating in the systems development effort, then it may be difficult to resolve potential problems and/or conflicts associated with user requirements and systems feasibility, among other issues. Any significant lack of cooperation between the two stakeholder groups may in the end contribute to the failure of the project. Again on this issue, numerous studies have confirmed end-user participation as a prerequisite to successful systems development efforts. The form this participation takes may, of course, vary depending on the project and organizational context. Still, it is important that end users be considered full members of the development team because of the knowledge and other insights—both as potential users of the future software and as users of the current system—that they bring to the development process. In chapter 7 I report on a case study of a failed project—CODIS—from the perspective of the end users and on the role they played in the project's development. In general, the social and organizational issues at the core of systems development efforts are embodied in the significant roles that the two stakeholder groups of end users and senior management are expected to play to ensure the success of the project. Their active participation and commitment to the development process is an accepted fact of good software development practice.

We now turn to specific cases of abandoned projects reported in the public domain. We will examine each of the cases in light of the framework for abandoned software projects developed in chapter 3. To the extent possible based on the available data, we will try to ascertain which of the factors identified in the framework as critical to abandonment occurred and at what stage(s) of the development life cycle this happened.

**Analysis of Abandoned-Project Cases: Socioorganizational Issues**

Chapter 3 presented a framework for analyzing cases of abandoned software projects. The following factors were identified as being dominant in cases of abandoned projects dealing with socioorganizational issues:

- Unrealistic project goals and objectives
- Changing requirements
- Lack of executive support and commitment
- Insufficient user commitment and involvement

These factors were shown to be particularly critical at the requirements stage of the development process, and mildly critical at the design and implementation stages. (See table 3.4.)

In this section I will use five reported cases of software projects that were either totally or substantially abandoned as a basis for discussing the socioorganizational factors critical to abandoned projects. The five cases—Confirm, Delta, TSM, DIA's BHS, and CODIS—reflect both public and private organizations. The cases represent projects from a consortium of four commercial organizations, a drug distribution company, a large public organization of the U.S. government, a public/private endeavor, and a medium-sized private commercial organization, respectively. The cases are illustrative of the incidence of abandoned projects reported in the public domain. For example, multiple secondary sources of data exist in the public domain dealing with the Confirm, Delta, TSM, and DIA's BHS projects, and the data for the fifth project, CODIS, are based on studies undertaken in the private organization. The examples were selected because each represents a case of abandonment or failure from which one can draw valuable inferences;

in addition, they share many of the same characteristics. The projects discussed here are drawn from published reports. Although the reports may appear dated, they provide useful insights into the pitfalls of software development. Software developers, project managers, and other stakeholder groups, including senior management and end users, can utilize these insights to improve the practice of software development in organizations.

In the case of public organizations, it is important to recognize how bureaucracy can constrain decisions that affect the entire software development process—the selection of which projects to fund, the composition of the project team, the selection of the project management, and the selection of contract consultants to work on the project. At times even the schedule for completing the project may be dictated by factors outside the control of the development team, as occurred in the Denver Airport Baggage Handling case.

The cases selected also reveal the increasing impact that IT projects have on the operations of various types of organizations. The failure of some projects can have significant negative effects on the organizations themselves. Cases of IT project failures now appear regularly in the popular press, confirming the increasingly critical role software systems play in the operations of both public- and private-sector organizations. Moreover, most of the cases analyzed here are not representative of traditional or routine IT projects but rather are highly sophisticated, complex innovations intended to provide strategic advantage to the host organizations. For example, Delta, DIA's BHS, Confirm, and TSM are all based on innovative client-server architecture and were intended to satisfy the needs of diverse and geographically dispersed end-user communities in the various organizations. Thus, though the various cases may seem old given the rapid pace of current IT developments, the facts and lessons they reveal transcend the time frames noted and so are widely applicable to current IT projects tackled in organizations. The cases seem representative of the variety of IT project failures that occur regularly in organizations—whether the failures are of cost overruns, schedule delays, reduction of functionalities, or even outright cancellations. In short, the cases provide us with the requisite data to validate the empirical results obtained on the incidence of software project failures in organizations. I give a brief synopsis of each project and then go on to use the socioorganizational factors to illustrate why I suspect the projects became abandoned. The projects are:

*Confirm Project*   In 1988, a consortium (Intrico) of three major corporations—Hilton Hotels Corporation, Marriott Corporation, and Budget Rent-A-Car Corporation—teamed up with American Airlines Information Services, Inc. (AMRIS) to develop and market what was intended to be "the most advanced reservation system in the combined industry of travel, lodging, and car rental."(Oz 1994, 30) AMRIS is an outsourcing subsidiary of American Airlines Corporation whose parent company, AMR, developed the SABRE reservation system. AMR entered into agreement with the three partners to develop Confirm. Five years later, after a number of lawsuits and countersuits and millions of dollars in cost overruns and schedule delays, the project, named Confirm, was finally canceled amid acrimonious and bitter accusations from some of the top executives involved (for detailed discussions see, for example, Halper 1992a, 1992b, 1992c; McPartlin 1992, 1994; Oz 1994; Zellner 1994). The lawsuits were finally settled out of court by the parties.

*FoxMeyer's Delta Project*   The Delta Information System was a distribution system for the drug wholesaler FoxMeyer Drug Company, which was intended to replace the company's aging mainframe system and enable it to leapfrog ahead of its competitors. The Delta project was a client-server system implemented on SAP software together with a warehouse system from McHugh Software International. The project, begun in February 1994 by Andersen Consulting at an estimated cost of about $18 million, was expected to be completed in eighteen months. Two and a half years after the project initiation, the company was forced to file for Chapter 11 protection from its creditors because of delays, cost overruns, and a host of implementation-related problems associated with the project (Bulkeley 1996; Jesitus 1997; LJX FILES, 1998). Despite this, the project was not abandoned, and major problems associated with it became a significant contributor to the demise of FoxMeyer Drug (LJX FILES, 1998). The case is included here to show that in some extreme situations, significant problems associated with a project may have disastrous consequences for the organization.

*TSM Systems* Tax Systems Modernization (TSM) was a U.S. government project begun in 1986 by the Internal Revenue Service (IRS). The project was estimated at the time to cost between $8 and $10 billion to develop and was scheduled for completion in 2001. In all, TSM was to consist of thirty-six systems development projects. By late 1996, a decade after it was initiated, TSM had cost over $4 billion and there was little to show for it (as was charged in a General Accounting Office report (GAO, 1995) and elsewhere—e.g., Anthes 1996a, 1996b; Neumann 1997). Some of the systems—notably Cyberfile, which was intended to enable taxpayers to file their returns electronically—had been canceled. Other systems—such as the Document Processing System (DPS), intended to convert paper filing to electronic images—had also been abandoned. Finally, twelve other systems in the TSM family were under review to determine whether they should also be abandoned. Several GAO reports have been critical of the IRS, and, in addition, both the National Research Council and the National Commission on Restructuring the IRS fault the IRS for failing to deal with the myriad problems associated with TSM. Notable among the criticisms were complaints of mismanagement, cost overruns, and most devastating of all, the "paucity of technical and managerial expertise" within the IRS to tackle the work of TSM (GAO, 1995, 17).

*Denver International Airport's Baggage Handling System* The Denver International Airport's (DIA) Baggage Handling System (BHS) was an automated airportwide integrated system intended to service the baggage handling needs of all the airlines using the new airport. The system was set up to "move any bag to any carousel or load point in less than 10 minutes" (Rifkin 1994, 112). The operation of the system was controlled by the Empty Car Management (ECM) software, a real-time control systems program that "dispatches empty carts [for carrying luggage] to any input point" where the carts may be needed. The program "coordinates the flow of carts to ensure that empty queues are replenished [with new carts] in time for arriving bags." About 4,000 individual carts make up the Telecar System, a miniature digitized railroad that moves carts from point to point and that is controlled by an Ethernet-based network in a client-server environment running under IBM's OS/2 operating system (Rifkin 1994, 114).

The DIA's BHS project provides a classic example of how not to undertake a software project development. The BHS project exhibited several of the factors that published studies indicate are major contributors to failed or abandoned projects. The factors that played a role in the failure of the project to achieve the desired outcome included the following: the large size of the project, its level of complexity, the newness of the technology and the inadequate technology base or infrastructure, the limited experience of even the company recognized as the world leader in baggage systems, the powerful stakeholders involved and the general uncertainties associated with the project outcome, and finally, the failure to recognize the potentially harmful effects that the unreasonably tight deadlines could have on the project outcome.

*CODIS Project*    CODIS (not its real acronym) was started in the late 1980s by a medium-sized electronics distribution company, located in Los Angeles County, California, with plans to become a billion-dollar company in the near future. The company realized the need to develop a new information system to cope with the increasing workload it was experiencing, which it expected would continue. After more than two years of investing in new IT resources, including new IS staff and new management to develop the system, it was forced to cancel the project and start again with a new IS staff and management (see Ewusi-Mensah 1998 for details).

The above cases are representative of many software projects that have gone awry. Glass (1998), Flowers (1997), and Collins and Bicknell (1997) have each compiled a collection of software runaways and failures that also includes abandoned projects. It is necessary to point out that because no formal official records are available in the public domain from which to reconstruct the facts of the development process, we are limited to speculation and inference from published reports and articles relating to the projects. Though I have tried to be accurate and careful in my recitation of the facts and circumstances of each project and of the various stakeholder groups involved, I do not claim, except possibly in the case of the CODIS project (which is based on field-study data), to have firsthand knowledge of the facts of each project. Still, I believe that the information I have been able to piece together from various sources is sufficiently credible to justify inferences and lessons from the cases. I hope that over time, more and more organizations will come to recognize the value to the software industry as a whole of their willingness to report fully and accurately, without attributing blame to any group of individuals, the facts surrounding their failed or runaway projects.

I now examine the reported facts of the above projects in the context of the socioorganizational factors discussed in the framework for abandoned projects (see chapter 3).

### Unrealistic Project Goals and Objectives

In the Confirm case, AMR Inc. charged in its suit that the consortium partners failed to "specify exactly what they wanted from the system" and that this "indecisiveness" of the partners had the effect of impeding progress on the project, as McPartlin (1992, 12) reports. In fact, John Mott, who led the Confirm project, is said to have asserted that the four years of Confirm's development involved "continuous debate" because the partners did not "know what they wanted in the first place." However, this claim is vehemently denied by James Yoakum, then chief information officer (CIO) of Marriott, who claimed that before the start of the project the other three partners provided AMRIS with a detailed list of specifications defining exactly what they wanted (McPartlin 1992). It is difficult, if not impossible, to verify which of the Confirm partners is right on this point, but it clearly shows there was no apparent consensus on what the goals and objectives of Confirm should be prior to the start of the project, other than the very vague and rather broad assertion that Confirm would constitute the first reservations system of its kind, combining airline, hotel, and car rental operations (Halper 1992a, 1992b, 1992c).

In its suit against Andersen Consulting, the bankruptcy trustee for FoxMeyer Drug charged that the Delta project was intended to be a technologically advanced, state-of-the-art distribution system. The over-arching goal of the Delta project set by management was to "push the technological envelope, and to do it fast" Bulkeley (1996, 2). The FoxMeyer chief operating officer (COO) who was reported to have championed the ambitious project indicated that the fast pace was needed and promised that within three years the company would be able to "accelerate sales growth without proportional increases in head count and operating expense, automating functions that now are manually driven, and improving the quality of our service" (Bulkeley 1996, 2). This unbridled optimism was shared by FoxMeyer's top management to the extent that they are reported to have "recklessly underbid contracts, expecting electronic efficiencies to lower costs enough to make the deals profitable" (Bulkeley 1996, 2). All of this was against the advice of their own independent consultant, who urged a slow approach, knowing full well the risks involved in undertaking a project of such magnitude and complexity. In addition, the consultant noted that SAP R/3 was really designed for manufacturing operations and in his view lacked "many features for the wholesale distribution business," as Bulkeley (1996, 2) also reported in his *Wall Street Journal* article. In time, when the computerization failed to realize the anticipated goals and benefits, the COO was removed by the board to atone for the errors and misjudgment of all top management.

The TSM, critics charged, had not created a comprehensive plan or blueprint outlining "what the system is supposed to do and how it would work," as the *Los Angeles Times* reported "IRS Computer Project Has 'Very Serious Problems,' Rubin Says," (1996, D1). This charge was echoed by Treasury Secretary Robert Rubin and by Representative James Lightfoot, chair of the U.S. House Appropriations Committee. In fact, Secretary Rubin was reported to have remarked that what existed or could be passed for a plan was rather a highly technical 6,000-page document that was not for a general readership. Most observers felt the project, was "too grand" and, furthermore, that the IRS had failed to prioritize the TSM projects, insisting that the projects were all of equal importance. This failure to prioritize the projects, was later cited by the GAO not only as "unrealistic" but also as potentially dooming the projects to be "generally unattainable." (GAO, 1995).

The BHS project, which is critical to the efficient operation of the new DIA, was inexplicably not part of the build-design plans until several months into the construction. Initially, DIA project leadership—that is, the city of Denver management—decided to leave the baggage handling details to the individual airlines. Unfortunately, none of the airlines using the old airport had committed themselves to using the new DIA, and consequently the baggage handling part of the DIA design was neglected. It was several months into the construction of DIA that first Continental Airlines and later United Airlines signed on to use the new DIA. It was only then that the DIA authorities, realizing that none of the potential airline users of DIA had committed to the design of a baggage handling system (with the exception of United Airlines, which had contracted with BAE for its concourse), moved to address this omission in the build-design plans of the airport. At that time sixteen bids were solicited from various companies for an airportwide automated baggage handling system. Of the sixteen companies solicited for the BHS project only three responded, excluding United Airlines' BAE company. However, none of the three responding companies was judged by the consulting firm asked to handle that task to be capable of undertaking a project of such magnitude and complexity within the time available before the airport was officially to be opened for operation. Thus it was quite late in the construction of DIA that United Airlines' baggage handling company BAE was brought in to undertake the BHS project. After several days of intensive negotiations between BAE and DIA management, the parties agreed on rather stringent conditions to provide BAE ease of access to facilitate its work and to make up for the time lost due to DIA's earlier inaction on the problem.

DIA management requested an automated integrated baggage handling system to serve the needs of all the airlines that would be using the new airport. The BHS was touted as the "most complex automated baggage system ever built" to "direct bags . . . from the main terminal through a tunnel into a remote concourse and directly to a gate" (Montealegre et al. 1996, 9). The efficient operation of the BHS for the entire airport was to be the hallmark of the DIA, enabling the airlines to maximize their hub operations and decrease the turnaround time for their aircraft.

Although the goals and objectives of the project were clear, the time frame in which the project was to be realized, coupled with the stringent conditions and operating environment in which the project was initiated, created much uncertainty. United Airlines, which had previously contracted with BAE to build the baggage handling system for its concourse, rightly anticipated the level of complexity involved in the project and estimated its completion to be no later than two and one-half years away. Yet when the BHS was expanded to cover the entire airport, the completion-time issue was not appropriately or adequately addressed. Instead, it was hoped that by placing "a number of conditions" on the contract—dealing, for example, with the freezing of dates for changes to software and giving BAE unhindered access to work sites—the project goals and objectives could somehow be achieved before the targeted opening day of the airport. With hindsight, it is apparent that consensus on project goals and objectives was not sufficient to guarantee project success. In this case, the other mitigating forces, namely, the size and complexity of the project, were so powerful that they conspired to nullify whatever benefit consensus on project goals and objectives conferred on the project. DIA management's failure first to deal with the baggage handling issue and then to make a realistic assessment of the time required to complete the project ensured that the state-of-the-art BHS would not get off the ground.

The data in the CODIS project suggested that although there was general agreement in the organization regarding the need for a new IS, there was no clear statement of what the new system's goals and objectives should be in order to satisfy the company's specific information requirements. The vice president of marketing, one of the project's participants, is reported to have indicated that "there were no firm, established goals and moreover no real consensus on what those goals should be." The only consensus existing at the time was that "the company was functioning with brute force—good people working very hard with little computing or information technology" (Ewusi-Mensah 1998, 7).

I have already reported elsewhere (Ewusi-Mensah 1997, 76) that "it is imperative that firm goals or objectives be established for the project to guide the information requirements phase of the development process.

Failure to satisfy this aspect of the project is likely to lead to fragmented efforts, and lack of team focus in assembling the facts to guide the rest of the development," as was the case in CODIS. Consequently, lack of "clear, measurable goals" at the start of the project is likely to lead to a vague set of systems requirements that can be harmful to the success of the project, as Curtis, Krasner, and Iscoe (1988) found in their study of large-systems design. I have further reported that "projects may still be canceled if the goals articulated as attainable in the original requirements document prove illusive," especially with changing requirements, which was the case in the Confirm project (Ewusi-Mensah 1997, 76). It is equally important that the goals specified not be perceived as overly broad or ambitious. In addition, the goals should be judged to be doable and within the capabilities of the project team. The Delta, TSM, and DIA's BHS were particularly vulnerable to this charge of being overly ambitious. The lack of priorities in TSM also worked against its success in the long run.

### Changing Requirements

Changing requirements may at times be a manifestation of a lack of consensus on goals and objectives prior to the start of the project. However, even when goals and objectives are agreed on before the start of the project, new clarifying information may be encountered at a later date that may cause changes to be made in the existing requirements and that thus may set the development process somewhat further back. Changes to requirements are, therefore, inevitable in any software development project. Because the more critical issue of concern is the frequency and intensity of those changes as the project proceeds through the development stages, there is always a need to control for such changes, which have the potential to wreak havoc in the development process.

In the Confirm case, Marriott charged in its suit that AMR began to eliminate functions from the system to help speed up the development process. AMR of course dismissed this charge as frivolous because it was confident that the project would come in on time (McPartlin 1992). Overly ambitious projects can be characterized by this problem of inevitable changes in the requirements as further knowledge of the problem domain is gained, and as what is and is not feasible is discerned.

For example, the TSM project was criticized as being "too grand," which may have played a role in the problems it encountered in, for instance, developing a blueprint to guide the development process. On the other hand, CODIS is illustrative of a project where the lack of consensus on what to do led to a scattershot approach to the development and the eventual, inevitable failure.

In May 1993, following the collapse of Phar-Mur Luc, a Midwestern pharmacy chain responsible for 15 percent of FoxMeyer's revenue stream, its top management felt added pressure to make up for the lost business and ensure its survival. As a result, FoxMeyer aggressively pursued University Health System (UHC) Consortium, a national network of major teaching hospitals, by underbidding the contract, expecting to make up for the smaller profit margin with the increase in volume they felt was assured by the Delta project. The successful acquisition of the UHS contract, however, set in motion a stream of actions that necessitated changes in the original requirements for SAP R/3 implementation. For example, because UHS hospitals are scattered across the United States, it required the opening of six new warehouses in the West. In addition, the implementation schedule had to be shortened "to get parts of the SAP financial software running three months sooner than planned" to accommodate the requirements of the UHS contract (Bulkeley 1996, 3). FoxMeyer's own CIO admitted that "the new contract [i.e., UHS] increased the difficulties of the already-ambitious plan" (Bulkeley 1996, 3). This fact is echoed by Jesitus (1997), who reported that the SAP contact on the project indicated that the new contract introduced a significant change in FoxMeyer's business. It added to the problems of Delta, because the focus of the project *changed* drastically from the original specifications to ensure that the UHS consortium's needs could be satisfied.

After the hasty start on the BHS by BAE, it was inevitable that the individual carriers would make changes to the specifications for the airportwide integrated baggage system drawn up by the DIA planners and consultants (once they committed to the project). While this was to be expected, the frequency of the changes and the set of problems they in turn introduced with respect to, for example, coordination with other contractors working in other areas of the airport for which BAE needed unimpeded access for its equipment, materials, and workers, was not anticipated by the project team and DIA management. Additionally, the freeze dates for changes to the design of the mechanical parts and the software involved, which BAE and DIA authorities had painstakingly negotiated, proved hollow and unenforceable, thus introducing another layer of problems to the project. For instance, after BAE took over the BHS for the entire airport, United Airlines requested design changes from its original specifications such that an entire loop was removed from its original two complete loops of track. This change saved United Airlines $20 million in its contract; it also required a redesign of the BHS, in the United Airlines section of the airport. As Rifkin (1994, 113) reports, "a flood of changes followed," including, for example, "relocation of outside stations, addition of a mezzanine baggage platform and Continental Airlines' request for a far larger baggage link." No sooner had these changes been acceded to than more requests came in. The head of BAE complained that six months prior to the airport's opening, requests for changes in software design, controls, and movement of equipment were still being dealt with across the board (Montealegre et al. 1996). In a complex system any change in design in one section is bound to have ripple effects on other sections of the project, which would require additional time and resources to tackle. Thus controlling for the frequency of the changes was a prerequisite to the project being completed on time. The DIA authorities painted themselves into a corner when they failed to heed the advice of their own consultants, other companies, and the technical advisors of the Munich Airport that BHS was so complex that "there was not enough time to build such a system" (Rifkin 1994, 113; Montealegre et al. 1996). Munich airport was contacted because of its experience in implementing an automated baggage sysem, albeit one that was considered much lesss complex than DIA's BHS (it is also the sister airport of DIA). It was therefore inevitable that, in order to accommodate the airlines, DIA and BAE agreed to changes in the design, which further delayed the completion schedule.

This factor is, quite frankly, tied to the project goals and objectives factor in the sense that both are linked to the issue of requirements for the system. Whenever there are excessive changes in the requirements resulting from, for example, ambiguous or ill-defined goals and

objectives, or incomplete requirements resulting from lack of understanding of the problem domain, the rest of the development process may
be affected. Depending on how far down in the life cycle the requirements changes occur and how extensive they are, the repercussions for
the development may be severe, affecting cost and schedule estimates
alike. In extreme cases, they may even cause the project to be abandoned
altogether, as DIA's BHS case illustrates.

### Lack of Executive Support and Commitment

The need for the active commitment and involvement of senior management in software development projects is well documented as a canon
of good practice. Senior management provide the necessary resources for
the project, and their commitment and involvement are viewed as evidence of their support for the goals and objectives of the project and its
contribution to the larger or broader organizational strategies. On the
other hand, "If senior management fail to become actively involved
in monitoring progress on the project" or otherwise fail to become
informed "on what is going on with the project on a regular basis, it
is likely that small unresolved problems will compound over time and
eventually contribute to the project's termination" (Ewusi-Mensah
1997, 78).

As reported in Ewusi-Mensah 1997, "The failure of senior management in the Intrico consortium to be actively engaged on a more frequent
basis in the development of Confirm" was cited by one AMRIS executive as partly to blame for the failure of the project. The AMRIS executive stated: "Confirm's 'fatal flaw' was a faulty management structure in
which no one group had ample authority over the project. . . . You
cannot manage a development effort of this magnitude by getting
together once a month. . . . Had they allowed the president of Intrico to
function as CEO in a normal sense and empowered their senior reps [to]
work together with a common goal and objective, it would have worked.
. . . A system of this magnitude requires quintessential teamwork. We
essentially had four different groups. . . . It was a formula for failure"
(p. 78).

The top executives of FoxMeyer Drug were actively committed and
involved, perhaps even overcommitted to the success of the Delta

project. As Bulkeley (1996) and Jesitus (1997) both reported, prior to the initiation of the Delta project, the board of FoxMeyer Drug as well as its COO realized that their current aging Unisys mainframe was not capable of handling the anticipated growth in the business. Consequently, they embarked on a search for a client-server-based system to do the job. This decision eventually led to the acquisition of SAP's R/3 software and its subsequent implementation on HP client-server hardware. FoxMeyer Drug hired Andersen Consulting to do the systems integration work based on the forceful representation the consultants made as to their level of expertise, experience, and resources for undertaking the arduous task (Bulkeley 1996; Jesitus 1997; LJX FILES, 1998).

Because top management saw the future of the company as being intrinsically interwoven with the success of the R/3 implementation, they perhaps did not pay adequate attention to other telltale signs of the potential for failure and thus became overly committed to the project until it became too late to withdraw. Their overcommitment to the Delta project caused the top executives of FoxMeyer—in particular, the COO—to lose their objectivity and thus fail to pay attention to the problems that their systems people were reporting with regard to the over-ambitious project. Systems people working on the project realized that it was not "appropriate to criticize SAP" because they were systematically "encouraged to minimize problems" (Bulkeley 1996, 3).

Another outcome of top management's dangerous overcommitment to the Delta project was their unwillingness to listen to the cautionary advice of their own independent consultant, who felt the schedule Andersen proposed for completing the work, even before the UHS contract was signed, was too ambitious and unrealistic (Jesitus 1997; Bulkeley 1996). The bankruptcy trustee charged that FoxMeyer was repeatedly "coerced" into paying additional fees to Andersen even when the "completed" work was riddled with flaws/bugs that needed to be fixed at the consultant's expense, demonstrating the extreme reluctance of top management to give up on the failing project (LJX FILES, 1998).

For TSM there is not sufficient documented evidence to attest to the extent of executive involvement. Consequently, we are left to infer the existence and nature of such high-level involvement and commitment from other sources. For example, Treasury Secretary Robert Rubin, the *Los Angeles Times* reported, had pledged to increase top-level attention to the project and to have it handled "much like a chief executive at a private corporation overseeing a major problem" during his appearance before the House Appropriations Committee ("IRS Computer Project Has 'Very Serious Problems,' Rubin Says," 1996, D1). At that meeting, Secretary Rubin was also reported to have announced the appointment of a new chief to head TSM with the experience and expertise to tackle the problems. All of these apparent senior-level activities with respect to TSM should have occurred throughout the project's development as evidence of senior-level support and commitment to the project, and to signal to the rest of the TSM project teams the strategic value of the project to the Treasury Department. The fact that these organizational changes were being discussed several years after the TSM project had started, while it was facing severe criticisms from Congress for its failures, showed at least that the project did not enjoy the kind of top-management commitment and support traditionally associated with a project of such magnitude in an organization.

As in the case of FoxMeyer Drug, the failure of the BHS to come in under budget and on schedule was not due to a lack of commitment and involvement by DIA's senior management, which included the mayor and other elected officials of the city of Denver. The case can be made that the apparent attempt by the city council to manage the project after the untimely death of the chief airport engineer—instead of assigning to his successor all the autonomy and authority to make decisions involving, for example, access control by BAE and other related issues—may have played a part in the difficulties BAE had in completing the project. Because the chief airport engineer had autonomy and authority granted by his stature in the organizational hierarchy of DIA, he was able to cut through any bureaucratic bottlenecks and provide the necessary assistance needed by BAE. Unfortunately, that level of decision-making authority was never conferred on his successor. So although she had some construction experience, it is not surprising that she was not able to achieve the same results as her predecessor.

The politics associated with the entire airport construction endeavor were also a significant factor in the problems encountered in the BHS project. DIA was a project on which much of Denver's political elite had staked its future, ranging from the mayor (who started it all with a campaign promise) to his successor (who inherited the built-in constraints associated with the project). For example, the revenue bonds the city used to partly finance the airport assumed the "date of beneficial occupancy" to be January 1, 1994, with the bond repayments scheduled to begin on that date. At the time the city believed it could meet its bond-repayment obligations if DIA opened no later than October 31, 1993 (Montealegre et al. 1996). Mayor Wellington Webb's failure to heed the advice of consultants and technical advisors with respect to the near impossibility of the BHS being completed by the time DIA was originally scheduled to open may have been for political purposes. Denver politicians' desire to please their constituents may have led them to jettison some of their objectivity regarding the readiness of the airport and the feasibility of completing the BHS project on schedule. For example, despite all indications that BHS testing was far from complete and that there were several bugs in the system that had to be fixed, the city of Denver in late April 1994 invited the news media (without BAE's prior knowledge or consent) to observe the first test of the baggage system, which turned out to be a major failure and embarrassment (Montealegre et al. 1996; Rifkin 1994).

The commitment and involvement of senior management of the DIA were in this case somewhat misplaced. The political elite would have served the city and citizens of Denver better if their role had been one of active support and participation, leaving management of the technical issues surrounding the BHS project to the people trained to handle such complex matters.

For CODIS, there is evidence to suggest that senior management failed to "request and enforce regularly scheduled management review meetings to monitor progress" on the project. As a result, senior management had no firsthand knowledge of the development process at any time and thus could not be informed of the possible completion time for the project. Consequently, far more resources were expended on the project than could be justified, as noted by the marketing director when he commented on "the inability of senior management to recognize they had a problem and delayed decision on it for so long" (Ewusi-Mensah 1997,

78). This lack of involvement led to delayed decisions on major issues, such as replacement of the nonperforming MIS director. Again, the marketing director commented that "Pete should have been let go sooner, and the MIS area should have been reorganized to deal with the project and its related problems earlier."

In both the Confirm and CODIS projects, senior management appeared to have been lax in managing the development by their conspicuous lack of commitment and involvement to the projects' outcomes. Specifically, in the case of Confirm, the lines of authority and responsibility for the success of the project were blurred, leading unavoidably to the passing of blame to others and failing to take decisive actions in situations where such actions would have advanced the course of the project. An additional factor may be the potential conflict of interest among the various stakeholder groups forming the consortium and, in particular, between AMRIS as project developer and the rest of the consortium. For example, AMRIS executives accused the other three partners in the consortium of failing to ask for copies of an IBM consulting report, which, it was suggested, carefully detailed problem areas that eventually contributed to the failure of Confirm. Finally, the other three partners accused AMRIS project management of "promising anything to keep the project moving" (Zellner 1994, 36). On the other hand, the Delta and BHS projects are examples of overcommitment on the part of senior management, impairing their objectivity and contributing to the difficulties the projects experienced.

Senior management, Krault and Streeter (1995, 80) have suggested, are supposed to be the "major beneficiaries of formal management procedures" in the software development process and are expected to use the procedures to gain feedback and exercise control over the process. In the cases of Confirm, TSM, and CODIS cited here, it is apparent that the requisite senior management involvement described by Krault and Streeter was nonexistent, which contributed immeasurably to the problems of cost overruns and schedule delays faced by the projects and led to cancellations in the long run.

## Insufficient User Commitment and Involvement
The key role of users in the development of organizational software is widely accepted in the software industry. Users can become involved in

the development process as participants in formulating the requirements and in helping the software personnel understand the users' problem domain. Users can also become involved by their continuous interaction with the systems personnel throughout the development process. The extent of the users' participation and interaction with other stakeholder groups in the development process may signal the depth of their commitment to the project's outcome. Through the study of users' views on systems development, I have suggested elsewhere that while user involvement in development projects is necessary, it is not a sufficient criterion for project development success (Ewusi-Mensah 1998). However, there is a significant risk of project failure, even abandonment, if the involvement in and commitment of users to the project are lacking.

In each of the cases under discussion there is no specific, direct information, except possibly with respect to CODIS, of users' active participation in the systems development process. For example, in the Confirm case the first mention of users in almost all the reports was when the system was initially beta-tested at the Hilton site in early 1992. This, of course, is not confirmation of a lack of users' involvement in the Confirm project; however, one is left to speculate as to the nature and extent of their involvement, if indeed they participated in the development of Confirm. The TSM systems also present a muddy picture of the nature of users' involvement in the entire development process. The GAO reports, for example, that in the area of requirements management, the involvement of the customers—that is, the users—has been rather limited and consequently has not had any appreciable influence on TSM systems (GAO, 1995, 36). The CODIS project is the only one of the three where active user participation in the development is documented. The users were the initiators of the project, and they stayed engaged through their constant interaction with the process until the end (Ewusi-Mensah 1998). Indeed, the CODIS project confirms the proposition that user involvement is, other things being equal, necessary but not sufficient to ensure successful systems development.

In the FoxMeyer Delta project, user involvement in the warehouse operations occurred when the frequent and persistent breakdown of the system forced users at the warehouse to carry out the tasks that were originally intended to be fully automated as a result of implementing SAP's R/3. However, prior to the implementation of the new system, employees at other warehouse locations where job layoffs were reportedly anticipated left in droves, making the entire warehouse operations vulnerable to the persistent system breakdowns (Jesitus 1997; Bulkeley 1996). Thus, although users are not explicitly cited in any of the sources on the Delta project, it is safe to surmise that they were probably never consulted on the viability or feasibility of the project and on what they could contribute to its successful completion. Both Bulkeley (1996) and Jesitus (1997) reported that one of the problems FoxMeyer faced that contributed to the delays was the unanticipated en masse departures of workers from Ohio warehouses, which the Washington Court House (i.e., the main warehouse) center was supposed to replace. It is apparent that once the workers realized their livelihood would be threatened whenever the Delta project became fully operational, they decided to leave rather than wait to be fired by management. The abrupt departures of many workers needed to handle the initial implementation stages of SAP for the UHS consortium imply that the workers were uninformed of the effect of Delta on their job security. The labor problems generated by the mass resignations could perhaps have been minimized if the workers had been fully consulted on the project and made to feel part of the decision-making process. There are no reports in the available and reviewed records to indicate that such an action was taken by management.

The decision to implement the airportwide integrated baggage handling system was made entirely by the DIA authorities without any participation from any of the potential users of the DIA project. To complicate matters further, the decision to construct the BHS was made in late 1991, when the DIA project was several years past the planning stage and construction had already begun. Originally DIA authorities left decisions involving baggage handling to the potential air carriers of the various concourses. It was only two years before the airport itself was scheduled to open when no carriers (except United Airlines) had contracted for baggage handling systems that the city scrambled to rectify the problem.

The BHS project was an example of top-down decision making with emphasis on cost containment and accelerated scheduling intended to catch up with the completion time frame dictated by the bond market.

The city of Denver and its agents on the DIA project never asked the airlines for their direct involvement in the decisions of BHS in the initial stages. This singular failure to involve the air carriers, in particular United and Continental, in the design, and implementation decisions of BHS from the beginning resulted in frequent design changes and contributed to increased costs as well as to further delays in the completion of the airport. The air carriers as important stakeholders in the successful outcome of DIA and, of course, BHS should have been assiduously courted with incentives to gain their support and commitment in the early stages of the planning, design, and implementation of DIA and the BHS project. The problems subsequently experienced could have been significantly reduced.

### Impact of Socioorganizational Factors on Systems Development Stages

In the preceding sections we have discussed the specifics of the four socioorganizational factors that dominate project-abandonment decisions. In each of the projects discussed—Confirm, Delta, TSM, DIA's BHS, and CODIS—we have illustrated the role played by the various socioorganizational factors in the development process. We now turn to the collective impact of the factors on the systems development stages of the life cycle.

In the abandonment framework discussed in chapter 3, we indicated the nature of the three factor categories and the influence they have on each phase of the development life cycle. In the case of the socioorganizational factors, the collective dominance of the factors in determining what the system is to do—that is, in defining the requirements for the software—makes them (i.e., the factors) critical in shaping the outcome of the requirements stage of the life cycle.

The critical impact of the socioorganizational factors also mildly extends to the design stage of the life cycle, because the products of the requirements stage are the drivers of the alternative "solution" approaches the designers may employ in determining how to satisfy the functional specifications embodied in the requirements documents. In addition, one-half of the factors in this category—unrealistic project goals and objectives, and changing requirements—are also present in the design stage of the development process, as shown in table 3.2. The design alternatives, which are the outcome of the design stage of the life cycle, are thus inextricably linked to the requirements documents, making the impact of the socioorganizational factors mildly critical to the design process as well. For example, in the CODIS project, the lack of consensus on project goals and objectives, coupled with the lack of senior management involvement, was particularly harmful in determining what the requirements for the system must be and how they would be realized in the design stage of the development life cycle. In the Confirm project, the design stage experienced difficulties partly as a result of the failure to address issues associated with the project's goals and objectives, partly because of the changing requirements of the project (which resulted in changes in the functional specifications), and, of course, partly because of the alleged hands-off approach reportedly exercised in the development by the senior management of the other three partners of the consortium. In the Delta project, design changes resulting from changes in the requirements brought on by shifting goals and objectives took their toll on the project's outcome. And in the BHS project, the frequent design changes brought on by changing requirements added to the cost overruns and completion-schedule delays.

In the implementation phase of the life cycle, the influence of the socioorganizational factors appears to be mildly critical to the outcome of the process, because they are not directly driving the outcome of the implementation stage. Even though the same two socioorganizational factors present in the design stage are also present in the implementation stage, their impact is dictated by the outcomes of the design stage. The impact of the socioorganizational factors, chapter 3 argued, is at most mildly critical to the implementation stage. In fact, this impact can be less severe if the outcome of the design stage does not generate ripple effects that negatively influence the implementation outcome. Thus although the impact of the socioorganizational factors on the implementation is generally mildly critical, it still does not directly affect the process outcome during the implementation phase. Therefore the implementation is somewhat insulated by whatever necessary corrections are made at the design stage, as a consequence of the critical impact of the socioorganizational factors in the requirements stage of the development.

## Conclusion

In this chapter we have presented empirical data highlighting the factors that contribute to decisions to abandon software development projects. We first discussed a profile of abandoned projects obtained from a study of Fortune 500 companies in the United States. A factor analysis of the abandoned-project data yielded twelve factors that contribute to abandonment decisions. Six of the twelve dealt with organizational and/or social issues pertaining, for example, to the commitment to and involvement in the project by management and end users. The empirical results were validated by case analyses of various reported projects from both the public and private sectors. These are projects that were either abandoned completely or that experienced severe difficulties that negatively affected their outcomes. We used the framework developed in chapter 3, which is based on the impact the various factor categories have on the requirements, design, and implementation stages of the project development process. We limited the case analyses of the projects to determining how each stage of the development process was affected by the socioorganizational factors. The remaining two categories—technological and economic factors—will be analyzed in chapters 5 and 6, respectively.

In summary, we can affirm that the socioorganizational factors as a whole have a significant impact on the entire development life cycle because of the behavioral, political, and other organizational influences they exert on the systems development process. For example, the lack of clear project goals and objectives tends to frustrate efforts to develop the software. Requirements volatility contributes to abundant "redirections" of projects, adding inevitably to project costs and schedule delays and even threatening the overall quality of the software itself. However, realistically speaking, stable and unchanging requirements, though highly desirable, are unlikely in a typical systems development environment. Consequently, the strategy must strike a balance in controlling the extent of the changes to minimize the fluctuations in requirements and thus help to control the costs and other factors associated with the development process. Lack of senior management commitment and involvement also contributes to lack of focus and may adversely affect the morale and commitment of the project team. Finally, lack of user involvement may carry with it a number of deleterious effects, such as the failure of the team to understand and fully appreciate the users' problem domain, which may in the long run contribute to an erroneous set of requirements and other problems.

# 5

# Technical Factors and Abandoned Projects

At the core of any software development project is the ability of the project team to convert a set of descriptive requirements, representing a sometimes-incomplete user understanding of the problem domain, into a technical artifact or product to be executed on the computer. The technical and technological problems associated with the challenge of creating software are often compounded by the social and organizational dimensions of the task. For example, the project team not only needs to concern itself with the purely technical issues of how to design the software but also needs to be attuned to the nontechnical issues that play a role in the development process, such as the commitment and involvement of senior management and users. Even the very important issue of project goals and objectives, which may be presumed to have been resolved at this stage of the development process, may have to be revisited. This sometimes occurs for nontechnical reasons—for instance, changes may be requested based on organizational structural changes taking place elsewhere in the organization.

There are also the purely social issues dealing with the group dynamics of the project team and its interactions with other stakeholder groups. The interactions of the technical members of the project team with the nontechnical members in requirements determination, and especially in designing alternative solutions to the requirements, are critical to successful project development. In chapter 4 we discussed the crucial role of socioorganizational factors in shaping the product outcome in software development. In this chapter we discuss the variety of technical and technological issues that can negatively affect software project outcomes. By *technical*, I specifically mean the general level of expertise and depth of experience in computer hardware and software, and in the ability of the design team to appropriately use those resources to achieve the design objectives of the project. *Technological* refers to the available computer hardware, telecommunications and networking facilities/infrastructure, software tools, and software development methodologies in the organization on which the project development is critically dependent. Inadequacies in either the technical or technological resources or both can be potentially harmful to the project's successful outcome. First we review the different technical factors derived from an analysis of data collected on failed Fortune 500 companies' software projects. We discuss the importance of each of the technical factors and the critical role each plays in contributing to the demise of software projects. The significance of each factor is evaluated qualitatively through case studies of five publicly reported software project failures (described in chapter 4), which teach major lessons about the pitfalls of software development. Finally, we discuss the impact each technical factor has on the stages of software development using the framework presented in chapter 3.

**Technical Issues in Abandoned Projects**

The investigation of the technical and technological issues that have significant influence on project outcome is based on an analysis of the data from the Fortune 500 study discussed in chapter 4, and the project cases that we use to illustrate the major contributions of the technical factors discussed in the abandonment framework described in chapter 3. I will deal first with the data analysis, which is based on the factored data from the Fortune 500 study described in chapter 4, the details of which can be found in Ewusi-Mensah and Przasnyski 1994. In table 5.1 I group

**Table 5.1**
Technical factors (extracted from table 4.10)

| Factor no. | Factor description |
| --- | --- |
| F2 | Lack of appropriate technical infrastructure and expertise |
| F4 | Technological shortcomings |
| F9 | Satisfy existing or emergent technology |

together the set of technical and technological issues, extracted from table 4.10, and use these as the basis for the analysis. The primary issues that comprise this factor category are technical and technological infrastructure, and technical expertise. Let us examine each issue in turn to determine its significance in project-abandonment decisions.

Technical and technological infrastructure encompasses issues of great importance to the development process, because they are at the core of the organization's ability to produce the required software. Factor F4 raises two major issues: a lack of available technical and technological infrastructure on which the project critically depends, and technical problems pertaining to project feasibility and to compatibility with existing hardware and software. Together these issues constitute the "technical and technological inadequacies and shortcomings" that may cause a project to be abandoned. During the design stage of systems development, technical issues dealing with the trade-off of available options to achieve the design objectives are necessarily constrained by the existing hardware and software infrastructure in the organization, or by what can reasonably be expected to be obtained from outside. However, if the implementation is based on a design for which the existing technological resources in the organization are inadequate, it is conceivable that the project will collapse. Similarly, if the project experiences technical problems with respect to its feasibility or its compatibility with existing hardware and/or software, it is equally likely that it may fail if the problems are not speedily and satisfactorily corrected. Indeed, as was argued from the study data, these "findings indicate that even in situations where the project is below cost and time of completion estimates, once deficiencies in the technological issues of the project are uncovered, which cannot be rectified, the project may eventually be terminated" (Ewusi-Mensah and Przasnyski 1994, 194).

Technical expertise deals specifically with the know-how and capabilities of the personnel engaged in the software development. In factor F2, these issues are directly addressed, because the factor elements that constitute F2 deal with the technical capabilities of the project team. For example, one of the factor elements states that "project implementation depended on level of technical expertise lacking in organization." That is, project abandonment is highly likely if an organization undertakes a project for which it lacks the requisite technical know-how to ensure successful development.

Another factor element is the following: "project too ambitious or technically difficult to accomplish." This element has multiple implications extending, for instance, to the project goals and objectives. In essence, what we have here is that even in some cases where technical expertise may not clearly be an issue, the risk of project failure can be high if the project is perceived to be too ambitious or technically beyond the capabilities and experience of the project team. This latter interpretation is also supported by the factor element "project was the first one of its kind or size attempted by the IS/user departments." The unequivocal inference we can make from these collective factor elements is that the goals and objectives of the project should be crafted within the parameters of in-house technical expertise, so that the project can successfully be carried out. That is, projects perceived by the technical staff as too difficult or overly ambitious are good candidates for failure unless one or both of the defects are corrected. For example, the level of expertise can be substantially raised prior to the start of the project by training or new hiring, and/or the project's goals and objectives can be adjusted to reflect internal staff capabilities.

The last factor element in this group was "project implementation depended on appropriate technical infrastructure lacking in organization," which affirms the conclusion reached in factor F4. Finally, factor F9 indicates that projects can be discontinued if there is an existing or emergent technology—for example, an available software package—that can be expected to satisfy the project's objectives and/or that can be considered a substitute for the project in question. Thus, in summary, based on the Fortune 500 study, projects are susceptible to cancellation for technical and technological reasons dealing primarily with the technical and technological infrastructures in the organization, and the level of technical expertise available in-house for carrying out the project. When these major criteria are not met, there is a high likelihood of project failure resulting in abandonment. The studies of software project risks reported on in chapter 2 generally support the finding that software projects are highly vulnerable to failure as a consequence of inadequate technical expertise and/or technological infrastructure.

## Analysis of Abandoned Projects: Technical and Technological Issues

In the preceding section we discussed the technical and technological factors contributing to abandoned projects in the Fortune 500 study of Ewusi-Mensah and Przasnyski (1994), discussed in chapter 4. In this section we undertake a qualitative analysis of the same technical and technological factors as presented in the abandonment framework of chapter 3. We are particularly interested in elucidating the nature of these factors and their impact on the different stages of the development life cycle. The dominant factors that comprise the group of sociotechnical factors in abandoned projects listed below are derived from table 3.2:

• Unrealistic project goals and objectives

• Inappropriate project-team composition

• Project management and control problems

• Inadequate technical know-how

• Problematic technology base/infrastructure

• Changing requirements

The two factor elements—unrealistic project goals and objectives, and changing requirements—have been discussed at length and illustrated with specific reference to the five project cases: Confirm, Delta, TSM, DIA's BHS, and CODIS. I do not wish to extend the discussion here except to point out that these two factors are both inextricably linked to the technical and technological directions a project may take. They provide the needed strategic vision and the corrective changes in direction respectively of the project development process from the technical and technological perspectives. Their particular relevance in this context is therefore in helping to formulate the functional specifications at the requirements stage of the life cycle, which will drive the rest of the project's technical development.

The factors were collectively described as having a critical impact on the design and implementation stages of the development life cycle, but as having mild critical influence at the requirements stage. Following the format laid out in chapter 4, we will take up the remaining four technical-factor elements, discussing their characteristics and illustrating them with supportive facts culled from the five project cases—Confirm, Delta, TSM, DIA's BHS, and CODIS.

### Inappropriate Project-Team Composition

Software projects are inherently team oriented and involve acquisition and sharing of problem-domain knowledge among team members, collaboration and coordination with individual members, and consensus decision making. The organization of the team is fundamental to a successful project outcome because it lays the foundation for the effective and efficient workings of the project group. The composition of the team becomes relevant in structuring the collective responsibilities of the participants to ensure the success of the development effort. Alan Howard (2001) alludes to the "development personalities" of the individual team members as an important factor to consider when putting together a software project team. Similarly, Klein Jiang, and Tesch (2002) discuss the varying professional orientations of the development team members as important to successful project outcome.

Team building becomes essential if the individual talents and capabilities of the members are to be molded and transformed into the collective expertise of the team in its thinking and interactions. Project success will largely be influenced to the extent that such team-oriented qualities and characteristics can be made transparent in the work of the team. Who becomes part of the project team is therefore of immense significance. For example, Boehm (1981, 688) describes "personnel attributes and human relations activities" as the two most influential attributes "for improving software productivity." Brooks (1987, 18) makes essentially the same point when he refers to "people" as the "great designers" on whose shoulders rests the "central question" of how to improve software development. In actual software development practice, Curtis et al. (1988, 1284) quote one of the vice presidents of the companies they studied to the effect that "the most important thing you do for a project is selecting staff. . . . The success of the software development organization is very, very much associated with its ability to recruit good people." We can thus surmise that the caliber of the team members and the contributions each member is expected to make to the project are significant issues that must be handled diligently by the project management in selecting the team.

In addition, as noted earlier, "The disparate backgrounds and goals of the team members make it critical that clear lines of communication be established within the team along with an enumeration of lines of authority and responsibilities of the team members" (Ewusi-Mensah 1997, 76). We have also seen that often the large size of the projects coupled with the inherent risks and uncertainties normally associated with systems development may require "special coordination techniques." This need underscores the critical importance of communication in the development process. Communication in project teams, Curtis, Krasner, and Iscoe (1988, 1280) have also found, is "necessary to resolve misunderstanding about requirements or design decisions among project members."

In the Confirm project, AMRIS alleged in its lawsuit that the other three partners in the consortium "made poor staffing assignments that harmed the . . . project" (Halper 1992, 8). McPartlin (1992, 12) reportes that AMRIS further charged that Hilton, Budget, and Marriott "impeded Confirm's progress by assigning personnel who 'lacked adequate knowledge of the industry.'" This charge was refuted by the partners. McPartlin (1992) maintains that according to several sources present at the original project meeting in 1987, AMR gave the impression to its would-be partners that it was going to use its experienced systems development experts responsible for SABRE's success on Confirm. However, the same sources confirmed to McPartlin that once the project agreement became final, "AMR began recruiting the development team from outside its organization. No one from SABRE was tapped for the job." Finally, James Yoakum—former head of IS at Marriott—is reported to have remarked that "the project was doomed to failure from the beginning" because "AMR hired people off the street and proceeded without the right project manager running it" (McPartlin 1992, 12).

What emerges from the above narrative is a picture of disarray as to the appropriateness of the team makeup for the project from the standpoint of the various consortium members. Each faction of the consortium essentially accused the others of assigning team members to the project who were not up to the challenge, and, consequently, as having partly contributed to Confirm's demise.

The bankruptcy trustee characterized the Delta project as one staffed by novices or inexperienced Andersen consultants "whose SAP expertise was insufficient to perform a proper installation in the first place. " Furthermore, the trustee charged that Andersen then "aggravated that problem through its reassignment practices" (LJX FILES, 1998, 45). FoxMeyer, in fact, alleged through its suit that Andersen used the Delta project for "on-the-job training" of its SAP personnel and then compounded the problem by often reassigning individuals who had gained valuable SAP R/3 experience on Delta to other Andersen projects such that, for example, "the building of interfaces and the archiving of data were not performed and monitored by the same person from beginning to end." At the height of the project, Andersen was reported to have brought in as many as seventy analysts and programmers (Bulkeley 1996, 3). This practice resulted, the suit alleged, in "delays and inferior work product." In addition, Jesitus (1997, 34) reports that FoxMeyer's own independent consultant, Kenneth Woltz, believed that the company "lacked available users on staff with the sophistication to handle a fast-track installation." That was why he questioned the eighteen-month timetable Andersen provided, which he believed to be "totally unrealistic" for completing the project. Thus the team made up of Andersen consultants and FoxMeyer's own in-house staff was described by many as lacking the experience and know-how to undertake the Delta project, especially on an accelerated schedule. In addition, the signing of the UHC contract changed the focus of the project drastically, adding significantly to the problem.

With respect to DIA's BHS, we do not know enough about how the team working on the project was put together to offer any analytic commentary on the team composition. DIA contracted with BAE to provide the integrated airportwide BHS. It was the only company with the expertise necessary to complete the project, although admittedly its experience was not as extensive in dealing with a project of this magnitude and complexity. The information available in the public domain does not hint at any problems within BAE itself that might have aggravated the problems the project experienced. All indications were that despite the technical complexities and size of the project, BAE was the only organization in the United States with the team capability to carry out the project.

In both the TSM and CODIS projects, we do not have access to data relating to the composition of the team. However, some critics of the TSM project failure assert that "frequent changes in leadership at IRS— three commissioners in five years and two deputy commissioners," all judged to be not technically oriented—may have contributed to the problems, because leadership by the commissioners is vital in creating continuity and ensuring the stability of the rest of the project team (Maglitta 1996, 30). The problem with CODIS was similar, with the changes in the MIS directorship that occurred at the company. Uncertainties as to the project direction occurred with each subsequent change, especially when the new leadership lacked the requisite skills and expertise to undertake the desired project (Ewusi-Mensah 1998).

Apart from the problems with leadership of the project team, the data also suggest that if the team is not broadly based—that is, drawn from all areas of the organization that may be affected by the new system— some sectors of the organization may not be heard from, which may not augur well for the project's success. As explained in chapter 4, the singular failure of DIA authorities to include the airlines on the team that put together the plans for the airportwide baggage handling system contributed mightily to the frequent design changes requested by the air carriers, which was a source of delays and cost overruns. In addition, lack of structure and organizational purpose to the team's efforts, aggravated by lack of leadership and active interaction among all three stakeholder groups—senior management, technical staff, and users—is likely to lead to problems at later stages of the systems development life cycle, as we will discuss later in this chapter.

### Project Management and Control Problems

Software development as a "goal-directed activity" needs to be managed and controlled with the intent of producing the desired artifact within an estimated time frame and budget. The technical dimension of this sociotechnical, purposeful activity requires that some structure be imposed on the development process. There are several variants of the systems development life-cycle model or methodology that are widely available and used in practice in organizations. The recognized advantages of using a phased life-cycle approach to new systems development are to help the project team realize what activities are to be undertaken and what the deliverables for each stage may be, enable different types of communication between the activities of the different stages, and determine whether the deliverables of each stage are satisfactory prior to proceeding to the next stage. These "intellectually demanding" and complex sets of activities are also frequently iterative, further complicating the development process. Still, the phased life-cycle approach has been instrumental in helping to manage and control the development of large software projects successfully. Bad project management practices are often at the heart of software project failure (Glaser 1984).

In the Confirm case, the CEO of AMR Corporation, the parent company of AMRIS, is quoted as having stated in a letter to the other three partners that "the individuals to whom we gave responsibility for managing Confirm have proven to be inept. Additionally, they have apparently deliberately concealed a number of important technical and performance problems" (Zellner 1994, 36). The above statements were later retracted by AMR. McPartlin reports that "there never was a cover-up, nor had there even been an investigation of a possible cover-up," and that the eight Confirm managers chose to resign en masse after problems were uncovered on the project. However, this view of the events and conditions surrounding Confirm is vigorously disputed by the Marriott Corporation, which alleged in its suit that the eight top AMRIS executives associated with Confirm "were fired for concealing information about the project" (McPartlin 1992, 12) McPartlin further reports that the Marriott suit alleged that "if employees spoke up about problems . . . they were quickly reassigned." The implication here is that there were attempts within AMRIS to present the most favorable picture regarding the status of the project and that dissenting or less favorable views were perhaps discouraged.

This dispute between AMR and the consortium partners with respect to how Confirm was managed is one of the core problems the project faced. It was hard to resolve in the aftermath of the project's demise as each side, perhaps for litigious reasons, tried to blame the other for the project's failure. Notwithstanding the veracity of each side's claims, it is apparent that management's failure to manage the project satisfactorily "created an environment" where the alleged concealment of the activities could have occurred (Ewusi-Mensah 1997, 78). Furthermore, it is worth noting that even if the alleged concealment of the activities on the project did not take place, the IBM review commissioned by AMRIS clearly urged a "more critical review and immediate corrective action by AMRIS management," and stated that neglecting to take these steps would "almost assuredly result in failure" (Zellner 1994, 36). Studies by Curtis, Krasner, and Iscoe (1988, 1284) have correctly asserted that in software development there is a "constant need to share and integrate information." Thus "communication [is] necessary to develop a shared vision of the system's structure and function, and the coordination necessary to support dependencies and manage changes on large systems projects." Unfortunately, this dispute about who concealed what vital information from whom indicates a lack of the information sharing and communication that a project of Confirm's size and magnitude desperately needed in order to succeed.

The available literature on the Delta project does not provide us with adequate information with which to assess how the project was managed. In its suit the trustee alleged that Andersen's management of the project was "marred by problems, defects, deficiencies and errors" (LJX FILES, 1998, 32). For example, the reassignment practices Andersen engaged in—specifically, the "shuffling of Andersen personnel"— "severely disrupted the project," by causing "delays and inferior work product, because various long-term tasks . . . were not performed and monitored by the same person from beginning to end, or even for substantial periods of time" (LJX FILES, 1998, 45). Moreover, the added time pressures that came with the acquisition of the UHC contract severely affected the management of the project. Bulkeley (1996, 3) reports that FoxMeyer was unable to reengineer its related business practices to make the software more efficient. The project even "skipped testing some parts of the system where the software hadn't been customized." All of this was done in a misguided effort to save development time. These decisions created problems that contributed to the operational difficulties experienced in warehouses servicing the UHS Consortium (Jesitus 1997). The trustee alleged that it was Andersen's "flawed project management" that contributed to the inventory-discrepancy problems that were at the heart of the SAP conversion (LJX FILES, 1998, 32, subsection ii). All of this is in contrast to claims Andersen allegedly made prior to gaining the contract, citing "unsurpassed project management techniques to structure and implement and ensure quality control of its work for FoxMeyer" (LJX FILES, 1998, 22).

The TSM systems project presented a far different picture. The GAO alleged in its July 1995 report that almost a decade after TSM was initiated, the IRS had failed to put in place "an effective process for selecting, prioritizing, controlling, and evaluating the progress and performance of major information systems investments" (GAO, 1995, 25). The GAO (1995, 27) further alleged that the IRS "lacked comprehensive decision criteria for controlling and evaluating TSM projects throughout their life cycles." We are therefore left to speculate as to which life-cycle stages the IRS was most vulnerable in in its various TSM systems projects. This failure is contrary to the best practices in the software industry, where organizations typically have in place criteria for evaluating the expected benefits of the systems under development, as well as their potential risks, uncertainties, and estimated costs and times of completion. The software development process at the IRS was described in the GAO report as "chaotic" at times and as "ad hoc." In an environment where about 2,000 people were working in software development, plus several hundred more from outside companies in contractual arrangements, the lack of detailed and repeatable procedures for developing software had a negative impact on the IRS's ability to build the TSM systems economically and on time and to have them perform as intended. At the end of the GAO study, the IRS had begun the process of developing draft criteria to tackle the problems associated with its software development practices. Although the GAO found these efforts commendable, it still considered them insufficient to deal with some of the issues associated with the review of projects for top-management decision-making purposes.

The management and control of BHS were assumed by the project management team of DIA, with the manager specifically assigned to handle various DIA structures, such as the people-mover, passenger-bridge main landside building complex, airside concourse building, and other structures dealing directly with BAE. However, despite the area manager's extensive experience in construction project control management, it was insufficient to deal with airport construction in general and with baggage system technologies in particular, or even with the introduction of new technologies into the implementation (Montealegre et al. 1996).

In addition to the area manager who had responsibility for the BHS project, each concourse had its own manager and a manager for the main terminal as well. The management setup proved unwieldy because of the integrated nature of the BHS, creating an additional bottleneck in the implementation, since BAE was therefore required to consult with each of the senior managers in charge of each concourse in order to resolve each issue. The problem is clearly stated by Gene DiFonso: "The bag system . . . traversed all of them. If I had to argue a case for right of way, I would have to go to all the managers because I was traversing all four empires" (Montealegre et al. 1996, 11).

This sort of arrangement for managing control of the BHS created problems with coordinating the various design changes taking place in each concourse. With the frequent changes to the design being proposed by the user groups of each concourse, it became particularly troublesome to manage the disparate units without a centralized decision maker with the authority to resolve conflicts and make systemwide decisions beneficial to the entire DIA project. With hindsight, it is apparent that this project management approach had a negative impact on the ability of BAE to properly manage and control the large and richly complex BHS project.

BHS itself was organized into three main areas—mechanical engineering, industrial control, and software design—for ease of management and control under DiFonso as the project manager. Before the untimely death of Chief Airport Engineer Walter Slinger, the DIA project's cumbersome coordination, control, and management setup did not have a significant effect on the ability of DiFonso to manage BHS, because Slinger was able to use his considerable influence to provide solutions to any ease-of-access problems the BHS project encountered. However, the situation changed significantly when Slinger's deputy, Gail Edmond, took charge. Because Edmond lacked Slinger's influence and was not given the same autonomy and authority he had had, DiFonso was not able to enjoy the same ease of access to work areas as was previously available. DiFonso offers a reason for the disparity: "[Slinger] clearly understood the problem the city was facing [i.e., with respect to BHS in the DIA project] and he understood the short timeframe under which we were operating. He was the one that accepted all of the contractual conditions, all the milestones of the original contract" (Montealegre et al. 1996, 11, 12). In DiFonso's estimation, Slinger's successor did not have the same understanding and authority, and as a result the project suffered various setbacks. He elaborates: "Not only did we not get the unrestricted access that was agreed upon, we didn't even have reasonable access." For instance, barely ten days after Slinger's death, a request for access to Concourse C by a BAE millwright was rebuffed by one of the DIA project contractors working in the area. Similar incidents prevented BAE from gaining access to other work sites.

In the CODIS project, the failure to provide any systems development methodology to guide the project resulted in the project being tackled as another systems maintenance problem. The vice president of marketing remarked that "there was no planning developed for the project; no meetings were held to discuss systems development efforts; and the project never moved beyond the level of what we wanted to do and could the computer do it." This view was echoed by another project participant, the vice president of strategic planning: "All we had at the end of the two years was a 'lot of paper documentation' to show for our efforts. . . . The MIS group always talked about the capabilities of the new system as having the ability to do what [the user] wanted [it] to do" (Ewusi-Mensah 1998, 12).

The review of project management practices, or lack thereof, attributed to the five project cases underscores the important role management has in ensuring that proper management and control practices are instituted organizationwide and enforced in software development projects. The evidence suggests that it should be the joint responsibility of management and technical staff to come up with a set of metrics and development methodology that can be used to monitor and manage progress on the projects. In particular, mechanisms need to be in place to induce compliance by the technical staff with accepted industry standards for reporting and dealing with problems uncovered in any phase of the development process. The absence of good measurement systems or metrics to gauge and monitor progress on a project will undoubtedly make it very difficult for any organization to identify and correct development problems early, before they blossom into major disasters. Still, management will be well advised to heed Krault and Streeter's (1995, 80) caution that managers should not be "misled by an illusion of control," because technical staff often view "software metric data and status reviews" primarily as instruments used by senior managers with little impact on the day-to-day activities of software development.

### Inadequate Technical Know-How

One of the technical dimensions of software development concerns the level of experience and technical know-how of the project team engaged in the development process. The team's technical capabilities and collective expertise must not be underestimated, nor should they be a matter for speculation. This is of fundamental importance to the success or failure of a software project. At the core of a number of failed and abandoned projects are insufficient technical experience and know-how. The fact remains that lack of familiarity with a form of information technology new to the organization is not uncommon in a variety of organizations undertaking a software development project. As the KPMG study (Cole 1995) found, "technology new to the organization" is one of the leading causes of project failures or runaways. It is also one of the major risk factors associated with software projects, as studies by Barki, Rivard, and Talbot (1993, 2001) and Boehm (1991) confirm.

In the Confirm case, the experience of the technical personnel was an issue of concern; James Yoakum of Marriott is reported to have alleged that "AMR hired people off the street and proceeded without the right manager running it" (McPartlin 1992, 12). McPartlin further reports that from the start the leader of the Confirm development team "was in over his head." However, the validity of these allegations cannot be independently verified; we are, therefore, left to speculate on their relevance in this context. The intent of these comments may have been to create an overall impression that the project team's experience and leadership were inadequate to take on a project of the size and complexity of

Confirm, with all its attendant risks, uncertainties, and pressures. A similar charge of technical incompetence was apparently made by Joseph Atteridge, the president of AMRIS, who is said to have indicated that "the task of tying together Confirm's transaction processing facility–based central reservation system with its decision support system proved to be overwhelming. . . . We found they were not integrable" (Halper 1992b, 20). Yet another former AMR employee connected with the Confirm project, the vice president of operations for Intrico, is reported to have attributed part of the failure to "design error." The DB2 database for Confirm was determined to be "virtually unrecoverable in the event of a crash" (Halper 1992a, 10). This was in addition to several applications that Intrico failed to complete, stating that "the fundamental issue is [AMR Information Services] didn't deliver." Are the problems raised above ones of technology or of the technical expertise of the development team? In a sense, the two issues are inextricably linked from the systems design and implementation perspectives. The systems design forced the implementation choices that were subsequently made. Consequently, the fact that the development team failed to anticipate the implementation problems constrained by the design choices and trade-offs made, raised some questions about the level of expertise and, perhaps, even about the competence of the development team.

Claims of a lack of experience and technical know-how on the part of the Andersen team involved in the Delta project were perhaps the most damning allegation made by the bankruptcy trustee. The suit specifically accused Andersen of misrepresenting its level of technical expertise and experience on SAP R/3 implementation to FoxMeyer in order to get the contract (LJX FILES, 1998, 25). And then after the contract was signed and the project was started, Andersen is alleged to have failed to properly staff the project with consultants with sufficient technical know-how to get the job done. In fact, even though Andersen was accused of using the Delta project for on-the-job training of its SAP consultants, the experience gained by the consultants did not benefit FoxMeyer, because the consultants were often reassigned to other projects. This practice prolonged the time required for the various tasks, since each individual reassigned to the project had to spend some time acquiring the requisite knowledge and on-the-job experience before becoming productive.

The problems associated with the Delta project did not stem entirely from Andersen's role. According to Jesitus (1997, 34), FoxMeyer's own independent advisor on the project felt the time estimated for completion was overly optimistic, and, more importantly, FoxMeyer "lacked available users on staff with the sophistication to handle a fast-track installation." As a result, the advisor urged a go-slow approach, advice that was ignored because of the added business pressures resulting from the collapse of the Phar-Mur business relationship and the subsequent acquisition of the UHC contract to replace it. Bulkeley (1996, 2) has also reported that the same FoxMeyer advisor indicated a high level of risk associated with "a relatively new product [such as SAP R/3] and processing high volumes in a client-server environment." All of these factors—the high level of risk, the technical complexity of the overly ambitious project, and the inadequate expertise and experience of the Andersen personnel working on the project—conspired to doom it from the beginning.

The TSM project has been criticized by several observers, internal and external to the IRS, for problems associated in particular with the technical competence of the development team. For example, the development team of 2,000 people in the IRS alone, not including the several thousand outside contractors, has been accused of failing to redesign IRS's business processes prior to beginning work on TSM. The GAO (1995) furthermore charged in its report that the IRS team did not have in place an overall systems architecture to guide in the development of such a massive and costly project. Some of these problems with TSM are blamed on the "chaotic" and somewhat "primitive" development practices in existence in the organization. Some outside contractors have even faulted the IRS technical staff for failing to acknowledge that TSM as conceived was "badly flawed." These criticisms were a source of friction between the IRS technical staff and some outside contractors, it is alleged, because of the former's unwillingness to follow guidance offered on the project. These conflicts and disagreements about the problems of TSM are partly attributed to the fact that the "IRS overestimated its ability to do much of the technical work in house" ("IRS Computer Project Has 'Very Serious Problems,' Rubin Says," 1996, D1). The charge of technical incompetence was also made by Maglitta (1996, 30), when he reported that "IRS balks at admitting when a job is beyond" its capability. He went on to cite one critic, Paul Strassmann, a private consultant, who has suggested that the IRS "has a 'congenital disability' in attracting and retaining qualified systems management talent, 'especially at the executive levels.'" Maglitta further charged that the IRS was unable to technically supervise the work of outside contractors, such as TRW. This was because the IRS's inferior technical capabilities allowed it to be somewhat easily "buffaloed" by those outside contractors. These charges of technical incompetence, painful as they are, were echoed by none other than Arthur Gross, the new chief of TSM, hired by Treasury Secretary Rubin to handle the problem-plagued TSM. Barely ten months after Gross took over he was quoted as acknowledging that the IRS lacked the "intellectual capital" for the job (IRS Admits Its Computers Are a Nightmare," 1997, A1). The cumulative effect of the above statements is to convey a broadly held view that the IRS technical staff working on TSM lacked the technical skills and experience necessary to ensure success in the venture.

It is generally reported that BAE is a "world leader in the design and implementation" of baggage handling systems (Montealegre et al. 1996, 8). For this reason, the DIA project leaders contacted BAE to take over the airportwide integrated baggage handling system when all the three companies that responded to the public bid on the project were deemed incapable of undertaking the project. The problems BHS experienced cannot justifiably be blamed on inadequate technical expertise on the part of BAE. Gene DiFonso, president of BAE, said of the BHS project: "When we arrived on the scene, we were faced with fully defined project specs, which obviously in the long run proved to be a major planning error" (Montealegre et al. 1996, 10). The project specifications were developed by the airport planners and consultants, apparently without any input from the major stakeholders and clients or users of the DIA project (Rifkin 1994). In addition to the above error, which resulted in frequent design changes to the BHS project, the schedule for completion of the project was considered by most experienced executives to be "too short given its complexity, size, and lack of structure and interdependence on project activities related to the airport construction project" (Applegate 1999, 6).

The lack of adequate time for fully testing the system and correcting any errors was a major contributing factor in the problems of BHS. This was a fact that DiFonso later came to acknowledge as a fundamental mistake BAE made in accepting the terms of the contract. For example, DiFonso explained that "although we had the technology developed, its implementation in a complex project like this would have required significantly greater time than the city had left available," because of all the testing required to correct the bugs in the system (Montealegre et al. 1996, 9). It is not clear what concessions BAE could have extracted from DIA project leaders other than assurances of greater ease of access to the concourses, given the time constraints under which the DIA project itself was operating as a result of the financing involved. Possessing adequate, even highly recognized expertise to undertake a particular software project without adequate provisions made for time of completion may doom the project from the start, especially if the design specifications are subject to frequent changes by user groups whose inputs were not represented in the original specifications.

The CODIS project was, from the point of view of technical expertise, no different from the Confirm and TSM projects. The new project director, hired to work on the project after previous attempts failed, said about the canceled project: "The major contributing factor was that most of the people hired to work on the project had *no real prior experience* [emphasis added] or knowledge of new systems development activities. Most of their experience had been involved with maintenance-related activities. There was a general lack of know-how on basic, indeed fundamental, activities like writing memos, taking minutes of meetings on user information requirements, and providing formal guidelines on how new systems development activities should be conducted or carried out" (Ewusi-Mensah 1998, 13).

The technical expertise of the project team must not be the only issue of concern here. As I have argued elsewhere, "The scope of the project is also a significant concern in abandoned projects. Projects that are excessively grand in scope tend to have built-in difficulties, higher risks, and levels of complexity that may frustrate even some competent teams" (Ewusi-Mensah 1997, 77). The KPMG study (Cole 1995) also confirmed that "overly ambitious" projects were good candidates for potential failure. This was arguably the situation with Confirm, Delta, TSM, and DIA's BHS, where the scope of each of the projects was generally viewed as being rather broad and overly ambitious. In addition, technical complexity may lead to compartmentalization of the various interacting parts of a project. This makes it imperative that adequate time be set aside for testing the various modules or components in order that all the identifiable bugs can be eliminated. A failure to allow sufficient time for testing, particularly of complex software projects, is often blamed for contributing to the problems the projects subsequently experience during their implementation. This was the case in both FoxMeyer's Delta and Hershey Foods' ERP projects briefly discussed in chapter 1. Effective coordination of the various subparts is therefore essential for project success, thus introducing another layer of complexity, risk, and uncertainty into the development process. The BHS project illustrates these challenges, because of the coordination difficulties BAE encountered in gaining access to various work sites. Indeed, the role of a competent project leader with "both application–domain knowledge and software knowledge" to guide and coordinate the activities of the various subgroups is vitally critical to the project's success (Krault and Streeter 1995, 69; also see Curtis, Krasner, and Iscoe 1988, for a similar view).

**Problematic Technology Base/Infrastructure**
Technology infrastructure includes the IT resources of the organization—that is, computer hardware, telecommunications and networking facilities, software tools, software development methodologies, the requisite technical personnel, and so on. The technology infrastructure provides a critical foundation for an organization's new systems development projects. It furnishes the essential physical structure on which the entire systems development effort rests. Any structural weaknesses in the technology are bound to pose a major threat to the viability of the systems development process. Consequently, it is incumbent on the project leadership to be unequivocally certain that the existing technology infrastructure is judged appropriate to the task prior to the start of any major systems development project. Similarly, the senior management of the

organization has a responsibility to satisfy itself that the organization's technology base is indeed adequate to the task. "Projects must not be approved for development unless and until senior executives are fully convinced that the organization's technology base is satisfactory to the task. Failure to get that assurance from the IT management unduly increases the risks and uncertainties normally associated with systems development work to an unacceptable level," laying the foundation for potential problems in the projects in the future (Ewusi-Mensah 1997, 77).

For the Confirm project, Flowers (1997) provides a schematic representation of the design architecture, illustrated in figure 5.1.

The Transaction Management Function (TMF) was to provide the interface to the various classifications of users—Airline Reservation Systems, Hotel Management Systems, Travel Agents, and Others—and to the two IBM mainframe computers. One mainframe computer would run the IBM MVS operating system and would be used to store data on

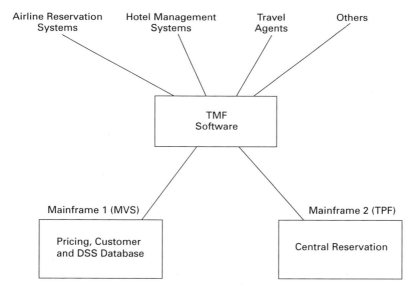

**Figure 5.1**
Structure of Confirm system. *Source:* Flowers 1997

pricing and customers in DB2 databases, together with decision-support system (DSS) data. The other mainframe computer was to use IBM's Transaction Processing Facility (TPF) operating system to process car and hotel reservations using C-language program instructions. The two mainframe computers were to be "connected to each other through a channel-to-channel bridge," as McPartlin (1992, 12) notes. However, the expected communication between the two computers did not work as planned. In addition, there were recovery problems associated with the DB2 relational databases in the event of a system crash.

The failure of the database to recover in the event of a crash was attributed, by the vice president of operations for Intrico, to the fact that "in the development of the DB2-based decision support system, the company mistakenly implemented a version of Texas Instruments' [TI] Information Engineering Facility (IEF) computer-aided software engineering tool in which IEF generates its own database structure." The vice president is again reported to have suggested that for Confirm's size, Intrico "should have implemented a version of IEF in which the structure is dictated [because] . . . the system was so big that what IEF generated would have been impossible to maintain" (Halper 1992, 10).

The decision to have a version of TI's IEF CASE tool generate its own database structure was indeed fateful because it became a major contributor to Confirm's failure. The failure should have been anticipated, since AMRIS had never used a CASE tool for that purpose before. It had no prior experience from which to determine if it would work, and in the event of a failure what the likely problems would be and how they might be corrected. As it turned out, the CASE tool did not work as expected and the failure became a basis for severe criticism of the project's management.

Another major source of the failure was the inability of TMF to handle the interface problems associated with the two mainframe systems, as well as with the Airline and Hotel reservation systems and the users' and travel agents' terminals connected to the Confirm system. The data overload the system experienced had not been previously tested or simulated to determine if the design could withstand that level of stress. Furthermore, the failure of the DB2 database to recover fully in the event of a crash compounded the problem. The orders-of-magnitude difficulties presented by the size of the project and the distributed system associated with the project should have led AMRIS management to be somewhat more cautious about trying out technologies not yet proven in the organization, or at least technologies with which they had no prior experience. In addition, if the charge that people were "hired off the street" for the project is valid, it further raises some serious questions as to the capacity of the project team to deal with the technology, and their likelihood of success.

At the core of the Delta project is a client-server system that was to be installed by Hewlett-Packard, and on which the SAP R/3 software was to be implemented. The client-server system was intended to replace the aging Unisys mainframe computer system on which the FoxMeyer distribution system was implemented. The move to the client-server system was necessitated by the company's business strategy and the anticipated growth in business, which top management envisioned would outstrip the mainframe technology (Jesitus 1997; Bulkeley 1996).

The SAP R/3 was originally designed for manufacturers, and FoxMeyer's own independent consultant suggested that it lacked "many features for the wholesale distribution business" because it had never been implemented to run an operation of that nature (Bulkeley 1996, 2). This concern about the software's capacity to handle the huge volume of FoxMeyer's business transactions led the project team first to run simulations to test whether SAP R/3 could handle the 500,000 lines of invoice FoxMeyer generated each day. Unfortunately, the simulations never came close to approximating the level of data involved in a typical operating environment (Bulkeley 1996; Jesitus 1997). In other words, the technology support that FoxMeyer management expected would lead them to create a more cost-effective and efficient operation (with anticipated savings of up to $40 million a year) had no proven record to justify their faith in its viability. The bankruptcy trustee accused Andersen of failing to inform FoxMeyer of SAP's volume limitations, which rendered it "incapable of running the sales distribution/order processing operations at each warehouse" (LJX FILES, 1998, 38). SAP R/3 had not even been proven capable of handling more than 10,000 lines of invoice a day. It was alleged that Andersen became aware of this fact soon after work on the project began, yet failed to disclose the information to FoxMeyer executives. Furthermore, the technical staff Andersen assigned to the project was alleged to lack the requisite technical expertise and experience.

The trustee specifically stated in his suit that Andersen had never "implemented any solution to allow SAP to meet the volume demands" of the company. For example, the allegation stated categorically that none of FoxMeyer's seventeen non-UHC warehouses were ever converted by Andersen to run/operate the SAP system (LJX FILES, 1998, 40). For an IT project to succeed, both the hardware infrastructure and the software to run on it have to be proven effective and capable of handling the volume of data in a typical operating day in the systems environment. This was not the case in the Delta project.

Furthermore, the computerized warehouse developed by Pinnacle Automation to provide "state-of-the-art computerized pickers" was reported to be "so bug-ridden" that it required several extra months of testing. Because the system kept failing and shutting down the conveyor belt additional manpower was required to put the orders together on the right track (Bulkeley 1996, 3). However, Jesitus (1997, 36) reports that Pinnacle accepted responsibility only for "problems of motherboard failure" and placed the bulk of the responsibility for the systems failure on the existing Unisys-based system. Pinnacle believed that integrating the Unisys-based system with SAP R/3 failed to give the Pinnacle-installed computerized pickers the right information in a timely manner (Jesitus 1997). Changes in the original design specifications requested by FoxMeyer after the project had been started were also fingered as contributing to the overall problems of the systems failure. For example, one of Pinnacle's executives claimed that "we were told to design a system that could ship in X number of hours, and we designed a system that could do that. Then, later, it became a requirement that they be able to ship in one-third to one-half that time" (Jesitus 1997, 36). These are some of the factors that contributed to the project's failure.

The GAO (1995) report on TSM found a number of deficiencies with respect to TSM technical activities. There was, for example, nonexistent systems architecture for TSM, and there were no defined interfaces and standards to ensure that TSM components would successfully integrate and interoperate. In fairness, GAO also found ongoing work on an integrated systems architecture for TSM, but it considered that to be of limited value since work on TSM was already in progress. In a Computer World article on Hank Philcox, then chief information officer for the IRS, Anthes (1996b, 28) writes that "the IRS computer systems were on the verge of collapse" in 1986 when Philcox took charge of TSM. Anthes also comments on Philcox's response to criticisms that the TSM project had "wasted $2.5 billion," claiming that they had made substantial progress and built an infrastructure where before "underpowered mainframes and inefficient software took five days to do 'weekend' file updates." By 1990 the improvements in infrastructure— "automation plus the network"—were credited with having reduced processing delays and manual effort in IRS operations. The productivity increases were such that a net of 4,000 clerical positions was eliminated.

The BHS project ran into severe problems as a consequence of several factors, which included lack of adequate infrastructure. Because the plans for the baggage handling system were drawn up rather late, insufficient consideration was given to some of the critical underlying infrastructure features needed for a baggage system. As DiFonso explained later, the city severely underplayed "the importance and significance of some of the requirements of a baggage system, that is arranging things for the space into which [the system] must fit, accommodating the weight it may impose on the building structure, the power it requires to run, and the ventilation and air conditioning that may be necessary to dissipate the heat it generates" (Montealegre et al. 1996, 10).

Whether the above-cited complaints can be explained away as the consequence of the BHS specifications being put together by airport planners and consultants, perhaps with limited knowledge and understanding of the type of infrastructure provisions that needed to be made for the BHS project, is unclear. Although time pressures constrained the work of BAE on the BHS project, the failure of the city to include any organization or persons with expertise and experience in baggage handling systems in the development of the BHS specifications was a critical omission that had severe repercussions for the project's outcome. Another major infrastructure issue was that of securing a smooth power supply for the project. According to BAE's DiFonso, the city of Denver had a problem supplying "clean" electricity to the baggage system. This created its own set of problems for the BHS project because of the extreme sensitivity of the motors and circuitry to power surges and fluctuations (Montealegre et al. 1996). Attempts made to resolve this problem became lost in a tangle of bureaucracy, which resulted in further delays on the project since the filters required to handle the current fluctuations were not received until March 1994—the second date for the scheduled opening of the airport. It is amply clear in this case that the lack of available infrastructure, including a smooth power supply for the BHS project, was a major factor in the problems BAE encountered in attempting to complete the project under the tight schedule.

The CODIS project was in an even more precarious position with respect to its technology infrastructure. The new vice president of MIS, hired to manage the MIS department, described what he found when he joined the company as follows: "The mainframe computer had reached its capacity; they were running three different operating systems, none of which was current; there was no documentation for the application programs which were 15–17 years old; there was a proliferation of PCs with end-users actively involved in finding 'PC kinds of solutions' to their problems without any input from the MIS department; IS personnel were not up-to-date on technology, they were preoccupied with maintenance and enhancements to the existing applications," among a host of other problems (Ewusi-Mensah 1992, 8).

The above cases collectively convey a stark picture of projects lacking the technology infrastructure to serve as a foundation prior to their onset. All the projects experienced difficulties that may be partly attributable to deficiencies in the existing technology base and/or physical infrastructure. It is conceivable, though highly unlikely because of other factors, that the projects could have succeeded had these infrastructure deficiencies been dealt with appropriately prior to the start of the projects. That the projects were allowed to proceed in spite of the weak technology bases speaks unfavorably about the failure of technical and managerial leadership in the respective organizations. Therefore, it is not surprising that management problems are often cited in studies of software failures, runaways, and abandonment as being among the leading causes (see, for example, Ewusi-Mensah 1997; Cole 1995; Standish Group 1995; Johnson 1995).

## Impact of Technical Factors on Systems Development Stages

We have, in the preceding sections, discussed the details of the specific factors that make up the sociotechnical-factor category with influence on decisions to abandon projects. We have provided appropriate descriptive details from the five projects that are illustrative of the significance of the technical and technology issues in the systems development process. The goal of the discussion in this section is to point out the collective impact of this factor category on the various stages of the systems development life cycle.

The framework for abandoned projects presented in chapter 3 described the collective impact of the sociotechnical-factor category on each of the three stages of the systems development life cycle. In the requirements stage, as indicated previously, because the emphasis is on deciding what the needs of the system must be, the sociotechnical factors play a limited role in making that determination. This is partly because of the critical role of the socioorganizational factors in the requirements determination. The project goals and objectives and changing requirements, which together constitute part of the sociotechnical-factor category, are also included in the socioorganizational-factor category. The cumulative impact of the sociotechnical-factor category is thus mildly critical compared to that of the socioorganizational-factor category in the requirements stage of systems development.

The design stage, which deals with the technical issues of how to satisfy the systems requirements, is typically dominated by concerns about what is technically feasible. As a result, the technical-factor portion, which constitutes the majority of the factors in this category, plays a more critical role in the activities of the design stage than in the requirements stage. The sociotechnical factors are thus seen to be critical in tackling problems related to the design of the systems of the respective projects. Issues dealing with the project-team composition, technical expertise, and technology infrastructure of the organization are central to the satisfactory resolution of design issues associated with the entire development process. The influence of the social dimension of the sociotechnical-factor category tends to diminish as the development process moves forward to the implementation stage.

The implementation stage deals more with the construction and testing of the designed systems, and with the integration of completed subsystems. The role of the project goals and objectives and changing requirements ideally should be quite limited at this later stage of the systems development process if the project is to be completed successfully. Any unresolved problems dealing with the scope of the project or its specifications cannot be responsibly addressed at this late stage in the development life cycle without severe delays in the schedule and possible increases in the estimated costs. Still, the dominance of the sociotechnical factors must not be discounted at the implementation stage because the issues that have a critical impact on the viability of the development process are fundamentally technical and technological. For example, the level of technical expertise and experience of the development team and project leadership combine with the available technical infrastructure to critically influence the outcome of the implementation stage. Consequently, the collective impact of the sociotechnical-factor category is deemed critical to the implementation success of the systems development process.

## Conclusion

In this chapter we have reviewed the technical and technological factors identified in published studies and discussed how they contribute to the abandonment of software projects. We have shown how each of the technical factors in the sociotechnical category can influence the outcomes of software projects. We have analyzed the critical impact of each technical factor on each project case presented in chapter 4. Finally, we have discussed the collective impact the technical factors generally have on the requirements, design, and implementation phases of the systems development process, using the framework presented in chapter 3 to illustrate the significant role the factors can play in the entire software development process.

As software projects become increasingly complex and intellectually demanding, application of more sophisticated technology becomes necessary to accomplish the task of creating the desired artifacts. Rapid advances in IT notwithstanding, the technical skills and experience of project teams in some organizations have not, in some instances, measured up to the demands of the technology. Still, it is at the design and implementation stages of the development process that the technology fault lines are unquestionably exposed. The project is most vulnerable here because of the demands the technology imposes at these critical phases of the development process. Hence, in the final analysis the sociotechnical factors have a more decisive influence on the project outcome at the design and implementation stages than at the requirements stage of the development process.

# 6
# Economic Factors and Abandoned Projects

Software development is in general a capital-intensive activity consuming substantial financial and other organizational resources over time. Estimates of software development costs and time of completion are based on a variety of factors, notably the following: the scope of the project; the frequency and breadth of changes requested after the project is initiated; the stages in the development life cycle at which the changes are anticipated to be made; the technical and technology resources, including the experience and level of expertise of the technical personnel and the project leadership available for tackling the project. The accuracy of the estimates is partly influenced by the size and complexity of the project, the newness of the project in the organization's technical experience and IT environment, the robustness of the estimating model, the objectivity of the estimators, and the identifiable risks and uncertainties associated with the development process.

In this chapter we analyze the factors that contribute to the cost overruns and schedule delays associated with abandoned software development projects. We analyze the influence of those twin issues on decisions to abandon projects. We use information from published reports on the five project cases presented in chapter 4 to illustrate how the decisions to abandon those five projects were significantly influenced by the economic factors. Finally, we discuss the collective impact of the economic factors on the requirements, design, and implementation stages of the systems development process and point out the vulnerabilities of each of the three stages to project-abandonment decisions.

The cost of software development is affected by the development schedule. As the time of completion is pushed backward due, for example, to changes in requirements and/or in the scope of the project, the estimated cost of the project may increase. On the other hand, attempts to keep to the original project schedule by increasing the size of the project team may sometimes have an adverse effect, due to the extra time needed to train the new team members and to bring them up to the functional level of the current team, thereby possibly increasing the overall cost of the project. Brooks ([1975] 1995, 25) succinctly makes the point with the aphorism that the effect of adding more people to an existing software project that is late is to make it later. Abdel-Hamid and Madnick (1990), on the other hand, caution against overgeneralizing that observation, because in their experience the results of adding staff to a project that is already late will depend on other attributes of the particular project. Still, "the added burden of communication" needed for each new team member "to be trained in the technology, the goals of the effort, the overall strategy and the plan of work" can contribute substantially to the cost estimates (Brooks 1995, 18). Thus, increasing the number of personnel involved in the project will likely increase the cost of the project and extend the time of completion. Alternatively, if the project is allowed to exceed its schedule estimates without an increase in the number of personnel involved, the cost of the project will also likely increase. Hence, the twin issues of project cost and time of completion constitute the main underlying economic problem in tackling project-abandonment decisions.

**Economic Issues in Abandoned Projects**

Software development as a capital- and labor-intensive venture is often governed by decisions having to do with the economic viability of the project. For example, organizations are likely to abandon a project when they anticipate that the expected benefits of continued development may be exceeded by the further costs to be incurred. Thus, strictly on a cost-benefit basis, a project may be abandoned if the organization runs into severe problems in the course of the project development. The cost overruns and schedule slippage may expose the project as being either "technologically or organizationally infeasible." Elsewhere, I have described technologically infeasible projects as projects that "may be highly innovative and may involve technologies not familiar to the enterprise" (Ewusi-Mensah 1989, 206). That is, in essence, the organization may discover relatively late in the course of project development that it lacks the requisite level of technical expertise and experience to successfully complete the project and, therefore, any additional costs incurred are not likely to affect the outcome. Organizationally infeasible projects "may be highly dependent on the existence of an appropriate socio-technical environment within the enterprise to ensure implementation success." In this case also, the organization may realize after the project has been underway for some time that the existing technology infrastructure is not adequate to meet the needs of the project and thus that any further expenditures may not be sufficient to correct the problem. In both cases, then, the economic issues may only be symptomatic of the more fundamental problems existing somewhere in the project development process and environment. Thus, although an abandonment decision may be justified on economic grounds, the real locus of the decision may be found among the sociotechnical and/or socioorganizational factors associated with the development process. In chapters 4 and 5 we discussed the socioorganizational and sociotechnical factors, respectively, contributing to abandoned projects. In this chapter we focus on the contributions of the two main economic issues of cost overruns and schedule delays to project abandonment decisions. The first part of the discussion is based on analysis of the data from the Fortune 500 study, the details of which are presented in chapter 4.

The category of economic issues shown in table 6.1 is derived from the collection of twelve factor categories listed in table 4.10. The three primary issues, which fall under the economic-factor category from the factor analysis of the Fortune 500 study data, are escalating project costs

**Table 6.1**
Economic factors (extracted from table 4.10)

| Factor no. | Factor description |
| --- | --- |
| F1 | Escalating project costs and completion schedules |
| F3 | Actual project expenditures and duration below estimates |
| F10 | Lack of funds |

and completion schedules, actual project expenditures and duration, and funds available to the project.

Software projects that are over cost and behind schedule always run the risk of eventual cancellation. However, the cost overruns and schedule delays should not be mistaken for the root causes of the project failure. In most instances the real problem may be socioorganizational and/or sociotechnical, the two contributing factors discussed in the preceding two chapters. Still, it is important for us to examine the basis of the economic issues involved in decisions to abandon projects because they provide valuable insights into the underlying problems that may have escaped the attention of project management, through either oversight or neglect.

Factor F1, dealing with escalating project costs and completion schedules, may in most instances mask a variety of unresolved and/or persistent problems associated with the project. For example, problems may be related to project goals and objectives that are somehow ambiguous or lacking consensus prior to the start of the development. Such problems may frequently manifest themselves in changing requirements on which the rest of the development may depend. Whenever such changes are uncontrolled or become excessive, they tend to drive up the original cost estimates and may also add to the time of completion. At other times, the estimates of costs and time of completion may be faulted because they were derived from an evolving and unstable project scope, due perhaps to some differing perspectives among the stakeholder groups. Thus, factor F1 may be partially explained by inadequate information or systems requirements prior to the beginning of the development. This finding was substantiated by the fact that the "project personnel [often underestimate] the IS requirements problem," as reported in Ewusi-Mensah and Przasnyski 1994, 197. We can, therefore, surmise that the root of the escalating costs and schedule delays contributing to project cancellation is the more fundamental problem of information or systems requirements failure.

Alternatively, where there are no problems with the project goals and objectives there may, however, still be problems associated with the design of the systems, which may not be uncovered until later in the implementation stage. The extra time and effort required to correct such problems may also contribute to cost overruns and schedule delays, and even worse, may have ripple effects on other systems integrated into the target system. Studies have shown that the later in the development life cycle such problems are uncovered (either in the design and/or implementation stages), the higher the potential additional costs to the project (see, for example, Ramamoorthy et al. 1984; Boehm 1981). Whenever such cost increments are substantial and/or the completion delays are found to be unacceptable, they may significantly influence the decision to cancel the project. For example, in discussing the Confirm case in chapter 5, I alluded to the design problems uncovered during the implementation stage—problems that eventually led to the demise of the project.

Factor F3 deals with "actual project expenditures and duration below estimates," on the other hand, and presents a different rationale for some abandoned projects. The analysis of the data "consistently showed that both the cost of the completed portion of the project and the time spent on the project at the time of abandonment were lower than the estimated values" (Ewusi-Mensah and Przasnyski 1994, 199). The negative factor loadings on some of the variables served to confirm that fact and led to the conclusion that "abandonment may not only be dictated by escalating project costs and time of completion schedules, but may in some cases be actually the consequence of other problems associated with the project" (p. 192). This is because the actual incurred cost and the expended time on some abandoned projects at the time of abandonment may actually be below the projected estimates.

Finally, factor F10 indicates "lack of funds" as the cause of the project's cancellation. As argued in Ewusi-Mensah and Przasnyski 1994. "It is obvious that once a project's funding is terminated, there is a high likelihood that the project may eventually be terminated. What is more interesting is determining the underlying causes for the 'lack of funds' leading to the project's eventual termination." It is suggested that perhaps the explanation resides with factors such as "escalating project cost and lengthening completion schedules" or with "loss of critical personnel and management changes associated with a project" (p. 195). The suspicion is that both of the above factors may be at the root of the "lack of funds" that may potentially lead to the project's termination. Thus merely stating that the project was terminated for "lack of funds" is insufficient to explain the project's cancellation. The underlying reasons why the project ran out of funds will provide a more meaningful explanation for why it was terminated. Organizations do not routinely embark on major software development projects without giving adequate consideration to the funding needs and schedule-completion estimates and the associated strategic and/or competitive benefits they expect to gain from the project's completion.

## Analysis of Abandoned-Project Cases: The Economic Issues

I have stated elsewhere that in the computer industry it is common knowledge that "projects are still over budget and behind schedule in far more cases than IS professionals and management find acceptable" (Ewusi-Mensah 1997, 78; also see Glaser 1984). Projects that are severely over budget and behind schedule may, in general, represent more fundamental problems than usual in the systems development process. Brooks has remarked in his influential book on project management titled *The Mythical Man-Month* ([1975] 1995) that projects fall behind schedule one day at a time, and similarly become over budget. We are therefore persuaded that any search for the underlying factors in the problems of cost overruns and schedule delays should always begin elsewhere in the project's development history. Thus, information on a project being severely over budget and behind schedule may force management to act by canceling the project, where previously there were delays and postponements of unpleasant decisions. The cost overruns and schedule delays must not be misconstrued as the root causes of the project's failure.

This section is devoted to an examination of the economic issues in the five example project cases—Confirm, Delta, TSM, DIA's BHS, and CODIS—under discussion. Issues of a noneconomic nature that may have an indirect economic impact on the development project will not be addressed in this context. For example, design and implementation errors that are technical in nature but that otherwise have a potential economic impact on the development process are excluded from the discussion. Interested readers should turn to the discussions in chapter 5 that bear directly on those problems.

The dominant abandonment factors that comprise the economic-factor category discussed in the framework of chapter 3 and listed in table 3.3 are:

- Cost overruns and schedule delays
- Unrealistic project goals and objectives
- Changing requirements

The last two factors—unrealistic project goals and objectives, and changing requirements—have been discussed in conjunction with the socio-organizational and sociotechnical factors that bear on decisions to abandon the projects. The factors resurface here because of the direct economic impact they have on the project's outcome. For example, the scope of the project—that is, the functional specifications derived from the project's goals and objectives—will be fundamentally relevant in estimating the cost of the project and its tentative completion schedule. To the extent that changes in the project's scope will lead to changes in the requirements for the project, such changes will most likely have implications for the estimated project cost as well as for the completion schedule.

As such changes become frequent and have wider impact on the rest of the development process, the overall cost of the project will be duly affected, and so will the completion schedule. Thus, in essence, such changes may be at the root of the escalating project costs and schedule delays. The breadth and depth of such changes in the requirements necessitated by a changing or unstable project scope and/or ambiguous or overly ambitious project goals and objectives have a direct impact on the sustainability of the cost estimates and time-of-completion schedules.

However, regardless of the loci of such changes in project costs and/or time of completion, the evidence in some abandoned projects is that cost overruns and schedule delays may contribute to the project's eventual termination. Evidence from other studies confirms that for about half of the respondents to a survey, the cost of the project and the time of completion do "not seem to play any significant role in subsequent decisions to abandon those projects" (Ewusi-Mensah and Przasnyski 1991, 77).

### Cost Overruns and Schedule Delays

The Confirm project presents us with a classic example of escalating project costs and time of completion. Analyses by Oz (1994) and Flowers (1997) provide us with the chronology of the facts with respect to project costs and schedule delays. The cost of the project was originally estimated to be $55.7 million in April 1988 with a completion date of June 1992, and was later revised to $72.6 million in September 1989. The latest cost figure was subsequently revised to $92 million in February 1991, and the completion date was pushed back to March 1993. This trend in escalating project cost continued until the project was canceled, as Oz (1994, 32) reports: "In July 1992, after three-and-a-half years, and after spending $125 million on the project, the Intrico consortium disbanded." It was during the period outlined above that "some of the failure . . . due to bad management practices of all the four partners in the Intrico consortium" occurred, as Oz notes. For example, it has been reported that "the client-partners team met with the developer's representatives *just once a month* [emphasis added]." This apparent shortcoming was later cited by AMRIS executives as a major contributor to the problems leading to the eventual cancellation of Confirm. An AMRIS executive is quoted as saying that "you cannot manage a development effort of this magnitude by getting together once a month."

The IBM review undertaken in April 1989 confirmed that this was evidently the case. Indeed, the IBM team found, in addition to other problems, that "project management was perceived as promising anything to keep the project moving" (Zellner 1994, 36). In fact, it is reported that Marriott alleged in its suit that AMR engaged in endless delays and cost overruns and, furthermore, that there was a deliberate attempt in the upper echelons of AMR to conceal "Confirm's countless problems from the rest of the consortium" (McPartlin 1992, 12). Sources familiar with Confirm indicated to McPartlin that "the development schedules were *overly optimistic* [emphasis added] and relied on outmoded and unrelated technologies that were not up to the task."

The FoxMeyer Delta project also experienced escalating project costs and schedule delays. The bankruptcy trustee provided a detailed analysis of the "coercive" tactics it alleged Andersen used to prolong the project while billing FoxMeyer for defective work that needed to be corrected at Andersen's expense. For example, the original contract estimated an ambitious completion schedule of eighteen months at an estimated cost of $15 million. Yet as the suit states, by the time of the bankruptcy filing in August 1996, Andersen had collected "approximately $30 million in fees, representing a 100 percent increase over its $15 million estimate" (LJX FILES, 1998, 51).

The fees and schedule escalation came about as Andersen repeatedly threatened to pull its personnel from the project and thus to cease all work on it unless FoxMeyer acceded to Andersen's demands to sign a letter Andersen had drafted indicating completion of various portions of the project FoxMeyer claimed were in fact not completed, and to pay Andersen several hundred thousand dollars for "remedial work" in July and August 1995.

Approximately eighteen months after Andersen began work on the Delta project at a cost of a $1 million per month, FoxMeyer felt it "could neither abandon the project entirely nor engage a new consulting firm to pick up in the middle" (LJX FILES, 1998, 54). Consequently, FoxMeyer felt compelled to give in to Andersen's demands rather than risk abandoning the project. Still, the trustee claimed in its suit that Andersen failed to convert even one of the remaining seventeen non-UHC warehouses at the time of the bankruptcy filing in August 1996, which was estimated to be "a full year after Andersen first announced its purported solution to SAP's volume problems" (LJX FILES, 1998, 58). The facts of the case as summarized above from the trustee's perspective are similarly described in the reports by Bulkeley (1996) and Jesitus (1997), with the exception of the alleged coercive tactics Andersen used to extract concessions from FoxMeyer.

As observed earlier in this chapter, issues of cost overruns and completion delays are almost always symptomatic of deeper problem(s) in the project. It is apparent that in this case the original schedule and cost estimates were overly optimistic and unrealistic, given the following conditions: the limitations of SAP, which was originally designed for

manufacturing operations; the need for the system in distributed warehouse operations to "handle hundreds of thousands of transactions
daily" (Jesitus 1997, 34); the newness of the SAP R/3 technology/system
both to Andersen—its representations of expertise and experience
notwithstanding—and to FoxMeyer's in-house staff; the changes in the
requirements brought about by the acquisition of the UHC contract; and
the enormous difficulties associated with the integration of three disparate technologies—the Unisys-based mainframe system, the SAP R/3
system, and the warehouse computerized automation system—difficulties that were grossly underestimated. All of these factors made cost overruns and schedule delays on the Delta project inevitable.

The TSM project was proposed in late 1986 at an estimated cost of $8
to $10 billion with a scheduled completion date in 2001. In fiscal year
1995, the GAO reported $2.5 billion of the budget had been spent or
obligated, and an additional $1.1 billion had been requested for fiscal year
1996. However, the GAO reported in January 1995 that the IRS advised
the House Budget Committee that TSM would cost about $13 billion to
develop and operate. This figure was based on an October 1992 TSM cost
model, which the GAO found unreliable because it did not adequately
reflect the systems added to TSM since that time and, in particular,
"changes in TSM systems development methods." In March 1996, the
*Los Angeles Times* reported a revised figure of $20 billion for the mod-
ernization of what it termed the IRS's "badly outdated computer systems"
("IRS Computer Project Has 'Very Serious Problems,' Rubin Says," 1996,
D1). In the same article, the Secretary of the Treasury, Robert Rubin, was
reported to have acknowledged that there was as yet no comprehensive
plan for tackling the problem. Up to that time approximately $4 billion
was reported to have been spent on TSM, yet there was "basically nothing
to show for it," as Representative Lightfoot, chair of the House Subcom-
mittee on Treasury, Postal Services, and General Government, of the
Committee on Appropriations (which approves IRS funding), was
reported to have remarked (Anthes 1996, 28).

The cost of the BHS project was estimated to be $195 million, the
figure BAE agreed to in the contract to build the airportwide integrated
baggage handling system. BAE signed the contract to complete the
project within about two years under some specified conditions includ-

ing, according to DiFonso, an agreement that the design would not change beyond a certain date and that "there would be a number of freeze dates for mechanical design, software design, and permanent power requirements" (Rifkin 1994, 113). The city also agreed to provide BAE with unrestricted access to work areas for its equipment and personnel to install needed systems in order to meet the tight deadlines for BHS's completion.

All of the above conditions in the agreement were hammered out with the support, cooperation, and active participation of the chief airport engineer, who had been a strong proponent of the integrated airportwide baggage handling system. But soon after BAE began work on the project in April 1992, the carriers asked for a number of design changes. For example, United Airlines requested changes to its concourse, reducing its original two loops to a single loop track, saving $20 million from its share of the cost. Continental Airlines requested "a far larger baggage link," and a host of other changes that required redesign of the system, adding to the schedule changes and increases in cost of the BHS.

On the issue of unrestricted access for BAE equipment and personnel, Rifkin (1994) reports some disagreements as to what the understanding was between BAE and the DIA authorities. However, what is not in dispute is the fact that until the death of the chief airport engineer, who played a crucial role in the talks to convince BAE to accept the contract, work proceeded quite well without much friction. But soon after Slinger's death, the problems concerning access surfaced and contributed to work delays, because his successor was not able to exercise Slinger's considerable influence to move the project along. After BAE lost its most powerful ally and champion in DIA's senior management ranks, its problems with the implementation of BHS began to spiral out of control, to the point that the mayor called a press conference to give a demonstration of the BHS, reportedly without even notifying BAE about it. The situation became so poisoned that the city and BAE ceased communicating with each other. The city eventually hired a consultant to assess its options; this led to the development of a backup baggage system and a request for BAE to pay a penalty of $12,000 a day for the numerous delays in completion of the BHS and postponements of the opening day for the DIA, in addition to paying for the backup baggage system at a reported cost to the city of $50 million. Naturally, as is almost always the case in such software development project failures, BAE countersued the city and, of course, the major carriers had their legal departments research their rights and options in future litigation involving the cost overruns and project delays.

What is unfortunate in the above scenario is that the BHS project might not have come to such an end if a number of prudent steps had been taken by the city and BAE early on to avoid the problems that ensued. Missteps included the failure of the city to include the baggage handling system in the initial planning stages of DIA, assuming that it would be the primary responsibility of the carriers using the concourses; the failure of both the city and BAE to recognize the major impact of the design changes on the final project outcome in terms of cost and time of completion; the failure of BAE executives to comprehend the size and complexity of the BHS project as being beyond anything in their past experience and therefore requiring considerable effort on their part; the failure of both BAE and the city to recognize that the tight deadlines required a different approach to managing the project than would have been the case under normal circumstances; the failure on both sides to anticipate loss of critical personnel who might be champions of the BHS project and to put in place mechanisms to ensure seamless transitions for their replacements. All of the above factors conspired to doom the project from the beginning.

In the case of CODIS, we do not have figures indicating what the estimated project cost and completion schedule were prior to the start of the project. This was not unexpected or surprising, given that the project was never treated as a new project proposal for which separate funding was requested. Instead, funding for CODIS was handled as part of the MIS department capital expenditure. Moreover, in the view held by the new director of MIS hired to develop CODIS from scratch, the project evolved, in essence, as a series of "fixes" to an already badly outdated system. He complained about the outmoded practices he encountered in the project group, which failed to approach the new project development as being separate and distinct from regular systems maintenance operations within the organization. Despite those misgivings, funding for the project was never considered problematic in the organization because it was prepared to spend whatever was needed to get the project completed, due to the importance it attached to the project with respect to the company's future growth and survival (Ewusi-Mensah 1998).

It can be inferred from the preceding discussion that economic issues, in the absence of other compelling contributing factors, may not be sufficient to cause a project to be discontinued. In fact, projects may be discontinued in instances where the expended project cost and time schedule are below the budgeted estimates. It is considered sound management practice to "know when to pull the plug" on a project that may not be over budget and/or behind schedule in order to conserve organizational resources on a problematic development process.

However, projects may be abandoned because the original cost and schedule estimates were badly flawed and/or because the cost overruns and schedule delays reflect deeper problems uncovered during the course of the development process (Ewusi-Mensah and Przasnyski 1994, 1991). For example, analysis of the Confirm case has shown that the underlying causes of the escalating project costs and schedule delays are primarily bad project management and decision making, as well as reliance on inadequate or inappropriate technology. In the TSM and DIA's BHS projects, the escalating costs and schedule delays can be attributed to a variety of factors including, but not restricted to, inadequate planning and inappropriate oversight in a highly bureaucratic organizational setting. Furthermore, Delta, TSM, and DIA's BHS were overly ambitious and highly innovative projects, the successful outcome of which depended on a technology base and technical skills and experience on the part of the project teams that were nonexistent in the FoxMeyer, IRS, and BAE cases, respectively, as noted in the previous two chapters.

The cost overruns and schedule delays were just inevitable manifestations of those problems. Unfortunately these are the issues that consistently rise to the surface, burying the real culprits: the problems that gave rise to them. This situation is not surprising, because the technical issues involved in software development are often elusive and opaque to senior management (leaving aside issues of cost and schedule completions). Cost and schedule issues are the issues that executives in charge of project development are able to react to and make decisions on, affecting the future of the endeavor and all those who were engaged in it for the organization. Consequently, technical and/or technological problems at the root of the software project's problematic development history often manifest themselves in cost overruns and schedule delays when not properly addressed. When such problems become apparent, senior management often react negatively to the situation and cancel the project. This is because cost overruns and schedule delays are two of the nontechnical critical factors in software project development that nontechnical senior executives can fully understand, which causes them to cancel the project in order to safeguard organizational resources.

### Impact of Economic Factors on Systems Development Stages

The issues of economic importance and relevance to decisions of abandonment in software projects have been enumerated and discussed in the preceding sections. In this section, we are specifically interested in examining the general impact the economic factors have on the various stages of the systems development process. The discussion will be within the context of the framework for abandoned projects developed in chapter 3. The primary issue of interest is to analyze what impact the factors comprising the economic-factor category have on each stage of the systems development process and the nature and significance of that impact.

How does the primary issue of cost overruns and schedule delays affect the outcome of the requirements phase of the systems development process? The three constituent issues of the economic-factor category—that is, cost overruns and schedule delays, unrealistic project goals and objectives, and changing requirements—collectively have insignificant influence on the outcome of the project's requirements at the start of the project. The only exception to this is the issue of unrealistic project goals and objectives, which in concert with other issues articulated in the socioorganizational- and technical-factor categories does exert critical influence in shaping the outcome of the project requirements. However, the influence of the goals and objectives is really limited to determining what the system must accomplish; otherwise they have virtually no impact in determining how much it will cost to produce the end product.

Estimates of project costs and completion schedules are rather vague at this early stage of the development and only become clear when the design alternatives are developed and discussed. Because software is a "design know-how" activity, it is at the design stage of the systems development process that the relevant issues dealing with how to satisfy the specified requirements get aired and debated in the project team. The cost of the project and the schedule of completion are ultimately affected by the design decisions made in the course of the discussions. At that stage in the development process, the estimates of project costs and completion schedules may have some impact on what design alternatives may be found acceptable by a consensus of stakeholders and approved for implementation. Until that phase of the development process is reached, the economic factors have limited or no impact on the requirements-gathering phase; therefore, we describe their collective impact as mildly critical to the requirements.

In the abandonment framework, we have described economic issues as mildly critical in influencing the outcome of the design and implementation stages of the development life cycle. The issues of cost overruns and schedule delays do not determine or contribute directly to the work of the project team during the design and implementation phases. Nevertheless, changes in requirements occurring at the design and/or implementation stages have a potential economic impact on the rest of the development process. For example, we have previously described how excessive or uncontrolled changes may significantly add to the project cost and schedule estimates. Cost overruns and schedule slippages occurring in the design and/or implementation phases may draw attention to more fundamental problems with respect to the development. Although cost overruns and schedule delays may not be the primary cause of project failure at the design or implementation stages, they may indirectly induce management to act in canceling a project if they determine that the root problems cannot be solved at an acceptable revised cost and completion schedule. The Confirm project and, to a lesser extent, DIA's BHS and the CODIS projects are illustrative of such cases of abandonment decision making. Overall we can infer from the above discussion that the issues subsumed under the economic-factor category collectively exert a mildly critical influence in determining the outcomes of the design and implementation stages of the project's development life cycle.

## Conclusion

We have explained in the preceding pages what factors in software development projects compose the economic category of project-abandonment decisions. We have analyzed cost overruns and schedule delays, project goals and objectives, and the influence of changing requirements on software project development. We have examined, in particular, how cost overruns and schedule delays may be symptomatic of systemic problems in the development process. We have used the five project cases to illustrate and confirm the analyses by demonstrating in each how cost and schedule-delay concerns influenced the abandonment decision. Finally, we have analyzed the collective impact the three constituent economic factors have on the requirements, design, and implementation stages of the systems development process. We have asserted that the collective influence of the economic factors has a mild critical impact on the three software development stages because socioorganizational and technical factors have more to do with project outcome. We have explained that typically when difficulties associated with software development projects manifest themselves in cost overruns and schedule delays, the problems have ceased to be mainly technical or technological issues and instead have become those of organizational resource usage, and of what may be in the best strategic and economic interest of the organization. It is precisely at such a juncture in the life of the software development project that senior executives may act to cancel the project, if appropriate, to safeguard further consumption of organizational resources.

# 7

# User Perspectives on Software Development Failures

In the preceding three chapters we have analyzed a variety of factors grouped into three major categories—socioorganizational, technical and technological, and economic—and provided some perspectives on the multiple roles these factors play in contributing to the abandonment of a variety of software development projects in organizations. In this chapter I will closely examine, through a case study of a failed software development project, the interactions of three major stakeholders involved in the project—users, IS staff, and senior management. The case analysis will primarily be based on the perspectives of the users in determining the factors that contributed to the project development failure. Software development projects undertaken in organizations are invariably intended to benefit the user community. Consequently, a significant number of studies over the years have been devoted to understanding the role of users in systems development (see, for example, Newman and Noble 1990; Tait and Vessey 1988; Ives and Olson 1984). Unfortunately, little is known about the role users may play in contributing to software development project failures in organizations. Hence, examining the role or involvement of users in the failure of software development projects will be instructive in helping us gain a better understanding and appreciation of how users' involvement and expectations can be managed to minimize the risks of project development failures and enhance the likelihood of implementation success. The case study is also intended to validate the relevance of the factors discussed in chapters 4 through 6 as contributing to abandoned software development projects.

As indicated above, the role of users in software development has been extensively studied and reported in the software development and information systems (IS) literature. For example, it is widely accepted in IS development practice that the involvement of users is a necessary condition for the successful implementation and subsequent acceptance of a new IS in an organization (Newman and Noble 1990; Tait and Vessey 1988; Ives and Olson 1984; Edstrom 1977). User involvement in IS development has been described by some as the "participation in the system development process by representatives of the target user group" (Ives and Olson 1984, 587). Newman and Noble (1990, 89), on the other hand, define user involvement as "a process of interaction between systems specialists and users or their representatives." They provide four models that capture the essence of the interaction process between users and IS staff in a case study of a university admissions system. The process may take the form of learning, conflict, political influence, or garbage can, depending on the stage of the IS development process. Tait and Vessey (1988, 105), also present the results of a field study asserting the effect of user involvement on successful IS development to be contingent on such factors as "system complexity and constraints on the resources available for system development."

What is missing in the literature are studies that attempt to shed light on the role users play in software development failures. This is despite the fact that software development failures are a common, although underreported, occurrence in the software industry, according to DeMarco and Lister (1987). They assert that a code of silence about systems failures exists among industry specialists (see, for example, McFarlan 1981; Glaser 1984; Keider 1984; Lyytinen and Hirschheim 1987). McFarlan (1981) was perhaps the first to report on the frequent abandonment of IS development projects among even Fortune 500 companies. Ewusi-Mensah and Przasnyski (1991, 1994) later confirmed the incidence of the problem in a survey of companies in Southern California and also among Fortune 500 companies in the United States.

This chapter presents a case study of a software development project failure that occurred in an electronics distribution firm. The data from the project—CODIS, briefly described in chapter 4—is used to examine the views and perceptions of the users group in order to assess the underlying factors or issues that presumably contributed to the "failure" of the systems development effort. I begin with a brief description of the company, followed by an analysis of the users' involvement in the systems development effort. The analysis will focus on a number of specific factors and discuss from the users' perspectives the role they may have had in the project's failure. Finally, I present an interaction model dealing with the roles of all relevant stakeholders involved in a software development project.

**Company Profile**

The electronics distribution company is one of the five largest companies in sales volume in the industry. It provides suppliers of electronic products and equipment with nationwide coverage of customers in both the United States and Canada. Its customers are mainly original equipment manufacturers in the major industries of computer mainframes and peripherals, capital and office equipment, communications, medical equipment and instrumentation, the military, and aerospace. The general product areas it handles for its customers include semiconductors, connectors, passive components, computer systems, and peripherals. It also provides value-added services ranging from component testing and assembly to sophisticated computer interface services such as electronic data interchange.

Its sales revenue over the three-year period from 1989 to 1991 inclusive ranged from about $534 million to $583 million. The company has only three tiers of management hierarchy. At the top is the CEO and president, at the next level is the executive vice president and COO, and below the COO are twelve senior executives, as follows: the vice president of finance, who also reports to the president, regional vice presidents (nine of them), the senior vice president of marketing, the vice president of MIS, and the director of human resources. The above corporate officers together manage a network of thirty-nine distribution facilities and three regional support and distribution centers in the United States and Canada. Some time during the later half of the 1980s the company became convinced of the need to develop a new IS to meet the growing business demands for its services. A small cadre of users in the marketing department was asked by the senior vice president of marketing to spearhead the development for a project that would satisfy the IT needs of the company well into the 1990s.

**The CODIS Study**

The study describes the history of the IS development project, from the perspective of the users. I will refer to this project as CODIS (not its real acronym, as noted earlier). The case focused on the users group that played such a pivotal role in the development process, tracing the evolution of the project from its inception in the requirements stage to the time at which the decision was made to cancel it. The study was based on interviews with four users who were part of the original project team. Five thematic topics—project goals, project-team composition, project management and control, project financing, and project cancellation decision—formed a basis for examining the views and perceptions of the users group in the systems development process. Successful systems development projects, in general, are able to reach consensus on project goals or objectives, have knowledgeable project leaders capable of molding the project team and setting achievable targets and strategies for attaining them, have satisfactory management and control of the project development process, and, finally, have active senior management involvement in the work of the team to convey both interest and commitment to a successful outcome of the project. What follows is the story of the CODIS development as told from the perspectives of the users group, without all the technical details typically provided by software professionals. The responses are based on interview notes the users reviewed, commented on, and edited for accuracy.

**Project Goals**

It is generally accepted that an IS must satisfy the specific information needs of the organization for which it is intended. Davis and Olson (1985, 6), for example, define an IS as "an integrated system designed to provide information in support of the operations, management and decision-making functions in an organization." Thus it is reasonable to expect a new IS project to have a set of well-articulated goals and objectives that the IS is intended to satisfy.

The data suggest that although there was general agreement in the organization on the need for a new IS, there was no clear enunciation of what the new system's goals and objectives were to be in order to address the specific information requirements the company had. This is a sample of what some users interviewed had to say on the subject of project goals:

*VPM*: There were no firm established goals and moreover no real consensus on what those goals should be. They [i.e., the group] had real conflicting agendas. If a consensus existed it was "the realization that the company was functioning with brute force—good people working very hard with little computing or information technology support."

*VPSP*: There was no established consensus on the project goals. People had divergent views of what the project needed.

*DCA*: The goal was to provide "a paperless order entry sales and customer service support system for the company." The goal was partly based on the need to improve the efficiency and the productivity of the business operations brought about by growth in the company's business volume.

*MD*: In essence, there were no established goals for the project besides the fact that senior management asked them [i.e., the users] as a group to come up with the design of a new system to replace the old [i.e., current] system. The employees constantly complained to senior management about the old system's deficiencies in helping them do their job well.

There is a general consensus, as can be surmised from the above responses, that the project had rather vague goals and lacked clear objectives as to the specific information requirements the new IS was expected to satisfy. The sense of frustration and exasperation the group felt was succinctly expressed by MD, who later commented that the group had the impression "they were being set up to fail" so they would quit complaining about the deficiencies of the old system. Analysis of the above responses leads us to the following contributing factor:

**Factor G**   Lack of consensus on the specifics of a new IS—that is, on its goals and objectives—is likely to have contributed to a vague set of systems requirements (which may lead to problems in later stages of systems development).

**Project-Team Composition**

The development of any IS project is the work of a team of individuals drawn from the following three stakeholder groups: the senior management, who are expected to provide the leadership, support, and resources needed to carry out the task; the user groups, which are expected to provide the operational and decision-making perspectives of the system to be developed; and the IS staff, who must handle the technical aspects of the task from requirements analysis and specification to design and implementation. Thus, the composition of the team is a crucial step in the process of new-systems development. Equally essential in the effort is a leader responsible for organizing and directing the activities of the team.

The absence of a project team leader definitely compounded the problem of a lack of specific project goals to create a disorganized and dysfunctional project environment. The "conflicting agendas" and the "divergent views" pointed to by VPM and VPSP, respectively, attest to the fact that there was no common identifiable organizational purpose to guide the deliberations of the team. Consequently, the team meetings became nothing more than regular office meetings. This is what users said on the question of project team leader:

*VPM:* George [i.e., senior VP of marketing] was "the leader" of the group, but since he did not stay involved, in essence "the team had no captain." What usually happened was that "the team would meet and discuss a few things and try to come to some decision. No structure existed for the organization of the project." The composition of the team remained relatively stable for some time.

*VPSP:* Pete [i.e., the VP of MIS] was not very much involved with the project; he did not attend any of the meetings. Pete was later replaced on the team by Mike, who joined the company as director of MIS. The team remained relatively stable through the duration of the project.

*DCA:* The VP of MIS was the one in charge of the project; the last VP was Mike. However, there were about two or three changes in the VP position. The last manager [i.e., Mike] stayed with the project until it was canceled.

*MD:*   There was no official leader of the group; perhaps Pete was supposed to be the team leader but he never really participated much in the work of the group after the first meeting. They [i.e., the users] all acted as surrogate leaders. There were no turnovers on the team.

Adding to the problem of lack of leadership was the fact that there was also a dearth of structure and organizational purpose to the team's efforts. The lack of formal documentation of the minutes of the meeting confirms the view that the formal requirements of information gathering in determining the systems requirements were not seriously observed. In essence, there was no sense of direction or purpose to the discussions on what the new systems requirements ought to be at the meetings. The stability of the team, coupled with the fact that it was mostly a marketing group (for example, as MD commented, "they had worked together for quite sometime and felt comfortable in relating to each other on that basis"), should have helped in making some progress in the requirements phase of the project. However, the lack of project team leader may be partly responsible for the lack of visible progress made on the project. The following contributing factor seems appropriate, based on analysis of the above data:

**Factor T1**   Lack of an active, official project leader, with responsibilities for the project's successful completion, is likely to have contributed to fragmented efforts and loss of direction or purpose on the part of the team.

The project was initiated and orchestrated by the marketing department, although it had implications for the entire company. The IS group was only superficially involved in a subordinate role as advisors or consultants without any real decision-making authority or responsibilities. The first VP of MIS did not help matters by failing to stay involved and offer the necessary technical leadership that a project of that magnitude needed. The lack of active senior management involvement, other than the professed support provided, was also a major contributor in that it created a somewhat erroneous impression on the part of some team members that setting up the team was an attempt to silence those within the organization who were criticizing the inadequacies of the current system. This is what the users said:

*VPM:* "Marketing was really pushing the automation and MIS was expected to deliver the product." The MIS group existing in the company at the time was a lower-level organization and had no involvement with the team.

*VPSP:* The team consisted mostly of people from marketing; there were no team members from accounting.

*DCA:* Not quite sure how many of the IS staff were directly involved with the project. [He thought the number quite large but had no facts to substantiate his claim. It is worth pointing out that DCA was not part of the corporate staff during most of the time the project was in progress. Thus his perspective on some issues tends to reflect that of an outsider at the division level.]

*MD:* The team was made up of six to seven people mostly from marketing, with one MIS person. There were, however, no persons on the project team from accounting, operations, or warehouse.

The peripheral involvement of the IS staff in the systems requirements phase is clearly a matter of concern. Although the users group had a sense of what their systems needs were, lack of formal participation on an equal basis and regularly by the IS group in the deliberations deprived the team of the benefits of the technical advice the IS group could offer to guide the discussions along a more fruitful and feasible path. Thus the role of the user in conceptualizing the system and as "an associate [together with the IS personnel] in the development of the requirements specification" (Sage and Palmer 1990, 89) was sacrificed or lost in the team arrangement set up to handle the project. This view is partly supported by the fact that there was general agreement among the users that the project lacked consensus on what its goals were for the organization. The data from the interview lead to the second contributing factor on project-team composition:

**Factor T2**  Lack of active interaction between the users group and the IS staff in the project development is likely to have contributed to communication and other problems in later phases of the systems development process.

**Project Management and Control**

The technical dimension of any IS development project demands that some structure be imposed on the development effort to help guide the system to successful completion. Several variants of the systems development life-cycle methodology are widely available and used in practice (see Boehm 1981; Modha, Gwinnett, and Bruce 1990; Olle et al. 1991; Sage and Palmer 1990; Pressman 1992). The most obvious advantage of using a phased life-cycle approach to new-systems development is to help the project team to realize what the deliverables for each stage are and to know whether they have been satisfied before proceeding to the next stage. The iterative nature of systems development notwithstanding, the phased sequential life-cycle approach has been instrumental in helping to manage and control the development of large complex systems successfully (Sage and Palmer 1990; Pressman 1992).

The users were interviewed for their perspectives on the development methodology used in the project and on how the project was managed, after being shown a sample of a systems development life-cycle model. Each of the users indicated on seeing an illustration of the systems development life-cycle model that no such formal guideline was provided by the IS group to guide or direct the development efforts. Their responses are summarized in the discussion below:

*VPM:*   The project "never moved beyond the level of what we wanted to do and could the computer do it." VPM explained this failure as due in part to the lack of planning on the part of both the company and the head of MIS. The situation unfortunately did not change when the head of MIS was replaced. VPM further explains that the project's surrogate leader, Bob, "did the best he could under the circumstances, given the lack of direction" from senior management.

*VPSP:*   All we had at the end of the two years was a "lot of paper documentation" to show for our efforts. Lots of equipment was purchased but nothing concrete was provided of the systems they requested during the meetings, just "a lot of paperwork." The MIS group always talked about the capabilities of the new system as having "the ability to do what [the users] wanted [it] to do."

*MD:*   "The team was able to generate different [computer] screens," which they felt they needed and would help them with their job. No tangible progress was made beyond that stage in terms of real systems design and implementation.

The views and experiences of the users reported above are supported by Sage and Palmer (1990, 50), who state that "the use of an appropriate life cycle model for software development is far better than development with no management organization or control at all." Saarinen (1990, 185), in a study of systems development methodology and its impact on project success, recommended that "the larger the project, the greater the need for formal planning and management control." The data on the CODIS project leaves no doubt that it was indeed a large and important project intended to support the operations, management, and decision-making functions of the company. The above narrative leads us to propose the following contributing factor:

**Factor MC1**   Lack of a formal systems development methodology to guide the new systems development effort is likely to have contributed to the project's failure to progress beyond the requirements phase, or to its treatment as just another systems maintenance problem.

Because no formal systems development life-cycle model was used to guide the project, it became apparent that either the developers were not aware of the need for such a systems development methodology or else they considered the new systems requirements as just another continued effort in the evolution of the current system. It was clear from the responses of all the users that what the IS department was engaged in was essentially continued maintenance of the current system. Here are some of their remarks:

*VPM*:   "From day one, the group [i.e., the users] sensed there was a problem. It was always as [they] started, nothing was getting accomplished." Nevertheless, they persisted in their efforts, partly due to the entrepreneurial spirit of the team members and to a desire to get something done.

*VPSP*:   The MIS group used a lot of technical jargon to impress the users about what they [i.e., the IS staff] were doing with the new system. The meetings were typically a rehash of things in the documentation that the users group had requested. There was a lot of going back and forth between the MIS group and the users on what the users wanted and what the MIS group felt could be accomplished system-wise. "The MIS group was working on the old [i.e., current] system and trying to improve on its functional capabilities instead of trying to develop a new system from scratch."

*DCA:* There was no effort made, in general, by the IS personnel to discuss with the users how the users' requests could be addressed by the systems development efforts except for the occasional phone call. In retrospect, "the complexity of the whole problem was beyond the capability and expertise of the people who were involved with the project at that time."

The users' views expressed above were later confirmed by the new IS personnel hired to reactivate the project. For example, the current project director, in commenting on the remnants of the IS group associated with the abandoned project, said that "the major contributing factor was that most of the people hired to work on the project had *no real prior experience* [emphasis added] or knowledge of new systems development activities. Most of their experience had been with maintenance-related activities. There was a general lack of know-how on basic, indeed fundamental, activities like writing memos, taking minutes at meetings on user information requirements and providing formal guidelines on how new systems development activities should be conducted or carried out." The following contributing factor seems relevant:

**Factor MC2**   Lack of technical know-how in a new systems development effort is likely to have contributed to continued maintenance of the current system as a substitute for the new system.

Systems maintenance in the form of enhancements to an implemented system is generally accepted as a beneficial way for an organization to extend the life of a current system. Thus major expenditures on new systems development can be deferred to a later time. However, at some point in the life of an implemented system, continued maintenance in the form of further enhancements becomes counterproductive, in that the cost of systems breakdowns and its concomitant effects on the operations of the organization far outweigh any benefits expected to be gained from the postponement of the new system. This was a recurring theme echoed by all the users interviewed.

*VPM*:  "The frequent systems failures resulted in the computers being down sometimes for a whole day . . ."

*VPSP*:  During that time [i.e., of new systems development] there were a number of system downtimes experienced due to frequent attempts to add new features to the old [i.e., current] system. "The situation got to be so bad that changes to the system were eventually halted and Mike [i.e., the then-new director of MIS] was asked to 'take the company back to the old system,' so new features to the system were temporarily put on hold."

*DCA*:  "What they [i.e., the MIS group] were doing was causing severe impact on the business. It was crazy; the computer was a piece of junk; work was slow and it was not getting better but worse; and what they were doing had no direct relation to the functionality of the business." He later learned through the grapevine that the president of the company had demanded the IS group "take us back where we were and for them to get their act together." [Again, later in the interview, in discussing the decision to cancel the project, DCA further remarked that] the constant fixes to the system had made it so complex that "any change attempted had an unforeseen ripple effect on some other parts of the system; that was how messy and complex things had gotten in the old [i.e., current] system."

The third contributing factor is based on the above user experiences with the performance of the system and its impact on their work:

**Factor MC3**   Further enhancement of a system that had reached the maturation point is likely to have contributed to significant further deterioration of the system's performance.

In assessing the costs and benefits of systems development, if the cost of new systems development efforts is not accompanied by a comparable return on the investment that senior management believe is justified, their likely reaction is to carry out wholesale dismissals of those they consider the potential source of the problem—that is, the IS staff, including the head of the department, if necessary. Such a drastic move is especially likely under the following conditions: when senior executives are convinced of the importance of the new system to the future of the company (there is general consensus among all the interviewees on the importance of the CODIS project to the company); when all the financial resources needed to acquire the technology that the new system is expected to bring to the organization are made available (again, there is agreement that this was done in this case); or when senior management perceive—rightly or wrongly—that the lack of progress on the new systems development is the fault of the IS leadership and personnel.

*VPM*: "From day one, [the group—i.e., the users] sensed there was a problem. It was always as [they] started, nothing was getting accomplished." Most of the MIS group were fired at the time because it was perceived in the company that they could not get the job done.

*VPSP*: The project changed leadership when it was approximately halfway to completion. A new director of MIS (Mike) was brought in to replace Pete. But when it became obvious after some time that the new director also could not deliver the new system, he too was let go together with a number of the IS personnel he hired to work on the project. Problems on the project first came to VPSP's attention when some colleagues in the IS group began to discuss the low-morale problem in the department due to lack of progress on the project. The situation, he felt, got so bad that some of the IS staff individually expected they "would be set up to be the fall guy for the problems of the group."

The other users essentially expressed similar views. For example, DCA indicated that the problems on the project surfaced when he learned "everybody associated with the project had either been terminated or resigned." The inference can thus be made that no amount of political maneuverings or gamesmanship would be tolerated by senior management for failing to deliver a new system that they considered crucial to the company's survival. As VPSP remarked, "Mike was so consumed with his desire to become VP of MIS that his actions on the project were politically motivated to please top management. He was more interested in 'creating an image in the boardroom' on what a good job he was doing on the project than he was in getting anything of substance accomplished." The pattern of behavior observed by VPSP seems to fit the conflict and political models of Newman and Noble (1990) quite well with respect to the nature of the users' interaction with the IS group. The evidence provided by all the interviewees supports the following factor:

**Factor MC4**    Senior management's displeasure at the lack of tangible progress in a systems development considered crucial to the company is likely to have contributed to summary dismissals of most of the IS personnel associated with the project.

The failure of senior management to request and enforce regularly scheduled management review meetings to monitor progress on the project was a major issue raised by all the interviewees. The consequences of this failure were as follows: senior management had no way of knowing what stage in the systems development process the project was at any given time, much less when the project would be completed: the IS personnel failed to come up with a formal systems development methodology to guide the project to successful completion or at least to monitor its progress (see, for example, factor MC1); the new systems development project was treated essentially as another series of "fixes" to the current system to satisfy the identified needs of the organization; and far more organizational resources were expended on the project than could be justified before senior management realized the project could not be delivered as expected (e.g., VPSP—more equipment was purchased and "at least fifty new programmers were hired to work on the project").

*VPM:*   There was no planning developed for the project; no meetings were held to discuss technical issues on how to satisfy the computing needs; no management review meetings were held to discuss systems development efforts; and the project "never moved beyond the level of what we wanted to do and could the computer do it."

*VPSP:*   Although lots of equipment was purchased and new IS personnel were hired, still nothing concrete was provided of the systems requested. All this was going on in spite of the fact that Mike (director of MIS) met with the senior management team "almost daily on a regular basis to inform them on the progress of the project."

Unfortunately, senior management never realized what was going on until very late, when performance of the current system had deteriorated to the point where the only alternative left was to force closure on the project by demanding the IS group "take us back where we were and for them to get their act together," a comment DCA said was purported to have been made by the company president.

*DM*:   No formal reports were made to management or requested by them. Some senior management personnel occasionally dropped in on the meetings to inquire about their progress, but it was more on an ad hoc basis than in any formal or systematic manner.

*DCA*:   The project meetings were random and aperiodic with the "users groups (at the divisional level) being told little, if anything, about the goings-on of the project by the MIS people." The project management, especially when Pete was in charge, was "very directorial." There was virtually no communication or interaction with the users groups; "everything had to be done Pete's way and if Pete disapproved then it could not be done."

This virtual lack of communication or interaction between the users group and senior management helped to conceal the problems experienced by the IS group from the rest of the company. There were problems that an individual like VPSP only became aware of later when he became "friendly" with some of the IS people on the team. It is indeed desirable for senior management to be supportive toward a project and to provide the resources needed to carry it out. However, if senior management fail to become actively involved in monitoring progress on the project or otherwise to inform themselves of what is going on with the project on a regular basis, it is likely that small unresolved problems may become magnified over time. This may eventually contribute to the project's termination (Brooks [1975] 1995). As observed by one of the IS personnel holdovers on the project, "The scope of the project kept changing all the time; the team could never show management how and what progress was being made on the project at any point in time." The evidence summarized above from the users interviewed lends support to the following factor:

**Factor MC5**   Lack of active involvement by senior management in monitoring the progress of the project may have contributed to concealment of the problems experienced on the project by the IS personnel associated with it.

**Project Financing**

As noted earlier, it is common knowledge in the computer industry that projects are still over budget and behind schedule in far more cases than IS professionals and management find acceptable. Often projects seriously over budget and behind schedule end up being abandoned (Glaser 1984; McFarlan 1981; Brooks [1975] 1995). This made the financing of the abandoned projects a logical area of investigation. Admittedly, in most instances users may not be the right people to be questioned on this issue; however, the facts suggest that in this case they were fully informed about finances—in particular, because the project was initiated by them and they had much to gain from its successful completion.

All the interviewees unanimously agreed that money was never an issue on the project. The MIS department was treated as a capital expenditure without its own separate budget at the time. They generally felt that senior management of the company were prepared to spend whatever funds were needed to get the project completed. This is because the company realized the importance of the project to its future survival and growth. It will also be recalled that when the new director of MIS (Mike) was hired and placed in charge of the project, he was able to hire new employees and purchase new hardware that he presumably felt were needed to complete the project. It is possible that his lack of new-systems development technical know-how contributed to his failure to realize from the beginning the magnitude and complexity of the project and the resources that were required to get it completed. For example, despite his lack of experience, he still failed to bring in outside consultants with the expertise and experience to help the IS group tackle the project successfully.

Part of the "blame" should be leveled at senior management for hiring someone of the director's caliber and for failing to stay fully engaged with the project as necessary to monitor its progress. Indeed, MD noted as a concern "the inability of senior management to recognize they had a problem and delayed decision on it for so long. Pete should have been let go sooner and the MIS area should have been reorganized to deal with the project and its related problems earlier." Here is a sampling of their comments on the issue of project financing:

*VPM:*   Money was not a big issue. The issue was one of competent people to do the job.

*VPSP:*   Money was not an issue on the project. The senior management of the company always provided whatever resources they felt were necessary to get the project completed.

*DCA:*   There were no funding problems on the project. The company was willing to spend money in the area. But the president also wanted the MIS group to get the work done as inexpensively as possible and to get the company running on the new system as quickly as possible.

*MD:*   Money was never an issue. There were no discussions during the meetings on how much the project would cost or how it would be funded.

We are led to offer the following proposition in light of the above narrative:

**Factor F**   The availability of adequate funds and other resources for a systems development project might not be sufficient to prevent the project from being canceled for other reasons.

## Project Cancellation Decision

In this section we examine the decision-making process associated with the termination of the project. We analyze the concerns that might have led to the decision and the role, if any, the users may have played in the cancellation of the project. The project, we learn from the information provided by the users, was suspended by senior management twice and restarted with a new set of individuals brought in from outside. The decision to terminate (i.e., "suspend") the project was always forced on the company when management was confronted with evidence of lack of progress despite the continued provision of resources for the effort. However, because the project was unanimously considered critical to the survival of the company, each termination decision was immediately followed by a new desire to restart from scratch with new hires. This is what each user had to say:

*VPM:*   The project was never really canceled; it went through an evolutionary phase. The project was temporarily put on hold to enable the company to concentrate its efforts on getting the computing systems to work. About one and one-half years after Mike (director of MIS) arrived, "the chaotic situation still existed" in the company with respect to computer accessibility. Most of the people fired in the MIS group were fired because of the constant downtime of the system. There was not much distinction made between systems maintenance and systems development in the company; they were considered the same activity. The desire was to regroup and to sort out the issues again because of the daily frustration resulting from the computer systems failure.

*DCA:* The project was not moving as scheduled; it was costing too much money and was creating too many performance problems for the business. It was a good decision to abandon the project. It was killing us; it was difficult to do business on a day-to-day basis. He felt disappointed because "the company had an old system which everyone knew was not doing the job. . . . The sense of frustration was quite deep within the company. Pete had boxed himself into a corner in the old system. The system had been enhanced and modified so much that it had become so complex [that] only a few people could understand [how] it worked. Any change attempted had an unforeseen ripple effect on some other parts of the system; that was how messy and complex things had gotten with the old system."

*VPSP:* The decision to suspend the project was made partly in response to the fact that middle management at VPSP's level went to senior management and made it clear to them what they felt was "needed by way of a new system to deal with the operations of the business." Whoever has had the Vice President of MIS position has been under a lot of pressure "from senior management to get the new system in place. The current system does not allow fast response to economic changes quick enough in today's market."

*MD:* The project was never really canceled. Things were in such disarray that there was no coding work undertaken. Mike brought "zero leadership" to the MIS group. A lot of people were let go at that time, including Mike, but (MD) was not sure what the reasons were for the downsizing of the MIS department.

The data gathered from the users form the basis of the contributing factor below:

**Factor TD**    Lack of tangible progress on a new systems development project considered critical to the company is likely to have contributed to the decision by senior management to terminate the project and reactivate it with a new cast of technical personnel.

"Zero leadership" was probably one of the more important difficulties the project experienced. It is highlighted by comments regarding such problems as the lack of distinction between systems maintenance and new-systems development, the complexity of the system, and the failure of the system to respond to changes in the marketplace for a market-sensitive industry. It can thus be surmised that the decision to terminate the project and to restart it was made partly in response to the sense of frustration generally felt in the company with respect to the performance of the current system. A further catalyst would have been the realization on the part of senior management, in response to the prompting of middle management, that the project was too critical to the company's future not to be reactivated. A summary of the contributing factors is provided in table 7.1.

**Stakeholders-Interaction Model**

As discussed in earlier chapters, software project abandonment is a multidimensional event with several interacting subcomponents. The CODIS case study has explored the factors relating to the role of users and their perceptions in the systems development process. The interaction of the users group with the other two stakeholders—that is, the IS staff and senior management—provides us with a framework for understanding the dynamics of the systems development process and for understanding the risks associated with systems development failure.

Figure 7.1 depicts the three main pillars of the stakeholder-interaction model (SIM) as constituting pairwise interaction and communication between the IS staff and the users group, between senior management and the users group, and between senior management and the IS staff. The software development literature is replete with articles indicating user involvement as a prerequisite to successful project development. What is not clear is the extent to which inadequate or inappropriate

**Table 7.1**
Summary of factors contributing to software development failure

| Project topic | Proposition |
| --- | --- |
| Goals (G) | G: Lack of consensus on the specifics of a new IS—that is, on its goals and objectives—is likely to have contributed to a vague set of systems requirements (which may lead to problems in later stages of systems development). |
| Team composition (T) | T1: Lack of an active, official project leader, with responsibilities for the project's successful completion, is likely to have contributed to fragmented efforts and loss of direction or purpose on the part of the team. |
| | T2: Lack of active interaction between the users group and the IS staff in the project development is likely to have contributed to communication and other problems in later phases of the systems development process. |
| Management and control (MC) | MC1: Lack of a formal systems development methodology to guide the new systems development effort is likely to have contributed to the project's failure to progress beyond the requirements phase, or to its treatment as just another systems maintenance problem. |
| | MC2: Lack of technical know-how in a new systems development effort is likely to have contributed to continued maintenance of the current system as a substitute for the new system. |
| | MC3: Further enhancement of a system that has reached the maturation point is likely to have contributed to significant further deterioration of the system's performance. |
| | MC4: Senior management's displeasure at the lack of tangible progress in a systems development considered crucial to the company is likely to have contributed to summary dismissals of most of the IS personnel associated with the project. |
| | MC5: Lack of active involvement by senior management in monitoring the progress of the project may have contributed to concealment of the problems experienced on the project by the IS personnel associated with it. |
| Financing (F) | F: The availability of adequate funds and other resources for a systems development project might not be sufficient to prevent the project from being canceled for other reasons. |
| Termination decision (TD) | TD: Lack of tangible progress on a new systems development project considered critical to the company is likely to have contributed to the decision by senior management to terminate the project and reactivate it with a new cast of technical personnel. |

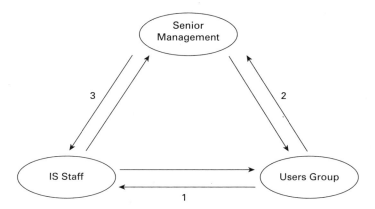

**Figure 7.1**
Stakeholder-interaction model

interaction with codevelopers of a project may act as a catalyst to its demise. We have already discussed the role each stakeholder plays in the systems development process. We now discuss the interactions each stakeholder must have with the others to ensure successful project development.

***1. Interaction between IS Staff and Users Group*** The level and frequency of interaction between these groups should be high, almost day-to-day, to keep everyone aware of the varied issues that are bound to crop up in the course of the project. The objective is to foster an environment of cooperation and collaboration, learning, and exchange of views on the technical capabilities of the system vis-à-vis the users' expectations and the information needs that the system is intended to satisfy. When the level of interaction, collaboration, and communication is judged satisfactory by both groups, the likelihood of project success may be significantly increased.

***2. Interaction between Senior Management and Users Group*** The frequency of interaction, collaboration, and communication between these two entities may be relatively low compared to that between the users and the IS staff. Still, this interaction is critical to effective project development in conveying the level of senior management commitment to and interest in the successful outcome of the development process to the users group. In addition, the value of the project to the organization can be more convincingly expressed by senior management, with its broad-based perspective on the organization's future direction and strategy. This interaction will also have the beneficial effect of reassuring the users of the significance of their role in the project and help motivate them to work more diligently and cooperatively with the systems developers toward a successful outcome.

**3. *Interaction between Senior Management and IS Staff***   This leg of the model is equally critical to successful project outcome. Depending on the prevailing organizational environment, interaction should be as frequent as necessary to achieve the following:

• Make the IS staff aware of senior management commitment to the project's success and its importance to the organization.

• Help resolve quickly and effectively project-related problems requiring decisive management action.

• Make the work of the IS staff on the project, as well as the project's significance to the organization, visible to the rest of the organization.

• Help assure the IS staff of the availability of the resources it needs to carry out the project.

• Enable senior management to learn as quickly as possible of any problems encountered during the development and of how they may affect the project's outcome.

Communication among all three stakeholders is essential to the success of the project development process. Consequently, if the level of interaction and communication required of any pair of stakeholders falls below what is expected depending on the size and complexity of the project, the entire development process may be affected. For example, inadequate communication between senior management and the users group may undermine the level of commitment users feel senior management attach to the project, which may in turn affect their own level of commitment to the project. Even more important, it will prevent senior management from learning firsthand from the users group of any project mishaps or foul-ups with the potential to inflict serious damage on the development efforts. It is therefore necessary that the level and intensity of interaction and communication existing among the stakeholders be appropriate to the task in order to ensure successful project development. We now discuss the factors derived from analysis of the data in the context of the interaction model to highlight the potential problems that a breakdown in any leg of the model may produce.

**Project Goals**

The relationship between IS staff and the users group fell somewhat short of the expected level of cooperation and collaboration in this case. The result was the lack of agreement or consensus on the objectives or goals of the project and how they could be jointly accomplished. The interaction between IS staff and the users group achieved in the project did not pass the minimum threshold essential to create a mutually supportive and productive environment for successful systems development to thrive. Consequently, the development efforts "never moved beyond the level of what we wanted to do and could the computer do it," as expressed by VPM. Senior management also share part of the responsibility for failing to engage with both groups and to make their members realize individually as well as collectively the value of the project to the organization and the need for joint action to create the desired systems product.

**Project Leadership**

Project leadership is an important issue senior management need to resolve early on in the development process. As Krault and Streeter (1995, 69) point out, "Large projects are more successful if a single, often exceptional, individual with both application-domain knowledge and software knowledge guides and coordinates the project," though such an individual may be hard to come by in most projects. In this instance the failure of senior management to fully engage with either the IS staff or the users group also made them unaware of the lack of leadership and progress on the project until it became obvious and much time had been lost.

## Project Interaction

The level of interaction and collaboration necessary for any user-initiated project to succeed should generally be high, as appropriate for a joint development project. Each participant in the project brings a level of expertise and experience critical to the success of the project. For example, the users will possess application-domain knowledge lacking on the part of the IS staff; similarly, the IS staff will possess software and systems-domain knowledge that may be lacking in the users group. Whenever the level of interaction between these two groups is too low to permit mutual interchange of ideas about the requirements of the desired application system, and the technical feasibility of the system is not properly communicated and understood by both groups, the potential for failure of the project is going to be significant. The statements from all the users have this underlying thread of lack of sufficient contact and collaboration between the two groups. Here again, if senior management had acted appropriately, the problems would have been observed sooner and suitable steps could have been taken to correct them.

## Senior Management Involvement

At the apex of the model sits the senior management of the company, playing the role of benefactor and supervisor to the project. Senior management's involvement in the project should thus be perceived throughout the project team as active and not passive. Hence the necessity of convincing the team members of management's commitment to the project's success. This sort of active commitment to the project on senior management's part may elicit from the rest of the team—principally the IS staff and users group—an equally significant commitment to project. Another benefit is that executives will become aware sooner than usual if the project is experiencing difficulties that, if not resolved appropriately and quickly, can lead to problems later. The data from this case suggest that senior management's failure to participate fully in the project during the tenure of the two MIS directors—Pete and Mike—was partly to blame for the disastrous results. Both directors were able to get away with less-than-full disclosure of the status of the project. Another point worth noting is the singular damage project cancellations bring to the IS staff and its leadership through mass dismissals and demotions. This makes it imperative for the IS staff to be especially vigilant in their role as technical experts on the project, because of the tendency for senior management to assign a disproportionate share of the blame for the project cancellation to the IS staff, as this case and others illustrate (see, for example, the Confirm case (Oz 1994)).

The stakeholders-interaction model has provided a framework for interpreting and explaining some of the underlying factors that contributed to the cancellations of the project during the tenures of both MIS directors. The model is useful in pointing out the need for communication, collaboration, and interaction among the stakeholders as necessary for successful systems development. However, because project cancellation is a multidimensional issue, the model is not sufficient for determining whether projects meeting these—that is, communication, collaboration, and interaction—requirements will be successful. What we can infer from the model is that communication, collaboration, and interaction among the major stakeholders may significantly improve the likelihood of the project being successfully completed.

**Project Development Risks**
In chapter 2 I highlighted some major studies that have contributed to our understanding of software project risks. I cited, in particular, the contributions of Boehm (1991), Barki,Rivard, and Talbot (1993, 2001), and Ropponen and Lyytinen (2000), whose studies have examined the risk factors associated with software project failures. However, none of these studies specifically examined risks associated with the role of users in software development. In this section I extend the analysis of project risks to specifically include risk factors involving the role of users in software development projects.

The stakeholders-interaction model has helped to explain how high the level of interaction and communication between the three pairs of stakeholders should be if project failure is to be minimized, if not avoided. It does not, however, fully discuss the risks of project failure where the level of interaction is deemed satisfactory for all pairs of stakeholders. In this section we use results from previous studies to try to describe the multidimensional nature of issues associated with failed or abandoned projects and to partially explain some of the risks associated with development projects, as illustrated by this case.

In a study of software project risk factors, Keil et al. (1998, 78) identify several risk factors associated with users, ranging from "failure to gain user commitment," "lack of adequate user involvement," "misunderstanding [user] requirements," and "failure to manage end user expectations" to "conflict between user departments," derived from an analysis of the perspectives of software project managers in Finland, Hong Kong, and the United States. Powers and Dickson (1973, 156) also conclude from an earlier study that "user participation is crucial to the success of the MIS project." They list a number of factors representing user participation that, in their view, are instrumental to user satisfaction with project results. These factors are as follows:

• "The origination of projects by users as opposed to IS staff"
• "The reported clarity of initial objectives and the specificity of user information requirements"
• "The existence of a project team consisting, in part, of the managers who were to use the products"
• "The managers' perception of their participation in project development" (Powers and Dickson 1973, 153)

The issue of projects being initiated by users as opposed to IS staff is indeed important; however, it is not clear to what extent this issue contributes to the project's successful completion. In the case of CODIS, the project was definitely initiated by the user group, which was involved in its development both "by doing" as well as "by control" (Ives and Olson 1984, 590 also see Tait and Vessey 1988). Still, the project never really progressed.

**Risks Associated with Project Objectives**    On "clarity of initial objectives," Powers and Dickson (1973, 153) found "several projects where the initial objectives were reportedly very vague." This situation, however, changed over time as users worked closely with IS staff to define "their objectives and information requirements as they learned more about their information/decision-making environments." This result is confirmed by Newman and Noble (1990) in their learning model of user interaction with IS staff. Keil and colleagues (1998, 78) also found that project managers considered "changing scope/objectives" of a project to be a risk factor threatening project success. Unfortunately, in the CODIS project there was no clear attempt on the part of the IS staff to facilitate the learning process or to create an environment where the project's objectives could be clarified and the information requirements better articulated as the users became more aware of their information needs vis-à-vis the technical feasibility of achieving those needs. Perhaps the level of technical competence and experience of the IS staff played a role in the failure of the learning model in this case, but so did the user attitude of claiming to be in full "control" over the IS staff, who the users believed to be acting as merely consultants in the initial stages of the project development. Here also the conflict and political-influence models of Newman and Noble (1990) seem to be at work. The users asserted their authority in some areas of the project development where they clearly would have been wiser to have deferred judgment to the technical experts. This attitude of the users might have created some conflicts in their relationship with the IS staff in terms of deciding what needed to be done, the order in which it needed to be done, and how it needed to be done.

**Risks Associated with Project Team**　A project team consisting of the "managers who were to use the products" is indeed necessary in helping to define the information requirements the system must satisfy. Nevertheless, it is not a sufficient criterion for systems success, as this case illustrates. All the users involved in the project were drawn from the ranks of middle management—the primary beneficiary of the system to be developed. Still, their failure to carefully articulate their information needs, coupled with the lack of experience and technical expertise in new-systems development methodology, almost guaranteed the demise of the project. As Keil et al. (1998, 78) also confirm, "Misunderstanding [user] requirements" was considered a major risk factor in project development by project managers. Similar findings are noted by Boehm (1991) and Ropponen and Lyytinen (2000) with respect to requirements changes. In the case of CODIS, the situation was exacerbated by the failure of senior management to stay engaged with the project at a level that enabled them to be sufficiently informed about problems encountered on the project. This fact is also confirmed in the study by Keil and colleagues (1998, 78), which lists "lack of top management commitment to the project" as being the premier risk factor perceived by project managers in the three countries they studied—Finland, Hong Kong, and the United States.

**Risks Associated with User Involvement**  The successful development and implementation of IS in organizations is influenced by several factors, including user involvement. Tait and Vessey (1988) present data contradicting the hypothesis that the likelihood of systems success increases as a function of the extent of user involvement in the development process. They are, however, able to accept the claim that "as the complexity of the system increases, the extent of user involvement increases." They explain this fact by suggesting that the "managers react to systems that are technically complex by involving users in their development" (pp. 99, 104). Indeed, as they subsequently suggest, the above two hypotheses are complementary in that without the equally active and committed participation of technically competent and experienced IS staff, systems success becomes illusory in the development process because the "likelihood of system success" will not significantly increase. This is what happened in the CODIS project—the users seemed to bear a disproportionate share of the burden for the development process without a matching level of commitment and participation from the IS staff and the senior management. Thus "lack of adequate user involvement" may be a risk factor that needs to be monitored, but perhaps a more significant risk to project development success may be "misunderstanding [user] requirements" (Keil, Lyytinen, and Schmidt 1998; Boehm 1991; Ropponen and Lyytinen 2000).

Tait and Vessey (1988) present two other hypotheses, one of which points to the likelihood of systems success as a decreasing function of the resource constraints on the development of the system. The other hypothesis, which was rejected, speculates that user involvement decreases as the resource constraints on systems development increase. The combined effect of the two hypotheses suggests that resource constraints can indeed be expected to "have a significant negative effect on successful CBIS design and implementation"; however, that fact may not lead to "a significant decrease in the involvement of users in the development process" (p. 104). Analysis of the users, statements confirms that resource constraints were not an issue in this case study, nor was the users' involvement in the development process. Thus the abandonment of the project could not be attributed to lack of adequate resources (e.g., several IS staff were hired and new equipment was purchased), nor can it be blamed on a lack of active user involvement. On the contrary, the project's abandonment can be attributed to a combination of factors, not least of which includes the lack of technical leadership in the IS group and management leadership from the ranks of senior management; the lack of satisfactory technical infrastructure in the MIS department to support a project of that magnitude, complexity, and significance to the company; and inadequate or inferior technical competence and expertise of the IS staff on the project team. The claim by Tait and Vessey (1988, 105) that the "information systems department has greatest knowledge of the complexities of the system to be implemented" is not confirmed in this case. Consequently, the risk of project abandonment was very high in this project in spite of the cluster of factors Powers and Dickson (1973, 156) have outlined as "crucial to the success of the MIS project." Several of the user-related project risk factors that Keil et al. (1998) identify are present in the CODIS project.

Finally, as noted, Newman and Noble (1990) discuss four models of user involvement: learning, conflict, political influence, and garbage can. They indicate how different models are appropriate to explain the nature of user involvement in different stages of systems development as well as within different contexts. With the exception of the learning model, which was clearly indicated to be absent, all the other interaction process models are exhibited in this case. In the learning model, the interaction between users groups and IS groups can take the form of one-way or two-way learning. In the case of the project in question, learning could have been the basis of interaction between the users group and the IS staff. However, the data does not support this model, in that the communication and therefore the learning between the two groups was at a bare minimum. No attempt was made by the IS staff to help the users group appreciate the technical complexity of the system to be developed and to help in refining the systems requirements. The users group, on the other hand, kept the IS staff at arm's length; they viewed them only as consultants who were "expected to deliver" the system, as VPM indicated. The failure of the IS staff to manage the expectations of the users group seemed to have indeed contributed to the project's failure.

The conflict model was present in their relationship, which stemmed, in part, from the "frequent systems failures" and "the chaotic situation" with respect to the computing facilities, a situation that had a serious negative effect on the ability of the users group to carry out their tasks. The users group attributed this condition to the technical incompetence of the IS staff for failing to keep the computers operating in any reliable manner. It was this sense of frustration that eventually forced the president of the company, after repeated complaints from middle management, to demand that the MIS department "return the company to the old computer system."

The political-influence model of the interaction process was also played out in this case, first in the attitude of Pete, which was described by DCA as "very directorial, . . . everything had to be done Pete's way and if Pete disapproved then it could not be done." Subsequently, Mike, who replaced Pete, tended to concentrate on his interaction with senior management in an effort to curry favor with them on his job performance. Eventually, when the situation did not improve, middle management also exercised their political option and forced senior management to stop the project, an action that led to the firing of Mike and several of his staff.

Perhaps the model that best typifies the kind of user interaction with the IS staff in this case is the garbage-can model. As Newman and Noble (1990, 93) describe it, "Randomness and accident play a large part. . . . Involvement and participation are fluid. Key players leave the scene, the composition of the team changes constantly, as do the goals." We saw earlier that the project changed IS leadership twice and that with the new leader, Mike, new IS staff were hired to work on the project. However, in most people's minds the project was still vaguely defined. For example, an IS staff member associated with the project from the beginning and who was still with the company at the time of this study recalled that "the scope of the project kept changing all the time; . . . People came in [i.e., joined the project] too soon when the systems were not set up; . . . New programmers were hired to do the coding even before the design specifications were completed." It was a classic case of "a decision situation" for which solutions were being proposed before the requirements problems had even been defined or at least identified and prioritized. Again, the same IS staff member noted that "there was no requirements analysis done as to how to get started on the project before even the new hires were brought on board the project. The team did not have that many design specs written, no true specs that a coder could code from." The Keil et al. (1998) study confirms most of the above problems as risk factors project managers view as detrimental to project success.

Consequently, the relative stability of the users group did not really matter because the technical development of the project rested with the IS staff only, which was constantly changing. Indeed, to cite Cohen, March, and Olsen (1972, 1), the project development effort exhibited all the properties of "organized anarchies," namely, "problematic preferences" (e.g., the requirements were unclear and undefined); "unclear technology" (e.g., no distinction was made between new-systems development and systems maintenance of an existing, mature system); and "fluid participation" (e.g., changes in the IS leadership and staff over the course of the project). It was in every respect a case of a project organized on the basis of "solutions looking for issues [i.e., requirements] to which they might be the answer, and decision makers looking for work" (Cohen, March, and Olsen 1972, 2).

## Conclusion

In the preceding pages we have analyzed the failure of a software development project—CODIS—from the perspectives of the users who were an integral part of the development process. The case-study analysis produced a set of hypotheses outlining the factors that may have contributed to the failure of the project. We have presented a stakeholder-interaction model stressing the need for communication among the three groups involved in the software project development in order to minimize the chances of minor problems evolving into bigger ones and thus threatening the viability of the project. The case also adds to the evidence discussed in the preceding chapters showing that software project failures are often the consequence of the failure of several interacting multidimensional factors, the most common of which are managerial and organizational.

The evidence generated from interviewing the four users has been organized in the form of contributing factors in an effort to understand, from the users' perspectives, the main issues that played a role in the decision to cancel or "suspend" the project. There are several lessons to be derived from this case study in spite of the prevailing "code of silence" among companies that have experienced abandoned projects. However, the limitations of the study should caution against broader generalizations of the results than is warranted by the facts of the project development environment. First, the lessons are based on the views of only four users associated with the project, though they were active participants in the process from the very beginning. Second, the users' views may have been colored by the passage of time and/or by their unanimous feelings of frustration and dismay about the whole experience. Third, the timing of the data collection, coming in the midst of a currently successful, and even more comprehensive, system being developed by a new set of IS staff with a new vice president of MIS, may have had a potentially negative influence on their perceptions of the previous IS staff's performance. Be that as it may, the lessons from the case appear worthy of further discussion.

Taking the particular circumstances and conditions of the company into consideration, a significant number of the factors discussed in this chapter may be at the root of most abandoned IS development projects. Despite the industry-accepted fact that a large number of development projects are often over budget and/or behind schedule, not all abandoned projects fall in to this category (see Ewusi-Mensah and Przasnyski 1991). The project was not abandoned for lack of resources and financing, even though it was getting further and further behind schedule. User involvement, which is widely regarded as crucial to successful systems development, may be necessary but is not a sufficient criterion for systems completion or implementation success. The data suggest that the project failed largely due to the lack of technical competence of the technical members of the team and due to the failure of senior management to actively monitor and manage the progress of the development team. Project success thus undoubtedly depends on the full participation of all three stakeholder groups, and anything less from any one of them may have potentially damaging effects on the project's outcome. Their joint effort should significantly contribute to two-way learning among all three groups—users, IS staff, and senior management—in order to minimize potential misunderstandings, conflicts, and the politics of the process. At all costs, the garbage-can approach to new-systems development should be resisted. There is, therefore, an unequivocal need to separate systems maintenance activities from new-systems development efforts. This distinction should particularly be insisted on when the technical competence, experience, and/or expertise of the IS staff are suspect. The use of a formal systems development methodology should be fundamental to the development of any particularly complex project. The clear management guidelines of such a methodology make it easy to monitor progress and uncover problems at various stages of the systems development process. This should prove quite beneficial, especially in inexperienced development environments.

We have shown through the views of the users that user involvement in IS development projects is a necessary but not a sufficient criterion for project development success and that there is still a significant risk of project failure if there is not equally active involvement from the IS staff and from senior management. For successful IS project development, the involvement of the users must be assured, the IS staff must be competent and committed to the project, and senior management must actively participate in the project as an equal component of the development team. Communication between the users group and the IS staff—often taken for granted—is extremely critical to successful development. In addition, collaboration among the stakeholders, in particular between the users and the IS groups, must be standard practice in all development environments if project success is to be achieved. Coordination within and between the users and IS groups is recognized as one of the critical facets of successful systems development. Software development is quintessentially a collaborative process. However, the collaboration is often erroneously perceived as only being required among the development staff. Collaboration that fails to involve all the interested stakeholders, in particular the users, only creates an environment in which minor issues can fester and contribute to project failure. Thus project development success is the joint responsibility of all three stakeholder groups. The process of IS project development may therefore be compared to the three legs of a tripod: a shortening of one or more legs will affect the stability of the entire tripod and may cause it to collagse. In a similar way, lack of full participation by any one of the three stakeholder groups in the systems development process may contribute to the eventual failure of the project.

# III

## Learning from Failures

# 8

# Postabandonment Review: Learning from Abandoned Projects

Software failures, runaways, or abandonment are all different manifestations of the combined effects of managerial and technical failures inherent in software development. Because it is a labor-intensive activity, software development will always be susceptible to human errors. Indeed, as Petroski (1992, 524) eloquently puts it in his discussion of engineering failures, "Human error, being part of human nature, cannot be expected ever to cease, but we might be able to reduce it." If human error were not widespread in software development, corrective software maintenance would not consume the substantial resources that are routinely allocated to it in organizations. It would, however, be unconscionable to dismiss the possibility of errors, say in design and other aspects of the development process, and subsequently fail to institute measures and procedures to tackle those errors. One of the major responsibilities of a competent software development team and of project leadership is to find ways to minimize the occurrences of the errors and to move expeditiously to correct them whenever they are uncovered.

Software development as a creative intellectual pursuit is also more prone to errors in the conceptualization of the problem, in the design, and in the subsequent implementation of the selected design alternative than some other endeavors are. The nature of software development requires team collaboration and coordination. The need for knowledge sharing and communication adds another problematic dimension to the mix and introduces other sources of errors into the development process. Moreover, software development must be always viewed as an experimental process, the outcome of which cannot be fully predetermined with any degree of certainty. As in any experimental process, errors are a constant challenge to be monitored and controlled. Every software development project presents its own set of problems as well as opportunities for learning and improvement of the process. It is, therefore, extremely important that the process be continuously monitored for deficiencies and ways in which improvements can be made.

The chance of major software failures, such as the examples discussed in the previous chapters, is likely to be significantly reduced, or in some cases the failures may even be avoided, if organizations and individual members of project teams make a concerted effort to constantly re-examine the circumstances surrounding each failed project and make the lessons learned part of the organizational record of improvements in software practices. Thus it is only through due diligence and continuous learning and striving for improvements in software development practices and methods that we can expect to make a difference in the "software crises." Just as the engineering profession has collectively made substantial progress by conscious and deliberate efforts to expose and learn from its failures—especially the spectacular ones—we (i.e., the software profession) can expect the same or better results if we become more candid and open about our failures and their causes. Until this level of maturity is achieved in software practice, the current level of software failures may turn out to be insignificant as we are confronted with more and more intellectually demanding and sophisticated projects.

In this chapter I examine the role of failure in organizational and individual learning in software development. I discuss what a postabandonment review is and why such a review is necessary and beneficial to the organization. I also discuss the postdevelopment review advocated in the literature on software development practice. The chapter offers a triangulation approach to inquiring about abandoned projects, in order to minimize bias and increase the accuracy of the information obtained and also to increase the likelihood of its acceptance by a majority of the stakeholders. I present and analyze the data from the same survey study on which chapters 4 through 6 are based but focus on the postabandonment review responses. I discuss the connection between the factors associated with failed projects and the practice of postmortem analysis in some of the reporting organizations. The chapter concludes with a discussion of how postabandonment reviews can be made part of the practice of software development and be beneficial to the organization.

## Postabandonment Review: Introduction

Historically, technical and technological progress has been made by examining failures in various endeavors in addition to extrapolating from successful precedents. However, progress in software development practice will not come about merely by inferences from an extrapolation of successful precedents. Attempts to improve the practice and methods of software development will only come about by concerted, collective, and open attempts to closely analyze the conditions and circumstances surrounding major failures in software development projects. Postabandonment review is a process of uncovering what happened in a software project failure as well as why and how it happened. Through this deliberate fact-finding process the major events and issues that contributed to the failure may be uncovered and conclusions may be extracted from which all can learn. For example, one of the purposes of design reviews and requirements reviews in software development is to ensure that proper and adequate communication has been achieved, that there is the requisite appreciation of the user requirements, and that a full understanding of the design concepts is derived from the functional specifications before development is continued. Having the users and other stakeholders participate in such reviews is of the utmost importance in ensuring that communication and understanding are achieved among all the stakeholder groups. These are considered good practices in successful software development.

The objective of a postabandonment review is to make the study of software development failures part of the education and learning experience of software practitioners. Software project failures can serve as catalysts to cause organizations to examine the processes, practices, and methods used in the projects. In this way, they can uncover the underlying problems associated with any of the major events or issues, learn from them, and ultimately avoid their recurrence in future projects. Failure to undertake such an analysis of why and how projects fail is to lay the foundation for possible repetition of the factors that contributed to the failure in the first instance.

Sometimes management and other stakeholders involved in the failed projects view postmortem analysis as a political process that they would rather not see undertaken in their organizations. This attitude is unfortunate, because it is important for an organization to understand what went wrong in turning a conceptual model of information requirements into a complex systems artifact. With the increasing levels of complexity associated with software projects being tackled in organizations, any failure to learn from the successes and problems associated with project development efforts will most likely pave the way for a repetition of the failures of the last project. Besides, progress in the practice of software development will only come about as organizations take the bold, and perhaps at times unpleasant, steps of carefully examining their project failures and making needed organizational changes. Organizations that fail to adopt the approach recommended by critics are not only failing to heed the lessons of history but are invariably shortsighted with respect to their management responsibilities and leadership.

What may be political in the process of postmortem analysis is the attitude brought to the exercise by project leadership and especially management. If the exercise is conducted in an open, nonthreatening, fact-finding environment by competent analysts without any other motives than to help the organization understand how to improve its software development practices, it will most likely be well received by a majority of stakeholders involved in the failed project. However, if the process loses objectivity and becomes a veiled attempt to find scapegoats or a witch hunt to assign blame to various individuals, most stakeholders involved in the process will be justified in viewing it as political and may try to sabotage it. Thus it is the negative or biased attitude toward project postmortem analysis that may be political and that therefore must be strenuously avoided by any organization intent on gaining new knowledge and insights into its software development practices.

The project environment is never static; it changes continually over time as new team members are added, sometimes to replace departing ones and at other times as additional expertise is needed. In addition, the technology of the software industry changes rapidly as new tools and techniques are constantly introduced into the marketplace with the potential to influence ongoing projects. The dynamics of such an environment add another layer of complexity, risk, and uncertainty to an already-difficult creative undertaking. Project development under such circumstances is undoubtedly fraught with the potential for failure, especially if the project is highly innovative and the organization has no prior experience with a project of its kind. For these reasons, it seems prudent for organizations to make project postmortems an essential part of their software development practices.

What makes software development qualitatively different from other types of engineering work is that the whole process, from requirements definition and design to implementation, is conceptual. Errors will always be part of the process because of the human element involved in the various stages of the development. The overarching objective of any organization, therefore, must be to identify and learn from the development failures resulting from these errors. However, organizational learning in software development will only come about when organizations are able to fully analyze and understand the problems associated with development failures. The learning that results from this process of organizational retrospection is intended to improve the performance of the organization in future projects and, in some sense, to change the environment in which the project development occurs so that there will not be a recurrence of the same or similar conditions. Because the project development environment is continually changing, this type of learning must be iterative to be of lasting value to the organization. The organization must continuously apply what it learns in the project development failures to improve its performance and practices in future projects. Organizational learning is emphasized because there is more at stake for the organization in determining the causal factors linked to the failed project than there is for the individuals involved.

The roles of the individual project team members are important in helping the organization achieve its desired objective—that is, the recovery of some of its investment in the project—by aiding in the search for answers to the questions of what happened and why and how it happened. However, because they have freedom of movement, individual team members may not have as much at stake in the failed project as the organization does. Even those whose careers may be intimately tied to the project can, if they choose, distance themselves from the failure by resigning. Only the organization is left with the task of picking up the pieces after the project's demise. Hence the compelling need for senior management to assume organizationwide responsibility for undertaking such postmortems as soon as the decision to abandon a project is made. To the extent that software failures serve as catalysts to organizational learning about methods and practices employed in software development, organizations should welcome the benefits they bring and not shy away from or be embarrassed by them. The benefits will come when the lessons learned from the failures are incorporated into the organization's revised software development practices. The reasons given for avoiding postmortems include an unwillingness to spend the extra money or time, the organizational embarrassment involved in the failure, a reluctance to open the organization up to potential lawsuits in contractual projects, and a general lack of appreciation of the benefits to be derived from the exercise as an investment in professional development for the organization and the individual project team members. However, the benefits in the long run seem to far outweigh the disadvantages sometimes cited for not going forward with project postmortems.

### The Postabandonment Review Process

The project postmortem is an attempt to institute a process of inquiry, knowledge dissemination, and communication among all the major participants in the project based on their retrospective observations and analysis of the problems surrounding the development. The process must not be used to apportion blame to the various stakeholder groups and the individual members involved in the development process. Rather it must always remain an honest attempt to uncover the problems associated with the project. Thus how the postmortem is undertaken will have obvious consequences for the reliability and accuracy of the diagnoses of what ailed the project, why the symptoms and ailments were not corrected or could not have been corrected, and why those ailments ultimately destroyed the project. The sensitivity and openness that the project investigators bring to the process will unquestionably influence the validity of their findings and, most important, whether these findings will be acceptable to the project participants.

Eliot Chikofsky (1990) and Bonnie Collier, Tom DeMarco, and Peter Fearey (1996) have advocated that the postdevelopment review process be made part of all software development projects—both the successes and the failures. Chikofsky, for example, believes this kind of "endgame strategy" will impart to each project team member at the end of the project not only "their own individual opinions and conjectures about workable or unworkable approaches," but even more significant, "knowledgeable experience that comes from thoughtful analysis, group input, and discussion" (p. 112). To achieve this goal he offers a sample of postmortem questions that can be used as a basis for analysis and discussion. I have grouped Chikofsky's sample questions into three broad classes:

*Project planning and initiation*

- What was the plan at the start of the project?
- How did the plan change?
- What do you know now at the end of the project that you wish you had known earlier?
- How would this have changed the project?

*Project management and control*

- What most noticeably went right on the project and why?
- What most noticeably went wrong on the project and why?
- What sorts of information came in too late, and what could have been done to get the information in on time?
- In what ways did the project backtrack or rework ground already covered, and how could the rework been avoided?
- What are the most important things you would point out to your manager or your staff if you joined a similar project in the future?

*Technical know-how and technology base*

- Did the project team have enough expertise or training at the start of the project? By the end of the project?
- What skills or knowledge turned out to be most important?
- How effective was the development method or approach used in the project? In what ways did it succeed or fail? Would you choose to follow that approach again?

• What tools were used on the project? For what were they most or least effective? How would you change the use of these tools to make them more effective? (Adapted from Chikofsky, 1990, 87)

The goal of the structured process illustrated by the above questions is to help the organization "to determine what went right, what went wrong, what worked, what didn't, and how it could be made better the next time" (p. 112). This will constitute the organizational learning that will in the long run prove beneficial to the software development practices of the reflective organization.

Collier, DeMarco, and Fearey (1996) also offer a five-step process for carrying out the postmortem review. The intention is to provide the organization with new insights with respect to the project in question and, most significantly, to find out which "behaviors need changing" in order to improve the methods and practices of the organization in future software development projects. The steps are summarized as follows:

1. Design and conduct a survey to collect relevant project information from all project participants.

2. Collect quantitative data on the overall project development process. For example, data such as the project cost at various stages, the schedule, and defect or error counts are considered to be valuable objective data to capture.

3. Conduct structured interviews or debriefings of the team members to expand on the survey data and to cover areas otherwise missing from the survey questionnaire.

4. Conduct a review of major events and issues (i.e., "Project History Day") in connection with the project with a select subset of project participants, presumably members in major leadership positions who will then be better informed on the events and decisions made on the project.

5. Document the findings in a report that will outline the lessons learned in the review and that can be beneficially used by the organization in new projects.

Finally, Collier, DeMarco, and Fearey strongly advocate that senior management create an open, sincere environment where such an exercise could be conducted in order to foster the kind of organizational learning that must take place and that must be disseminated throughout all levels of the organization.

## Postabandonment Review Triangulation Process

In an earlier work I proposed a three-pronged strategy for investigating software development failures resulting in abandonment (Ewusi-Mensah 1991). The three approaches consist of survey questionnaires, structured open-ended interviews, and archival data. I believe that this is an appropriate way of dealing with the several dimensions of the software project abandonment issue in organizations. Every postabandonment review must be approached as a case study of the failed project. Thus the inquiry must strive to "minimize bias, maximize accuracy, and report impartially, believing that 'inaccuracy and bias are unacceptable in any case study'" (Patton 2002, 93). The design strategy advocated is triangulation, which will enable the project investigators to take advantage of the strengths and minimize the deficiencies associated with each approach to data collection. The purpose of this triangulation approach is to make it possible for the inquiry to "test for consistency" of the information obtained in the study: "Different kinds of data may yield somewhat different results because different types of inquiry are sensitive to different real-world nuances" (Patton 2002, 248). This is particularly important with respect to software development because of its inherent abstraction and the levels of complexity that are encountered in the process of translating the organization's real-world information requirements into an implemented software artifact (Lehman 1989). The two parts to the triangulation strategy are as follows: *Methodological triangulation* (Denzin 1978; Patton 1987) will allow the investigators to use the methods of structured interviews, questionnaires, and documents to study and evaluate the abandoned software project. *Data triangulation* (Denzin 1978; Patton 1987) will enable the investigators to collect data from the different stakeholder groups on their perceptions and retrospective analysis of the development process for the abandoned project. Denzin (1978, 28) makes the plausible point that for this sort of evaluation research "no single method ever adequately solves the problem of rival causal factors. Because each method reveals different aspects of empirical reality, multiple methods of observation must be employed."

I now discuss the details of how the two strategies (i.e., methodological and data triangulation) can be applied in practice to determine what happened with respect to the abandoned project, why it happened, and how it happened in an effort to prevent recurrence in future software projects.

## Methodological Triangulation
This part of the triangulation strategy involves several approaches to data gathering.

*Questionnaire*    Like Collier, DeMarco, and Fearey (1996), I suggest that a survey questionnaire be designed and used in the investigation to collect data on the abandoned project. The questionnaire should be appropriately designed to reflect the type of project and its characteristics. It should be widely distributed to all the participants in the project team from all the stakeholder groups. The purpose of the questionnaire, especially in a very large project with large numbers of participants, is to enable the investigators to gather diverse opinions and perceptions from the different stakeholder groups and to aggregate them for statistical analysis in order to identify any general trends or broad patterns relating to the abandoned project. Over time, the historical record from such collections will enable the organization to assess its progress with respect to its performance in project development. However, it is important to note that the questionnaire is not intended to obtain in-depth information from individual project participants on any aspect of the abandoned project. That task is the focus of the structured-interview part of the data collection.

*Structured Interviews*    The structured, open-ended interviews will enable the investigators to get more qualitative in-depth information about the major events and issues surrounding the abandoned project. From the information thus gathered one may be able to surmise from the stakeholders' viewpoints which of the varied issues and events that transpired might have contributed to the project's termination. The data collection must therefore not be constrained by the predetermined categories of analysis that the questionnaire approach forces on the investigators (Patton 1987). More important, this strategy offers the investigators the only viable means of obtaining a wealth of data for this purpose. I especially agree with Lyytinen (1987, 37) that "IS problems are often confidential, and not easily disclosed as, for example, in questionnaires." My colleague and I have found this to be the case in our own work (Ewusi-Mensah 1997; Ewusi-Mensah and Przasnyski 1995). I therefore believe this qualitative approach will give free reign to the stakeholders to open up to a "neutral" person, preferably from outside the organization, or at least outside the project team, and reveal some of the frustrations as well as the excitement experienced in the course of the project development.

***Archival Data***    Although the previous two approaches will provide the investigators with satisfactory data, the need to corroborate the results should lead the investigators to pursue this third approach. In today's business environment, voluminous records are almost always kept of all major undertakings, including software development projects. Moreover, people's memories fade over time, and hence archival data will be extremely useful in helping the investigators reconstruct the facts of the project's development. All documentary evidence generated in the course of the project from its inception to its cancellation such as memorandums, project notes, minutes of project meetings, and any other records and documents providing basic information on the project must be requested and examined for their relevance. The wealth of information that can be gleaned from an analysis of such project records and documents has been shown to be invaluable in getting to the "hidden" agenda that may be at the root of some of the failed development projects in organizations (Markus 1983).

The three approaches to data gathering advocated here will offer the investigators a unique opportunity to collect a wealth of data of both a quantitative and a qualitative nature. The broad and diverse data generated by the quantitative method as well as data of sufficient depth and detail available through the qualitative method will give insights into the underlying "causes" or factors at play in the software development process environment with respect to the abandoned project. These two types of data can be richly supplemented by following the trail of documents generated in the course of the project in question.

## Data Triangulation (Stakeholder Groups)

The three sources for data collection are from the stakeholder groups of management, software developers, and users. We discuss the specific role of each in the data collection process.

*Management*    They will be able to provide a unique perspective on the issues, including causes and factors, associated with the abandoned project, the reasons that led to the abandonment decision, and some overall insights as to how such decisions are handled from the management perspective in the organization. Management will be an invaluable source of data because it may perhaps be solely responsible for authorizing the project to be canceled by taking appropriate action, with or without the concurrence or input from the other two stakeholder groups. The investigators must seek to determine if the views of management will be influenced more by economic, organizational, behavioral, and political considerations and less by technical and technological issues surrounding the project development.

*Software Developers*    This stakeholder group will be especially qualified to make their views on most of the technical issues surrounding the project known to the investigators. Perhaps more than management and users, they will have been responsible for the technical details associated with the project. Consequently, the investigators must try to assess to what extent their perceptions will be colored by their commitment to their profession and not by economic and other organizational/political issues that may be equally important in decisions of abandonment. For example, did the software developers push the state of the art in the project development beyond what their collective expertise and experience suggested could be reasonably justified to enable them to fulfill the project's requirements? Or did they engage in the process to enhance their own professional development and advancement despite the risks of project failure to the organization?

In addition, the investigators should uncover the software developers' perceptions of the role of the other two stakeholder groups in the development process. This includes, for example, the contributions the user groups made or were allowed or encouraged to make in the project and, in the case of management, the kind of support and commitment they provided to the project and whether this support was considered adequate.

*Users* User involvement in project development is a necessary but not a sufficient criterion for project development success, as the case study in chapter 7 illustrated. However, user involvement results in a significant reduction in risk of abandonment for some projects (Ewusi-Mensah 1998). What the investigators must diligently try to determine is whether the lack of active user involvement contributed to the demise of the project. The investigators must learn from this stakeholder group the level of involvement they were encouraged to have in the development process. For instance, were their views actively solicited on issues of potential interest to them at critical stages of the development, or were they simply informed of decisions after the fact without prior consultation? What role did they play in the abandonment decision, or was the decision made without their input? This stakeholder group should offer the investigators a unique chance to "prove" a negative corollary to the standard prescription that user involvement is essential to the success of software development, because the investigators can compare the level of participation of users in different abandoned projects in the organization over time (De Young 1996).

The data collection from the three stakeholder groups, using the methods described, will provide sufficient data to the investigators for subsequent analysis to determine the multiplicity of factors that may have contributed to the abandoned project. Later we will see how the results of the analysis can be used to influence software development practices in the organization.

## Abandoned-Project Postmortems in Organizations: Survey Results

Software as a "design know-how" activity will always exhibit innate characteristics, which are independent of whatever "state-of-the-art" development methodology is used to realize the conceptual model. Studies of past software project failures will continue to remain our best source of insights into software design problems and how to learn from past failures in their various manifestations. But that will not happen unless and until there is an openness and willingness in the software engineering community, and in the organizations that pay for their services, to consciously make the history of those failures part of the public record for the benefit of the industry and society at large.

In this section I report on a detailed survey of organizational practices with respect to abandoned projects. The data is from the same Fortune 500 study described in Ewusi-Mensah and Przasnyski 1995, and discussed in chapters 4 through 6. The results discussed here are broadly adapted from the responses of fifty-seven senior IS executives (labeled top computer executives or TCEs) and twenty-five systems managers (labeled SYS) who reported abandoned software projects in their organizations. Interested readers should consult Ewusi-Mensah and Przasnyski 1995 for further details of the study. The central issues raised in the study are "whether organizations keep records of abandoned IS projects and what, if anything, do they do with those records" (p. 5). The results discussed here, as in the article, are based on the TCE group, whenever necessary contrasted with the responses from the systems managers group. I only report the results of the study in this section. I defer the drawing of inferences from the results to the next section.

As table 8.1 shows, approximately half of the TCE respondents indicated that "sometimes" the organizations undertake a formal postmortem appraisal to ascertain the reasons for project abandonment, while one-third indicated that no such analysis was undertaken. Another

**Table 8.1**
Formal postmortems carried out in the IS department or elsewhere in the organization

|  | TCE ($n = 57$) | | | | SYS ($n = 25$) | | | |
|---|---|---|---|---|---|---|---|---|
|  | freq. | % | cumul. freq. | cumul. % | freq. | % | cumul. freq. | cumul. % |
| Usually | 7 | 18.9 | 7 | 18.9 | 3 | 16.7 | 3 | 16.7 |
| Sometimes | 18 | 48.6 | 25 | 67.6 | 10 | 55.6 | 13 | 72.2 |
| Never | 12 | 32.4 | 37 | 100 | 5 | 27.8 | 18 | 100.0 |
| Missing | 20 | | | | 7 | | | |

19 percent of the TCE respondents indicated that "formal post-mortems were 'usually' carried out with respect to the abandoned projects." The responses from the systems group were fairly similar. But as table 8.2 reveals, almost half of the TCE respondents indicated that the circumstances of project abandonment were never documented for future reference anywhere in the organization, with approximately 40 percent of the systems managers expressing similar views.

Table 8.3 shows that more than 60 percent of the TCEs and approximately two-thirds of the systems managers indicated that more than one project had been abandoned "for more or less the same reasons" in their organizations. Table 8.4 provides a detailed breakdown of the number of projects abandoned "for more or less the same reasons." According to the detailed breakdown of the data, 45 percent of the TCE group reported that three to five projects were abandoned for the same reasons. An additional 20 percent indicated that six to ten projects in their

**Table 8.2**
The circumstances of projects abandonment documented

|  | TCE ($n = 57$) | | | | SYS ($n = 25$) | | | |
|---|---|---|---|---|---|---|---|---|
|  | freq. | % | cumul. freq. | cumul. % | freq. | % | cumul. freq. | cumul. % |
| Usually | 4 | 10.8 | 4 | 10.8 | 1 | 5.6 | 1 | 5.6 |
| Sometimes | 15 | 40.5 | 19 | 51.4 | 10 | 55.6 | 11 | 61.1 |
| Never | 8 | 48.6 | 37 | 100.0 | 7 | 38.9 | 18 | 100.0 |
| Missing | 20 |  |  |  | 7 |  |  |  |

**Table 8.3**
More than one project abandoned for the same reason?

|  | TCE ($n = 57$) | | | | SYS ($n = 25$) | | | |
|---|---|---|---|---|---|---|---|---|
|  | freq. | % | cumul. freq. | cumul. % | freq. | % | cumul. freq. | cumul. % |
| No | 14 | 38.9 | 14 | 38.9 | 6 | 33.3 | 6 | 33.3 |
| Yes | 22 | 61.1 | 36 | 100.0 | 12 | 66.7 | 18 | 100.0 |
| Missing | 21 |  |  |  | 7 |  |  |  |

**Table 8.4**
Number of projects abandoned for more or less the same reason

| | TCE ($n = 57$) $n' = 22$ | | | | SYS ($n = 25$) $n' = 12$ | | | |
|---|---|---|---|---|---|---|---|---|
| | freq. | % | cumul. freq. | cumul. % | freq. | % | cumul. freq. | cumul. % |
| 1–2 | 5 | 25.0 | 5 | 25.0 | 3 | 27.3 | 3 | 27.3 |
| 3–5 | 9 | 45.0 | 14 | 70.0 | 7 | 63.6 | 10 | 90.9 |
| 6–10 | 4 | 20.0 | 18 | 90.0 | 1 | 9.1 | 11 | 100.0 |
| 11–15 | 0 | 0.0 | 18 | 90.0 | 0 | 0.0 | 11 | 100.0 |
| 16–20 | 1 | 5.0 | 19 | 95.0 | 0 | 0.0 | 11 | 100.0 |
| 20–25 | 0 | 0.0 | 19 | 95.0 | 0 | 0.0 | 11 | 100.0 |
| >25 | 1 | 5.0 | 20 | 100.0 | 0 | 0.0 | 11 | 100.0 |
| Missing | 2 | | | | 1 | | | |
| N/A | 35 | | | | 13 | | | |

organizations were abandoned for essentially the same reasons. Only a quarter of the TCEs reported that one to two projects were abandoned for the same reasons. More than 60 percent of the systems managers group said that three to five projects were abandoned for the same reasons. But slightly over a quarter reported only one to two projects, and about 10 percent reported six to ten projects, being abandoned for similar reasons. Finally, when the issue of record keeping of abandoned projects is raised, just over a quarter of the TCEs indicated that records of these projects were kept, while more than 70 percent stated that no records were maintained. The figures from the systems managers are comparable, as summarized in table 8.5.

In the rest of the questionnaire, respondents were asked what the abandoned-project records were used for and what lessons, if any, the organizations derived from examining those records. This part of the analysis is based only on data from the respondents who indicated that records of abandoned projects were kept in their organizations. As table 8.6 shows, the TCEs indicated that all the IS management have access to those records, together with 80 percent of the systems developers, 50 percent of both senior management and new-project leaders, and 40 percent of management in other departments as well as of programmers. The responses from the systems managers group show that 75 percent

**Table 8.5**
Does organization keep records of abandoned projects?

| | TCE (*n* = 57) | | | | SYS (*n* = 25) | | | |
|---|---|---|---|---|---|---|---|---|
| | freq. | % | cumul. freq. | cumul. % | freq. | % | cumul. freq. | cumul. % |
| No | 25 | 71.4 | 25 | 71.4 | 14 | 77.8 | 14 | 77.8 |
| Yes | 10 | 28.6 | 35 | 100.0 | 4 | 22.2 | 18 | 100.0 |
| Missing | 22 | | | | 7 | | | |

**Table 8.6**
Those in IS department of organization with access to abandoned-project records

| | TCE (*n'* = 10) | | SYS (*n'* = 4) | |
|---|---|---|---|---|
| | freq. | %* | freq. | %* |
| Senior management | 5 | 50.0 | 1 | 25.0 |
| IS management | 10 | 100.0 | 2 | 50.0 |
| Management in other departments | 4 | 40.0 | 1 | 25.0 |
| Systems developers | 8 | 80.0 | 3 | 75.0 |
| Programmers | 4 | 40.0 | 2 | 50.0 |
| New-project leaders | 5 | 50.0 | 3 | 75.0 |
| Other | 0 | 0.0 | 12 | 25.0 |
| Missing | 0 | | 0 | |
| N/A | 47 | | 21 | |

*Multiple entries permitted

of systems developers and new-project leaders, but only 50 percent of IS managers, have access to the records of the abandoned projects in their organizations. Only 25 percent of senior management and 25 percent of management in other departments have access to the abandoned projects' records.

Table 8.7 indicates that 80 percent and 70 percent of the IS managers and systems developers respectively "actually consult" the abandoned-project records, according to the TCE respondents. But only 30 percent of new-project leaders and 10 percent of senior management, management in other departments, and programmers actually consult those records. The systems managers group indicated that about two-thirds of

Table 8.7
Those in IS department or organization who consult the abandoned-project records

|  | TCE ($n' = 10$) | | SYS ($n' = 4$) | |
|---|---|---|---|---|
|  | freq. | %* | freq. | %* |
| Senior management | 1 | 10.0 | 1 | 33.3 |
| IS management | 8 | 80.0 | 2 | 66.7 |
| Management in other departments | 1 | 10.0 | 0 | 0.0 |
| Systems developers | 7 | 70.0 | 2 | 66.7 |
| Programmers | 1 | 10.0 | 0 | 0.0 |
| New-project leaders | 3 | 30.0 | 2 | 66.7 |
| Other | 0 | 0.0 | 0 | 0.0 |
| Missing | 0 | | 1 | |
| N/A | 47 | | 20 | |

*Multiple entries permitted

IS management, systems developers, and new-project leaders—compared with only a third of senior management—consult the abandoned-project records. Table 8.8 deals with the length of time abandoned-project records were kept, with more than 40 percent of the TCE respondents indicating a maximum of more than six years and one-third of the respondents indicating a minimum of about two years. The systems managers group indicated that 25 percent of records were kept in some cases for more than six years, and in others for two, four, and five years, respectively.

When the organizations were asked why those abandoned-project records were kept, about one-third of the TCEs indicated the records were "usually" utilized to minimize the chances of repeating problems that led to the project's abandonment, with the remaining two-thirds indicating that "sometimes" the records were used for the purpose just stated (see table 8.9). The breakdown of the data from the systems managers group regarding whether the abandoned projects are used to minimize repetition of the problems leading to the projects' abandonment, as summarized in table 8.9, is as follows: 50 percent "usually," 25 percent "sometimes," and the remaining 25 percent "never." In contrast, table 8.10 summarizes the responses dealing with use of the abandoned-

**Table 8.8**
Duration of abandoned-project records kept in organizations

| | TCE (*n* = 57) *n'* = 10 | | | | SYS (*n* = 25) *n'* = 4 | | | |
|---|---|---|---|---|---|---|---|---|
| | freq. | % | cumul. freq. | cumul. % | freq. | % | cumul. freq. | cumul. % |
| <= 1 year | 0 | 0.0 | 0 | 0.0 | 0 | 0.0 | 0 | 0.0 |
| 2 years | 3 | 33.3 | 3 | 33.3 | 1 | 25.0 | 1 | 25.0 |
| 3 years | 1 | 11.1 | 4 | 44.4 | 0 | 0.0 | 1 | 25.0 |
| 4 years | 0 | 0.0 | 4 | 44.4 | 1 | 25.0 | 2 | 50.0 |
| 5 years | 1 | 11.1 | 5 | 55.6 | 1 | 25.0 | 3 | 75.0 |
| 6 years | 0 | 0.0 | 5 | 55.6 | 0 | 0.0 | 3 | 75.0 |
| >6 years | 4 | 44.4 | 9 | 100.0 | 1 | 25.0 | 4 | 100.0 |
| Missing | 1 | | | | 0 | | | |
| N/A | 47 | | | | 21 | | | |

**Table 8.9**
Abandoned-project records used to minimize chances of repeating problems

| | TCE (*n* = 57) *n'* = 10 | | | | SYS (*n* = 25) *n'* = 4 | | | |
|---|---|---|---|---|---|---|---|---|
| | freq. | % | cumul. freq. | cumul. % | freq. | % | cumul. freq. | cumul. % |
| Usually | 3 | 33.3 | 3 | 33.3 | 2 | 50.0 | 2 | 50.0 |
| Sometimes | 6 | 66.7 | 9 | 100.0 | 1 | 25.0 | 3 | 75.0 |
| Never | 0 | 0.0 | 9 | 100.0 | 1 | 25.0 | 4 | 100.0 |
| Missing | 1 | | | | 0 | | | |
| N/A | 47 | | | | 21 | | | |

project records to plan and manage new projects better and to ensure their successful completion. Only one-third of the TCEs said that the records were "usually" employed for that purpose, with the remaining two-thirds indicating that this was "sometimes" the case. The figures show a proactive use of the information derived from the abandoned projects to improve the planning and management of subsequent projects, as confirmed also by the responses from the systems managers group. However, a quarter of the latter group indicated that the records were "never" used to better plan or manage new projects.

**Table 8.10**
Abandoned-project records used to better plan or manage new projects

| | TCE ($n = 57$) $n' = 10$ | | | | SYS ($n = 25$) $n' = 4$ | | | |
| | freq. | % | cumul. freq. | cumul. % | freq. | % | cumul. freq. | cumul. % |
|---|---|---|---|---|---|---|---|---|
| Usually | 3 | 33.3 | 3 | 33.3 | 1 | 25.0 | 1 | 25.0 |
| Sometimes | 6 | 66.7 | 9 | 100.0 | 2 | 50.0 | 3 | 75.0 |
| Never | 0 | 0.0 | 9 | 100.0 | 1 | 25.0 | 4 | 100.0 |
| Missing | 1 | | | | 1 | | | |
| N/A | 47 | | | | 21 | | | |

**Table 8.11**
Abandoned-project records beneficial in establishing management procedures in new projects

| | TCE ($n = 57$) $n' = 10$ | | | | SYS ($n = 25$) $n' = 4$ | | | |
| | freq. | % | cumul. freq. | cumul. % | freq. | % | cumul. freq. | cumul. % |
|---|---|---|---|---|---|---|---|---|
| Usually | 3 | 33.3 | 3 | 33.3 | 1 | 25.0 | 1 | 25.0 |
| Sometimes | 6 | 66.7 | 9 | 100.0 | 2 | 50.0 | 3 | 75.0 |
| Never | 0 | 0.0 | 9 | 100.0 | 1 | 25.0 | 4 | 100.0 |
| Missing | 1 | | | | 0 | | | |
| N/A | 47 | | | | 21 | | | |

The next two tables, 8.11 and 8.12, focus on whether the abandoned-project records were judged "beneficial in establishing management procedure for new projects" and on what the respondents thought these records contributed to the eventual success of new projects. As table 8.11 shows, the TCE group indicated that about one-third of the abandoned-project records were "usually" beneficial in managing new projects, and the remaining two-thirds felt that this was "sometimes" the case. About half of the systems managers group felt the records were "sometimes" beneficial and another quarter found the records "usually" beneficial, with the remaining one-quarter stating that the records were "never" beneficial. Table 8.12 indicates that the overwhelming majority (nearly 90%) of the TCEs felt the abandoned-project records were "somewhat

**Table 8.12**
Contribution of abandoned-project records to the success of new projects

| | TCE ($n$ = 57) $n'$ = 10 | | | | SYS ($n$ = 25) $n'$ = 4 | | | |
| --- | --- | --- | --- | --- | --- | --- | --- | --- |
| | freq. | % | cumul. freq. | cumul. % | freq. | % | cumul. freq. | cumul. % |
| Highly beneficial | 1 | 11.1 | 1 | 11.1 | 1 | 25.0 | 1 | 25.0 |
| Somewhat beneficial | 8 | 88.9 | 9 | 100.0 | 2 | 50.0 | 3 | 75.0 |
| Not beneficial | 0 | 0.0 | 9 | 100.0 | 1 | 25.0 | 4 | 100.0 |
| Missing | 1 | | | | 0 | | | |
| N/A | 47 | | | | 21 | | | |

beneficial" in contributing to the successful completion of new projects. Half of the systems managers group considered the abandoned-project records "somewhat beneficial" and another 25 percent found them "highly beneficial." However, another 25 percent indicated the records were "not beneficial."

Finally, box 8.1 summarizes the respondents' own descriptions of how abandoned-project records are used in their organizations. Analysis of the responses shows the records are used for the following four main reasons:

- To avoid future repetition of errors
- For learning purposes and as an aid in planning new projects
- To improve performance on future projects
- For historical review and analysis of what went wrong

In the next section we consider the implications of these findings and their relevance to the crisis in software project developments.

### Discussion of Survey Results

What do organizations collectively learn about the causes and circumstances of project failures? How is such information obtained and communicated in the organization? In the preceding paragraphs we have presented data based on the perceptions of a number of top computer

---

**Box 8.1**
Respondent's statements of how abandoned projects records are used in organization or IS Department*

• Records make it possible to review what was done previously.
• Documentation accumulated during project development life is retained for possible future use.
• Records help prevent future failed projects.
• Records are used to compare with new project requests to see if some research can be used; they are used in statistical reports to management to justify management involvement in systems planning.
• They are utilized for historical reference only.
• Records can be helpful as part of the software development life-cycle process. They are used as lessons learned to improve the process and as baseline measurements (function points) to give indicators on current projects.
• Abandoned = project records are filed with other project records; they are looked at if there is a possibility of reopening the original project or a related project.
• If a user group that has had a project abandoned requests a new project, the abandoned project's postmortem is reviewed in IS and then discussed with the user group.
• Records provide information on projects and end users that were unsuccessful and why; they are used as a test for starting new projects.
• Project records usually contain detailed descriptions of current business functions, requirements, and aspects of the organization. Subsequent maintenance, enhancement, or even partial new development projects could save time and money by using the past work.

*Statements lightly edited

---

executives and systems managers in Fortune 500 companies. A review of the data suggests that although most respondents indicated that postmortems are undertaken in their organizations to understand what went wrong and why (see table 8.1), a disturbing half of all the TCE respondents indicated that the circumstances of the abandoned projects are "never" documented (see table 8.2). It is therefore not surprising that more than 60 percent of the same respondents indicated that more than one project has been abandoned for more or less the same reasons (see tables 8.3 and 8.4). Even more disturbing is the fact that more than 70 percent of the TCEs said their organizations do not keep records of abandoned projects (see table 8.5).

The picture that emerges from the data is one of organizations "cursed to repeat past mistakes" because no effort is made to understand what went wrong or to learn from the past mistakes. The failure of organizations to document their project failures and to use that information to avoid a repetition of similar problems, perhaps more than any other single fact, attests to the continuing problem of project abandonment in organizations. As Hedberg (1981, 3) points out, "Organizations increase their understanding of reality [e.g., of software development projects] by observing the results of their acts," and these are often experimental. When such organizational learning is lacking, the result is a dearth of viable formal mechanisms for "detection and correction of errors" and a failure to engage in "repeated testing, construction and reconstruction of knowledge" in those organizations (Hedberg 1981, 7). It is therefore not surprising, as Lyytinen (1987, 9) claims, that "IS development is fraught with recurrent problems caused by poor, undisciplined and incomplete development practices."

In short, organizations that operate under such circumstances are, indeed, more likely to repeat past mistakes, especially as members come and go and leadership changes take place. There will be no organizational memory to warn against the behaviors, procedures, operating practices, and standards that may be at the root of the project failures. Thus the likelihood of repeating the same problems looms large, especially if new personnel are assigned to new projects. The data clearly support Boddie's (1987, 77) assertion that "we talk about software engineering but reject one of the most basic engineering practices: identifying and learning from our mistakes." As a result, it is not surprising that "errors made while building one system appear in the next one." The failure to keep records on the abandoned projects robs the organization and its future leadership of an opportunity to learn about the mistakes of the past, thus creating organizational memory loss for the long term. It is apparent that in most of these organizations, management treats project failures as "embarrassing moments to be quickly forgotten," not as opportunities for a concerted effort to uncover the causes of the failure, nor as opportunities to acquire new knowledge and discard obsolete information or practices (Boddle 1987, 82; Abdel-Hamid and Madnick 1990; Hedberg 1981).

For the respondents who indicated that records of abandoned projects are kept by their organizations, the picture that emerges is neither encouraging nor hopeful for the future of software project development practices. For example, even though table 8.6 indicates that quite a wide range of individuals have access to the abandoned-project records, only the systems developers and IS management generally consult those records (see table 8.7). New-project leaders (only 30%), senior management, management in other departments, and programmers (10% each) do not make as much use of the records as might be expected (based on the TCEs' responses). Thus, although the records are kept in some instances for as long as six years or more, little use is made of them (see table 8.8).

As pointed out earlier, the data also indicate that organizations experienced project abandonment for more or less the same reasons (see tables 8.3 and 8.4). Therefore, in an effort to avoid these pitfalls, some organizations took the prudent step of evaluating the abandoned projects. They probably undertook the evaluations primarily to ensure that the underlying factors or reasons for the abandonment of the projects were clearly understood and communicated with project developers. The results also suggest that some organizations chose to evaluate their abandoned projects to account fully for the expenditure of resources on the project, and to learn from the variety of interacting factors. For example, factors such as a lack of well-defined project goals, poor project-team composition, inadequate technical infrastructure, a shortage of technical know-how on the part of the project team, poor project management and control, a lack of end-user participation, and inadequate senior management support have the potential to negatively affect the project's outcome if they are not properly understood and dealt with in the project development process.

When the respondents were asked to indicate the benefits derived from the stored records, the majority of both TCEs and systems managers cited the potential to avoid repeating past problems or errors and improve performance on future projects through better planning and management (see tables 8.9 through 8.11). While these objectives are commendable, they are unlikely to be realized if a majority of the responding organizations do not routinely keep project records, much less consult them on a regular basis (see table 8.5). This singular "failure to learn from mistakes has been a major obstacle to improving software project management," as Abdel-Hamid and Madnick (1990, 39) charge. We are, therefore, doomed to "continue to produce too many project failures, marked by cost overruns, late deliveries, poor reliability and user dissatisfaction" (Abdel-Hamid and Madnick 1990, 39).

In contrast, respondents who indicated using the abandoned-project records overwhelmingly expressed the view that the records were beneficial in establishing management procedures in new projects as well as contributing to the success of the new projects (see tables 8.11 and 8.12). The problem of software project failure is therefore presumably not an intractable technical issue but rather one of failure on the part of both senior management and software/IS management to institute enforceable guidelines and procedures for undertaking postmortems of failed or abandoned projects and making proper use of the lessons learned from those experiences in subsequent projects.

**Learning Paradigm**

It is apparent that improvements in software project development can be made if organizations show a willingness to learn from past project failures. Consequently, a study of how and why a particular project failed will, in essence, be the best safeguard against a repetition of the same or similar problems. I believe organizations, to paraphrase Petroski (1992, 523), must incorporate a treatment of software failures in their software development history for the "measure of humility" it will bring to the "innate hubris" of developers and, even more significantly, for the inherent features of the organizational software development methods and practices that they can so effectively reveal. Thus organizations should allow the problems underlying the causes of the failed project to serve as a catalyst for a deeper understanding of the entire systems development process. Learning takes place when the results of the analysis of the failure, uncovered largely through postmortems, lead to changes and modifications of organizational practices and procedures.

The type of learning just referred to is similar to that described by Lehman (1989, 1980, 1062) in discussing the laws of software evolution, with specific reference to program types "P" and "E"—that is, programs that attempt to solve real-world problems and programs that "mechanize a human or societal activity," respectively. For the "P-programs," the solution's value and validity as compared to the real-world environment or context in which the problem emanated is the main concern. Whenever differences are detected in the course of the comparison, "it causes the program, its documentation or both to be changed." Thus, "P-programs are very likely to undergo never ending change or to become steadily less and less effective and cost effective." However, for the class of "E-programs," change is intrinsic. Lehman (1980, 1063) describes the changes involved: "Once the program is completed and begins to be used, questions of correctness, and appropriateness and satisfaction arise . . . and inevitably lead to additional pressure for change." In other words, as organizations begin to learn more about the strengths and weaknesses of the implemented systems, change becomes a necessary consequence of that knowledge and experience, which in turn leads to better systems. The costs incurred in effecting the changes are generally accepted as essential to the organization in the long run, because the changes help to prolong the useful life of the system.

Figure 8.1 presents an organizational learning-cycle paradigm appropriate to software development projects. The figure is an adaptation of the organizational learning cycle of March and Olsen (1976), applied in the context of software projects. There are essentially two parts to the paradigm. The first part deals with successfully completed and implemented software projects, and the second part deals with abandoned IS development projects. For completed and implemented projects, learning takes place in the form of maintenance and enhancements of the system (Blum 1987). In both instances, positive feedback is generated as a result of using the implemented system and learning about its deficiencies and shortcomings. Thus, through maintenance and enhancements, organizations have come to accept postmortem appraisals of even

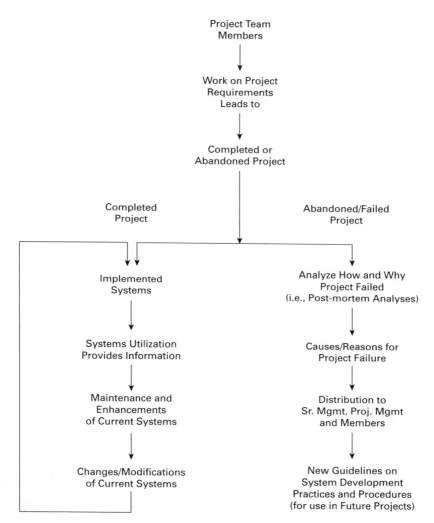

**Figure 8.1**
Learning cycle for software project

successfully implemented systems as an appropriate means of improving the performance and operation of such systems. In other words, organizations accept as normal the roles individuals and collective learning can play in "perfecting" the IS development process. Lyytinen (1987, 15) puts it succinctly when he writes: "A successful IS [or software] development process is more a matter of social learning. The information system is an incremental outgrowth of this learning, and it continues to *evolve* [emphasis added] over time owing to new learning." It is this type of evolutionary learning that takes place as successfully implemented systems are subjected to maintenance and enhancement changes as a consequence of users' increased learning and experience with the capabilities of the implemented system.

The model presented in figure 8.1 seeks to make such organizational learning standard practice for failed or abandoned software development projects through formal postmortems performed on those projects. An abandoned project is analyzed at the project-team level, using the methods and techniques discussed in earlier sections, to determine the underlying causes of the failure. The results of such an analysis should be widely communicated to all individuals associated with the project, including those who managed it. In addition, documentation of the analysis of the failure must be stored and made readily accessible to future project team members for regular consultation. The results of the postmortem should lead to the creation of guidelines calling for modifications to some organizational practices and procedures in project development in order to avoid the recurrence of the problems and/or to improve the overall performance of future project teams on subsequent projects. Such new guidelines should also be widely communicated to project team members and other individuals with responsibilities for future projects. Individual as well as organizational learning is likely to be achieved when postmortem analysis is routinely performed on each failed or abandoned software development project, and when the lessons learned are widely communicated to all concerned.

However, any discontinuity in any leg of the cycle will amount to a failure on the part of the organization to undertake a postmortem appraisal of the abandoned project. It is therefore critical that each leg of the learning cycle be maintained, if the learning process is to result in the necessary changes to the way the organization or individuals approach subsequent projects and if the organization is to fully realize the benefits from the lessons of the postmortems for later projects.

## Conclusion

This chapter has provided a rationale for why organizations must carry out a postdevelopment review of software projects, particularly failed projects—a necessary activity that should be undertaken on a regular basis. We have considered some approaches that organizations can institute to learn from their past project development failures. We have discussed the results of survey data that reveal a disturbing fact: most organizations do not place a high premium on this aspect of their software development practice, and thus are vulnerable to possible repetition of prior development errors and problems. The chapter concluded with a learning paradigm for improving software development practices in organizations.

The need for more organizations to undertake formal postmortems of their failed or abandoned projects is quite apparent, even from the limited evidence presented in this chapter. The facts suggest that organizations need to do more to learn from past errors in systems development efforts. The postabandonment review discussed earlier is intended to aid organizations wishing to institute formal mechanisms for uncovering the underlying causes of failed or abandoned projects on a regular basis. Both the methodological and data triangulation approaches advocated will enable organizations to develop a systematic way of collecting relevant information on what happened in the course of project development, why it happened, and how.

In chapter 3 we discussed factors contributing to abandoned software projects. For any particular project, it is conceivable that only some of the factors will coalesce to cause failure or abandonment. However, finding the critical combination of factors that may be responsible for the project's demise is essential if the organization is to learn from its problems and thus have a chance of avoiding their potential repetition in future projects. The science and experience of the software development process must be cumulative, or we will be cursed to continually repeat the failures of the past. The specific factors discussed in chapter 3 that are potential contributors to project abandonment decisions can serve as a rallying point in the search for underlying problems. Specifically, in the structured interview the postabandonment review should seek to elicit information on

• Project goals and objectives

• Project leadership and involvement of senior management in the project

• Project-team composition, and coordination and communication among the team members and/or groups

• Project management and control from requirements definition to the stage in the life cycle when the project was canceled

• Allocation of resources such as personnel, money, technology, and time/schedule for the project

• Degree of involvement and cooperation of user groups in the project

• Technological infrastructure issues of the organization that have particular relevance to the project

• Technical expertise and experience of the development team and the project leadership

Using the open-ended interview approach to elicit the views of the project participants will produce beneficial information, which can be utilized in conjunction with other data collection methods to piece together the multiplicity of factors possibly responsible for the project's demise.

The survey questionnaire can concentrate on a broad-brush approach to data collection, focusing on the fundamental factors of socio-organizational, behavioral, and political issues, the sociotechnical and technological issues, and economic issues such as project costs and the time-of-completion schedules. In fact, the archival data may be a valuable source of the less subjective information on project costs and schedules at any phase of the development life cycle.

Until now we have been silent on who should be the designated investigator charged with the responsibility of helping the organization learn from its project failure. The issue of the chief investigator should be handled with the utmost care and sensitivity to convey a sense of objectivity and constructive fact finding, as opposed to an interest in assigning blame or finding fault with individual project team members. No single individual, with the possible exception of the project leader, is capable of single-handedly causing a project to be canceled. The selection of the chief investigator, either from within or outside the organization but with the definite exception of project team members, must be seen and appear to be seen by all concerned as impartial, without any hidden agendas or biases and with the sole objective of determining the multiplicity of factors responsible for the project's failure. The chief investigator must be promised full cooperation by all concerned, from senior management and technical personnel to users, and must be given access to all archival documents needed to successfully carry out the investigation. Through this painful process of soul searching, the organization is likely to recoup some of its investments in the failed project and to learn to do better the next time around on a similar or even on a different project.

# 9

## Software Development: A Strategic Paradigm

As the preceding chapters have emphasized, the process of software development is fraught with risks and uncertainties that often result in cost overruns and schedule delays and even in outright project failure and abandonment. What is surprising is not the cost overruns and schedule delays, which are almost routine even with successfully completed development projects. Instead what is most disturbing is the frequency of the software project failures and their inevitable toll on organizational resources—in particular, on the technical personnel associated with the development effort, who often are demoted or even let go to atone for the failure of the development/project. But the main focus of this chapter is not on the process of software development—that is left to the individual organization and its project leadership. Besides, a voluminous literature on software development methods already exists. Instead the chapter tackles the question of what drives good software development practices to maximize the chances of successful outcomes. I do not use the concept of maximization in the classic optimization sense, in which a set of criteria for development practices exist that will permit us to compare all other alternatives and come up with one alternative that must be preferred because it will guarantee a successful outcome. Instead I expect in a pragmatic way to provide a set of guidelines that describe "minimally satisfactory" development practices that will enhance the chance of a successful project outcome.

In this chapter we will discuss the major dimensions of software development practice, the success of which is necessary for the success of the entire project. We will specifically examine the role users play in assessing the requirements for systems development. We will also explore the three interacting elements of a project—that is, the features or function-alities of the system, the resources needed to complete the development, and the quality of the project outcome. The discussion will highlight the need for active user participation and involvement in the development process—from requirements gathering to systems implementation—to provide needed input and feedback to the development team. The chapter stresses the need for flexible design architecture—especially for highly innovative projects—to enhance the development team's ability to control for changes in requirements and systems functionalities arising from user feedback. We consider the role audits can play in monitoring progress on the project, the use of consultants on the project, and how organizational politics can influence project development efforts. Finally, we emphasize the need for a broad-based development team represent-ing stakeholder groups with differing perspectives, perceptions, orienta-tions, and experiences on the project. This broad composition maximizes chances for a successful project outcome and system acceptance after implementation.

## Maximizing Successful Project Outcomes

What does the maximization of successful project outcomes entail? It means managing the project to control for desirable outcomes by avoid-ing, or at least minimizing, the risky behaviors that are the potential death knell of projects. Successful project outcomes can be achieved by paying attention to the factors that are known contributors to the risks of project failures. Thus, for example, when project objectives are clearly articulated and understood, are arrived at by a consensus of all stake-holders involved, are realistic, and are not overly ambitious relative to the organizational capabilities for achieving the project goals, an aspect of the maximization of successful project outcomes is achieved and in the process a potential failure risk factor is minimized, if not eliminated. A successful project outcome involves a triangulation of the interaction between the resources (that is, people and budget), the schedule for com-pleting the project, and the desired features or functionalities and quality of the completed product (McCarthy 1995). Successful project outcomes will always entail maintaining the right equilibrium among the three interacting elements of the project during the development.

**Project Triangulation**

In chapter 7 we discussed the stakeholder-interaction model (SIM) as a framework for creating a satisfactory project development environment, which is crucial to successful project outcomes. The underpinnings of the framework are pairwise communication and interaction between the IS/technical staff and the users group, between senior management and the users group, and between senior management and the IS/technical staff. The drive to maintain proper balance between the three elements of the project triangle can be controlled within the context of SIM. Successful project outcomes invariably entail maximizing, in a satisfactory sense, the desired features of the completed product under the constraints of the given or available resources and schedule for completion.

The project-interaction triangle of resources, features, and schedule is analogous to the SIM model of chapter 7. The distinctive difference is that in this case all the elements are to a large extent controllable, or at least can be manipulated, by the project leader to achieve the desired project outcome. On the other hand, the project triangle is also similar in its interaction behavior to the stakeholder-interaction triangle, in the sense that changes in any one of the elements has repercussions for the remaining elements, hence the need to always maintain proper balance among the elements in the triangle. For example, any new significant functionality resulting from changes in the project requirements may have a direct impact on, say, the schedule, and possibly on the resources already budgeted to tackle the project. It is therefore imperative for the project leader to ensure that proper balance is maintained among the three interacting elements of resources, features, and schedule at all times during the development process. This need to maintain proper balance among the three project entities requires that their determination at the start of the project be a joint effort developed from the ground up—that is, among all the stakeholder groups, especially those with direct responsibilities for the actual project development. Thus, for example, the schedule should not be developed from the ranks of senior management and passed down to the development team. Instead, it must be the responsibility of the project team, and the individual members involved in each phase must be held accountable for their specific role in achieving the expected outcomes (McCarthy 1995). Cost overruns and schedule delays, which are the bane of many software development failures, can at times be traced to the ill-advised effort of some stakeholder groups, in particular senior executives, to usurp the responsibility for determining the completion schedule and associated budget from the project team and its leadership. The DIA's baggage handling system is a case in point. The schedule for completion of BHS was essentially dictated by the opening date for the airport and not by the complexity of the features of BHS and the adequacy of the resources available to handle it.

**Project Features**

One of the three elements of the project triangle is the project features and the quality of the project outcome. Underlying this element is the project requirements, which are derived from the project goals and objectives. The preceding chapters have detailed how important it is for a consensus on project goals and objectives to be arrived at early in the development process in order to set the proper course for the project. It is crucial that participants demonstrate an adequate understanding of overall project goals and objectives so as to minimize the problems created by the requirements changes that can result from initial misunderstandings of the project's direction. All the stakeholder groups must play a role in helping to define the desired systems boundaries for the project before further development work is undertaken. The ability to complete the project on time and within the estimated budgeted resources may be partly dependent on the clarity of the project goals/objectives, which shaped the definition of the systems boundaries. Some of the crucial factors affecting the chances for maximizing successful project outcomes are:

· Project requirements
· Project audits

- Senior management support
- Project consultants
- Project politics

We now focus on some of these issues to highlight the important role they play in the project triangle to maximize successful outcomes.

**Project Requirements**

Understanding the problem domain of the project is crucial to successful software development. However, it is important to recognize that the problem-definition process is an evolving one and that full comprehension, no matter how much effort is put into it, may remain elusive at the start of some particularly complex projects. Once a project has begun, clearer understanding is attained as subsequent layers of the problem domain are uncovered and other matters not thought of due to oversight or misunderstanding are forced into the mix of issues to be tackled. The users play a crucial role in determining the requirements for the project because of their understanding of the application problem domain. Still, with particularly complex projects, even the users' understanding of the problem domain may be limited and thus may give rise to periodic revisions during the development. Eventually changes to the project's requirements and systems functionalities may become necessary to reflect new insights into the application problem domain. The development team must tap the differing perceptions and orientations of the various user groups represented, in order to obtain broad perspectives on the requirements and functions of the system.

The software requirements derived from the initial comprehension of the problem are bound to be modified in the course of the development. However, while requirements volatility is to be expected, controlling for the changes in the requirements becomes critical to successful project outcome. Not all aspects of the requirements that an evolving understanding of the problem domain uncovers should be allowed to factor into the current development effort. Some of the new requirements can be appropriately deferred to later enhancement efforts. Only the requirements changes that can be placed at the core of the system and its desired functionality, and that help clarify the team's understanding of the project objectives, must be allowed to affect the outcome of the current development phase. Thus knowing where to draw the line on what to include or leave out of the requirements as the team's comprehension of the problem domain evolves over time is of major importance to the eventual success of the project. Prioritizing what features the software must have that can be developed within the budgeted resources and schedule must be carried out jointly by all the stakeholders based on what the user groups determine to be critical to their needs, what the IT personnel determine to be attainable within the estimated budget, and what the schedule can accommodate. Thus, scoping of the project becomes a major follow-up to the initial effort of forging a consensus on the project goals and objectives, because scoping enables the project leadership to define what the appropriate systems boundaries are for the project. Features designated as high-priority features must clearly have a major impact on the attainment of the project goals and objectives; if they do, they must be included in the current development cycle.

Research by MacCormack (2001) and MacCormack, Verganti, and Iansiti (2001) provides evidence in support of the need for flexible design architecture to accommodate the requirements changes that are inevitable in the course of systems development, especially for innovative projects in a dynamic technology environment, because users' feedback on early systems features can lead to further clarification of the systems functions. Their work suggests that investing in flexible design architecture can be profitable; it permits changes to the project development to be controlled and prevents them from disrupting the development process. Furthermore, having a broad and diverse representation of stakeholders on the project team will also ensure that differing perspectives and orientations are heard and accommodated in arriving at a consensus on the requirements and subsequent changes to systems functionalities as the project proceeds through the various development stages (Klein, Jiang, and Tesch 2002).

**Innovative Projects**   It is suggested by some—for example, Bronzite (2000, 136)—that because a large proportion of project failures are usually characterized as highly innovative, with the potential to advance the state of the art of the technology, organizations must in general refrain from tackling such projects. Admittedly, these tasks invariably prove challenging; however, this prescription seems extreme. Not undertaking any such projects because of the risk of failure is unacceptable in a technology environment that is by nature highly dynamic and where innovations are the norm. Even the usually routine software projects, like those involving payroll, can be unique and different from other such projects attempted in the past because of the changing IT environment. For example, the technology products and the techniques and procedures for project development may themselves be new and innovative. A more constructive and prudent approach is for the organization to know how to undertake highly innovative projects and simultaneously minimize the risks of failure. For this reason it is important to closely monitor the underlying project factors that contributed to the failure of projects like Confirm, FoxMeyer's Delta, Denver International Airport's BHS, and the others analyzed in the preceding chapters. It is the prevalence of the failure factors more than the innovative nature of the projects per se that must be blamed for the high incidence of project failures. Their uniqueness and innovation suggest the need to manage these types of projects differently from others to maximize the chances of successful outcomes. Risks associated with highly innovative projects can be minimized by the active engagement of a diverse user community in all stages of the development process, by the active participation and support of senior management in making decisions deemed critical to the desired project outcome, and by the development team's use of flexible design architecture more amenable to necessary design changes in the course of the development (MacCormack 2001; MacCormack, Verganti, and Iansiti 2001).

Chapters 3 and 8 have discussed in detail the nature of the failure factors, their impact on the software development process, and lessons organizations can learn from their own and others' past experiences with failed projects. Incorporating the lessons of past experiences into software development practices is critical to the success of the enterprise because it will minimize the likelihood of mistakes being repeated. Highly innovative software projects can and must be undertaken by organizations so long as such projects are not beyond their financial and technological capabilities.

## Project Audits

Sound project management is critical to maximizing successful project outcomes. One of the tools available to project leaders is the use of regular audits to uncover problematic issues and/or error patterns with the potential to create problems later on. For example, the audits may be able to uncover emerging patterns of imbalance between the elements of the project triangle—that is, resources, features, and schedule—giving the project leader sufficient time to take corrective action. How the audits are carried out and who is entrusted with the responsibility (whether an internal or external auditor) is of no particular concern, as long as the integrity of the process and of the auditor are uncompromised. When that can be ensured, the results of the audit can be expected to provide valuable information to help in managing the project successfully. For large and complex projects, the audits must be frequent to ensure that potential problems are uncovered soon enough to be corrected. User feedback in such projects can also play an important role in the audit process. Active user participation and involvement in the audit may provide important information to the auditors on the progress being made, or lack thereof, on the desired systems functionalities in the project development. Thus, involving the diverse user communities and the development team in the audit may uncover potential sources of problems with the project.

Keil and Robey (2001) describe cases where auditors fearing for their job security often preferred not to be the bearer of unpleasant—but constructive and potentially valuable—information on the status of the projects being audited. When project audit information is compromised to this extent, it renders the process useless. Auditors will only be able to do their job honestly and faithfully if they feel there is no perception of their being misconstrued as the bearer of bad news, or even worse, as outsiders because of the unique role they play in helping to uncover potential problems hidden within the many layers of the project. For projects where the vested interests of higher-ups in the organization are likely to challenge the work of the auditors, the intimidation factor alone may be enough to lead some auditors to shade the results so as to curry favor with those in senior management who may also be champions of the project. Escalation of senior management commitment to failing projects is often a combination of auditors failing to do their job honestly and/or project champions failing to heed whatever information auditors may provide regarding problems associated with the project. "Blowing the whistle on troubled software projects" can indeed amount to a courageous act, which some auditors would rather not carry out given the slightest hint that their superiors are unlikely to heed their warnings or are apt to blame them for the negative information (Keil and Robey 2001, 87).

## Senior Management Support

Senior management's understanding of the project and its particular strategic value to the organization is also crucial to maximizing successful project outcomes. Such understanding should entail a high level of support and commitment to the development effort. The form the commitment and support take can be observed as elements of the project triangle impact each other. Senior management's understanding of the project and its strategic importance with respect to the organization's long-term prospects will influence their decisions on the project schedules, the resources needed to realistically meet the completion-time estimates, and the quality of the product that will be produced in the end. Such delicate balancing of decisions with significant import for the project cannot be deferred to anyone else in the organization. No one else in the organization possesses the kind of overall vision of the organization's strategic goals and objectives or has the authority and responsibility to realize them.

However, senior management support and commitment, though extremely critical at times in resolving problems, must also be tempered with caution and guided by pragmatic realism. For example, if project information provided by a competent auditor shows trends that are not responsive to various corrective measures proposed and duly implemented, further escalation of that support and commitment will only lead to further unjustifiable expenditure of organizational resources. It is important that under such a scenario senior management take appropriate measures to deescalate their level of support and commitment in order to safeguard organizational resources. In essence, senior management should not be afraid to withdraw their support and commitment (undoubtedly spelling failure for the project) if such a decision is justified by all appropriate indicators provided by the project audits. Unrestrained support and commitment on the part of senior executives who are strong advocates or champions of a project often draw organizations into difficulties. The FoxMeyer Delta case discussed in the previous chapters is a poignant example of how overcommitment of senior management to a project can contribute to the bankruptcy of the company. Consequently, deescalation of senior management support and commitment to a troubled project should be welcomed and respected as indicative of their comprehension of the delicate balance among the elements of resources, features, and schedule that constitute the project triangle.

In addition to the project audits, other sources must be developed or identified to provide additional confirmatory information to senior management. Multiple information sources and channels are essential to provide a level of redundancy to the system of information feedback between senior management and project teams (including project leadership), and to maximize the chance that senior management will stay informed about project status at all times. Multiple information channels will allow project-related problems and setbacks to be readily communicated upward to senior management and thus enable them to take corrective action to forestall further damage to the delicate balance of the project triangle. This type of bottom-up feedback information will not be achieved, however, if senior management is widely perceived on the project team to be "dictatorial" in their interactions with project team members. For example, whether decisions involving elements of the project triangle are arrived at by consultation or by executive fiat may signal to subordinate team members how to react to management on project-related problems—whether to be candid or to censor themselves.

## Project Consultants

The use of consultants on projects is especially important in cases when the skill and experience levels of the members of the project team are judged inadequate or do not meet the requirements specifications of the project. The decision to engage the services of a consultant on a project must be made early in the course of the project development, soon after the requirements have been determined and the capabilities of the organization for undertaking it have been assessed to be inadequate to the task. The search for qualified and experienced consultants to join the project team, or if necessary to take over the entire development, must begin with thorough research on the background of potential candidates even before requests for proposals (RFPs) are sent out. The background research will help weed out qualified but inexperienced candidates and focus the search on those with the experience deemed relevant and appropriate to the requirements specifications. How the RFPs is written is also important in making sure only candidates with the requisite technical and technology experience and qualifications will respond. Well-written RFPs will save the organization valuable time as it reduces the number of unqualified and/or inexperienced candidates who respond.

The selection process must begin soon after the deadline for the RFPs has passed. A thorough vetting of the proposals submitted must start with close attention being paid to the responses dealing with critical areas of the requirements specifications for the project. All claims made by the candidates in their responses to the RFPs must be thoroughly checked and independently verified for accuracy (something FoxMeyer Drug failed to do with Andersen Consulting on the Delta project). The strengths and weaknesses of each candidate vis-à-vis the project's requirements must be fully documented and thoroughly discussed in the meeting held to select the candidates. The time frame for deciding on the candidates should be set so the vetting of the candidates' RFP responses does not carry on for too long. It may be useful to develop a metric that can be used to rank order the candidates, when all the factors have been considered, before making the final selection. As much as feasible, the decision must be based on objective standards of what will be in the best interests of the organization and the project.

The winning candidate should be invited to come and discuss the project, suggesting possible strategies for tackling it. If the organization is satisfied with the in-house presentation and discussion, the selection can be finalized with a contract detailing what the consultant's and organization's responsibilities will be on the project, and how the consultant's work will be monitored for adherence to the contract. Both parties must approve any changes to the contract before the changes are appended to the original contract.

The writing of the contract will benefit from the services of an attorney who specializes in IT contracts. It is important for the organization to ensure that all important issues are clearly spelled out in the contract to protect the interests of both parties, especially those of the organization. Besides, it is good policy to ensure that the organization's and the consultant's liabilities in the agreement are spelled out to forestall any possible litigation resulting from termination of the agreement by either party. In addition, it is always important to have an escape clause dealing with noncompliance issues, so that in the event that the consultant fails to live up to the requirements provisions in the agreement, the organization can terminate the agreement and not have the project held hostage, as was the case with FoxMeyer's Delta project. A designated contact person must be selected from the consulting organization and the project organization to handle complaints and other matters related to the work on the project and to be a liaison to the other party. Typically in the project organization, the project leader or his or her designee can play that role. Projects may not succeed if the decision to engage the services of a consultant and the process used to select one are not handled properly, and if the work of the consultant on the project is not consistently monitored to ensure compliance with the terms of the agreement and performance expectations at all stages of the development process. In this regard, the work of the auditors will be important in ensuring that the consultants comply with the terms of the contract and make sufficient progress toward the desired project outcome.

### Project Politics

Project development politics often begin in the selection process, when several projects may be competing for scarce organizational resources. Projects with powerful sponsors and/or champions may sometimes be selected for development over worthier ones with less powerful advocates. The stakeholders involved in the process of project selection often work behind the scenes to ensure that their choices are viewed more favorably by others, even if the objective merits of their project are not clear. Often the raw exercise of political power may be camouflaged by specious arguments purported to demonstrate the project's benefit to the entire organization. Organizational alliances may play a significant role in winning over others who might otherwise be opposed, or at least non-committal, to the project(s) in question. Prioritizing projects for selection and development is thus a matter of the way organizational politics play out among competing stakeholders.

Once the selection process is resolved, how development proceeds is to some extent controlled or influenced by a different set of political norms often dealing with project-triangulation issues—that is, the availability of adequate resources, the project features, and the schedule for completion. Here again powerful organizational interests may control the agenda unless senior executives step in and impose an organization-wide vision on the stakeholders. For example, the control of the requirements for the selected project(s) will be greatly influenced by the powerful interests of the stakeholder groups as each tries to influence the outcome in its favor. How the issue of requirements is resolved obviously has implications for both the resources needed to tackle the project and the time frame for completion. Therefore, project triangulation has substantial political undertones as each stakeholder group stakes a claim to its vision of what is in the overall organizational interests. For example, the technical personnel will present their vision of the requirements in terms of what they perceive or argue may be technically feasible, thus exerting control over what should be the accepted set of requirements for development. Similarly, the project sponsors and champions may view the requirements from a budgeting perspective, defining the decision as a resource-allocation issue. Finally, the users groups may try to influence the requirements from the perspective of what is in their best interests as potential users of the completed system. All of these competing stakeholder interests may seek to control the development outcome by pushing their particular agenda. Sometimes consensus may be arrived at through the interaction process, which may serve the overall organizational interests. But more often the most powerful stakeholder group—and this may vary from project to project within a particular organizational context—carries the day, whether the resource controllers, the controllers of the systems functionalities, or the controllers of the technological dimensions. Thus the stakeholder-interaction model described here as played out in the project triangle reflects to some extent the power relationships that often exist in the context of systems development (Sillince and Mouakket 1997).

How power is shared among stakeholders on the project to match individual and/or group responsibilities and accountability is important in ensuring successful outcomes. Regardless of the power distribution and decision-making centers on the project, communication channels among all stakeholders, from the top to the bottom, must always be open, free, and unencumbered to allow for the free exchange of ideas and the sharing of information to guarantee smooth cooperation on the project. Also, allowing for free and open access to communication channels among project stakeholders has its own benefits, as discussed earlier. For example, it makes possible quick airing and resolution of potential problems and conflicts. It will allow for control of requirements volatility even as the loci of power and decision making change with the changes in the makeup of the project stakeholders. Free and open communication also creates an operating environment where superordinate decision makers are encouraged to act in a consultative manner and are less inclined to be coercive or dictatorial in relating to subordinates on the project. Subordinate stakeholders are also less likely to be inclined to censure themselves by filtering out bad news on a project before communicating their findings upward because of their perception of how their superordinates will react to them. The support and commitment of individual stakeholders on the project may be inversely proportional to their perceived power to act, and may also reflect their perceptions of responsibility and expectations of accountability on the project team. The focus in decision-making contexts will always invariably be on maintaining the correct equilibrium among the three elements of the project triangle. Thus stakeholders will be less inclined to accept changes in the requirements, for example, since such changes could significantly impact the features or functionality of the system, which could in turn significantly alter the schedule and the resources needed to achieve it.

## Conclusion

What are the drivers of good software development that will maximize the chances for successful project outcomes? In the preceding pages we have provided an analysis of the critical issues to which project stake-holders must pay attention to ensure successful outcomes. In particular, we have emphasized the need to maintain a proper balance at all times among the elements that make up the project triangle of resources, features, and schedule. The chapter's focus has not been on processes, because these may vary from one organization to another and from project to project. Instead the thrust of the discussion has been to bring to the fore fundamental issues that have the potential to distort the balance of the project triangle, limiting the likelihood of a successful project outcome.

To be successful, software development must begin with a clear focus on the goals and objectives the completed project is expected to achieve. These goals and objectives in turn drive the requirements analysis and determination process. Successful requirements are always the product of a clear, comprehensive understanding of the problem domain by all stakeholders involved in the development effort. Senior management will come to appreciate the resources needed for the project; the technical personnel will come to appreciate the desired systems features as appro-priately derived from the requirements analysis and specifications, as will the potential users of the completed system; finally, the schedule will be based on a realistic assessment of the impact of both resources and fea-tures on the completion time frame.

Once the project is launched, the active involvement in the form of support and commitment of all stakeholders, from senior management to end users, will be needed to maximize the chances of a successful outcome. In putting together the project team, it is important that atten-tion be paid to the "development personalities" of people selected as well as to their technical and/or organizational skills and capabilities to con-tribute to the work of the team (Howard 2001).

Earlier chapters discussed the fundamental need for the appropriate technology infrastructure to provide a foundation for the project devel-opment. Lack of the requisite technology infrastructure can create significant obstacles in the development effort, such that the chances for successful outcome are substantially reduced. The technical skills, experience, and capabilities of the design team will, to a great extent, influence or determine the quality of the design, and the design of the software will invariably reflect the existing technology base. However, the work of the team should be guided by sound industry practices and must stay within the technical capabilities of the organization. This means the level of innovation should be such that it can be sustained within the group and supported by the available technology infrastructure. Attempts to reach for the most advanced features are often the source of software development failure. This pragmatic attempt at innovation should not stifle the creativity of the design team in arriving at a design solution that fully satisfies the accepted goals and objectives of the software. The design will undoubtedly be subjected to changes in the course of the development. The critical issue is to be able to manage the change control process so as not to unduly introduce wide variations in the design, which significantly affect the resource requirements and the completion schedule. The schedule must not be dictated from on high but must be set by those actually doing the development working in close consultation with other stakeholders, especially those who control project resources, including the budget. When consultants are used in the development, their selection must be made objectively and their work monitored closely for adherence to the project's requirements.

In general, superior designs are likely to lead to superior software if there are processes in place to guide the development. As always, comprehensive knowledge and understanding of the problem domain will be critical to a good design. Good design, though always crucial, will not automatically produce the quality software desired; managing the development process is every bit as important. Because software design is essentially a creative learning process, as the team becomes more familiar with the requirements, incremental steps can be taken to incorporate the various functionalities that need to be satisfied and still maintain the requisite balance among the elements of the project triangle. Project management begins with the selection of projects and the choice of project leadership, whose guidance and ability to maintain the requisite balance among the elements of the project will maximize the chances of a successful outcome. The operating environment for software development is also not devoid of organizational politics. The stakeholder-interaction model makes explicit the political processes associated with software development. An open, flexible environment that encourages the free communication of ideas, problems, and solutions is the crucial ingredient that every software development project needs in order to succeed. Further, the sharing of power, the spreading of responsibilities, and the holding of individuals accountable for their actions are the hallmarks of a good software development team likely to succeed in creating high-quality software within budget and on schedule.

# 10
## Project Failures and Aftermath

The abandonment of software projects, including information systems (IS) projects under development, has not gained enough attention in either software/IS practice or research to have any significant impact, yet it is an important aspect of the general problem of software failures or runaways. In contrast, there have been several studies by researches, particularly in IS, dealing with IS "failure" from either the usage or operations viewpoint after a system has been implemented (Lucas 1975; Ives, Hamilton, and Davis 1980; Lyytinen 1987; Lyytinen and Hirschheim 1987; Kumar 1990). For example, in a major work on IS problems and solutions, Lyytinen (1987, 8) has characterized IS "failure" as "multidimensional" with "several subcomponents: technical, behavioral, political, etc." He attributes this to the fact that "IS development is fraught with recurrent problems caused by poor, undisciplined and incomplete development practices." We in the software industry are therefore faced with a genuine need to understand the nature of the problems associated with software development and to devise effective methods for tackling them in order to minimize the risk of project failure. Past studies have confirmed that IS project abandonment is indeed "a complex, multidimensional issue that defies simple explanations" (Ewusi-Mensah and Przasnyski 1991, 83; also see Ewusi-Mensah and Przasnyski 1994). This chapter summarizes the main issues involved in software project failures, providing recommendations on how to minimize project cancellations and deal with the aftermath of project cancellation decisions.

**Project Failures**

The preceding chapters have discussed the extent and nature of the recurrent problems of cost overruns, schedule delays, reduced functionality, and at times outright abandonment of software projects, with a devastating impact on the operations of organizations and the morale of project employees. Robert Glass (1998, 250) has eloquently captured the feeling of despair that usually accompanies project failures, runaways, or abandonment when he writes: "A team of people, probably operating in crunch mode on a death march quest, went down to defeat. Their hopes and plans for the future were probably dashed. There was probably blame and recrimination as the end approached, and relationships were bent or broken." He goes on to explain that "perhaps because software is a project built from no physical resources, a product constructed purely out of intellect, it is especially devastating to the psyche when it fails."

The central theme of this book is that factors that contribute to the failure of software projects are multidimensional and defy simple explanation. The factors can be grouped into two broad categories: managerial and organizational behavioral issues on the one hand and technical and technological issues on the other. The factors include ill-conceived and/or ill-defined project goals and objectives, inferior project-team composition, poor management and control of the development process, lack of active user participation and senior management support and commitment, and inadequate technical expertise and technological infrastructure. A combination of any of these has the potential to cause the project to fail, through excessive increases in project costs and completion delays, substantial reductions in systems functionalities, or termination of the project.

The technical and technological problems of software projects continue to receive research attention in the software engineering literature, as evidenced by advances in object-oriented technology, modularization of software development, and other developments. Software development problems attributable to managerial and organizational behavioral factors seem to be the most intractable and will require active research into their causes to help minimize their recurrence. Well-organized and concerted efforts to learn from every instance of project failure offer the only chance of increasing the odds of future project successes. The conceptual nature of software development suggests that progress in the practice of software development can only result from sustained efforts to continually examine the problems associated with project failures. Industrywide dissemination and application of the lessons learned in project-failure cases will help improve the overall practice of software development.

Nevertheless, because software development is an innovative process, it is fraught with unavoidable risks and uncertainties, which despite the best efforts of project development teams and their supporters may still result in failures. The fact that project failures may be inevitable in some instances should not diminish our continued attempts to understand the root causes of the failures and thus to minimize their occurrence in organizations. This concluding chapter discusses steps executives can take to minimize the risks of project failures. The chapter stresses the need for organizations to institute procedures that will enable them to learn from project failures in order to minimize their recurrence in future projects. Finally, the chapter cautions against the practice of reflexively blaming project teams and their leadership for project failures; this hinders learning from the mistakes of the development process.

The main contributing factors in project failures and runaways were illustrated using the cases of five abandoned projects—Confirm, FoxMeyer's Delta, TSM, DIA's BHS, and CODIS—in the public and private sectors. In each of the five cases, a combination of dominant factors coalesced to cause the demise of the project. The particular combination of factors that will prove fatal to a project is dependent on the project's characteristics and on the organizational development environment, among other things. Nevertheless, out of the despair of failure, especially in the case of abandoned projects, something of lasting value to the organization and its project development teams can be salvaged if they are willing to seize the opportunity. The opportunities come in the form of the postabandonment review, in which the organization undertakes a systematic study of what happened in the course of the project's development, why it happened, and how. This review presents the organization with its finest opportunity to recoup some of its lost investments in the abandoned project by learning from its failure and incorporating the lessons learned into its software development practices to benefit current and future developers. The learning paradigm discussed in chapter 8 is intended to assist organizations in making this aspect of software development part of standard organizational practices.

As more and more organizations adopt this method of introspection and individuals move from one organization to another, carrying the message of the benefits of this strategy for learning from organizational software failures, I anticipate a wider benefit to the software industry as a whole. Still, my hope is that as more and more organizations learn from their past mistakes, the incidence of failed projects will diminish over time, even as organizations attempt more complex and challenging projects. Nonetheless, software development as a creative intellectual endeavor will always entail the prospect of failure, including abandonment, as one of its inherent possibilities. Thus the suggestions for dealing with the incidence of abandonment in organizations are offered in the hope that they will provide some constructive ways of managing rather than eliminating the problem.

Chapter 9 offered some strategic guidelines for software development that are intended to maximize the chances for successful project outcomes. The chapter discussed some of the critical issues in software development that project leaders and project team members must pay special attention to in order to maximize chances for project success. We referred, for example, to issues dealing with project requirements, support of senior management, the use of auditors to monitor progress and spot potential problems, and the use of consultants whenever appropriate to make up for any expertise or skills lacking on the part of the project team. The chapter stressed how important it is for the project leader to strive to maintain the correct balance among the elements comprising the project triangle. Thus the impact of a change in the project features, for example, can be analyzed in terms of its possible repercussions for the remaining two elements—resources and schedule—and corrective action can be taken to keep the elements in balance.

## How to Minimize Project Cancellations

As intimated previously, the pattern that emerges from a synthesis of the data from my research and that of others is quite clear: software/IS project cancellation is a multidimensional or multifaceted issue with numerous and/or various interacting parts. There are, however, steps executives can take with respect to project selection and management in their organizations to minimize the likelihood of a project cancellation decision. To ensure successful development of software/IS projects, senior executives should be prepared to take specific steps to guide the process, and when all else fails, they should be ready to cut the organization's losses on the project by terminating it. In the five cases discussed in the book, I have focused on the factors that contributed to the decision to terminate or substantially limit the scope of the projects. My intention was to highlight the significance of the issues raised by the factors in order to instruct senior executives and project leaders on the pitfalls and other telltale signs to watch out for in the design, development, and management of large, complex software/IS projects. I now discuss the specific guidelines executives and/or project leaders can adopt in managing projects to minimize the threat of project cancellations by drawing attention to the key issues in project development that are critical to success.

## Project Goals and Objectives

The first critical issue is to have general agreement on a well-articulated set of project goals and objectives. Without a consensus on what the project is expected to achieve in satisfying the specific information requirements the company has identified, the development effort may revolve around a vague and immeasurable set of systems requirements. In a field study of large software systems, Curtis, Krasner, and Iscoe (1988, 1275) have determined that "fluctuations or conflict among systems requirements caused problems on every large project." They attribute the problem partly to "incomplete analysis of requirements" and/or lack of sufficient application-domain knowledge on the part of the analysts. They further argue that, at the project level, unstable requirements "usually resulted from the absence of a defined mission," leading them to state that "without a sense of mission the motivation for the project could not be translated into clear product requirements." These findings are echoed by Krault and Streeter (1995), who describe the problem under the general rubric of software complexity and uncertainty. It is clear that reaching a consensus on the goals and objectives of the project is paramount in providing an agreed-on basis on which the requirements can be developed. Thus one major contributor in the problem of creeping or fluctuating requirements may be controlled if not eliminated. This, in turn, will contribute to ease of communication among the team members in describing the essence of the problem complexity and the systems requirements to be satisfied.

In addition, sponsorship of the project should, as far as possible, be broadly based. Research data suggest that projects that enjoy broader support from other managers or are more consensus based tend to avoid the common pitfalls that characterize canceled projects (Ewusi-Mensah and Przasnyski 1991). Curtis, Krasner, and Iscoe. (1988, 1277) have reached a similar conclusion; they report that "for projects started for political reasons requirements fluctuated with the prevailing attitudes of those who approved funds." The consensus-based projects are better able to withstand the changing fortunes of organizational politics and their effects on project goals and requirements.

This is not to suggest that projects associated with one manager or sponsor should be taken less seriously than usual. On the contrary, sponsors of such projects should be compelled or encouraged to sell the merits of the project to other senior colleagues in other organizational units as well as to subordinates within their own organizational unit. In other words, it is important to build a supportive base in the organization for such a project so that in the event of the original sponsor's departure, the project will not risk cancellation because of the lack of internal organizational support.

## Project Team

The composition of the project team must be another issue of concern to executives overseeing systems development efforts. Inasmuch as it is beneficial to have broad-based support for and agreement on the goals of the project, it is equally essential that the team members be drawn from all the diverse organizational units expected to be affected by the project. The idea is to get as many people as necessary to not only buy into the project, but more importantly, to become actively involved in taking credit and responsibility for the project's successful completion. Individual ownership of the project is vitally important to the success of the entire team. The composition of the three groups of people—the technical staff, end users, and senior management—should, therefore, be carefully determined to maximize the contributions each individual can and will make to the project.

Research by Walz, Elam, and Curtis (1993) and Curtis, Krasner, and Iscoe (1988) speaks to the learning that takes place within a project team. Howard (2001) refers to the need to assign members to project teams based on their development personalities in order to maximize chances for successful outcomes. And Klein, Jiang, and Tesch (2002) report on the need for the project team to include a diverse group with three major orientations—technical, end users, and sociopolitical—to ensure that all views are heard in the course of systems development. This emphasis on the need for a balanced project team recalls the stakeholder-interaction model discussed in chapter 7; in each, members of the various orientation groups on the development team play representative roles. In fact, the length of time that a team is reported to spend in the requirements phase of the project is partly dependent on "the breadth and depth of knowledge the team members bring to the project" (Waltz, Elam, and Curtis 1993, 69). Consequently, one must be selective in deciding on the composition of the team to facilitate the project development efforts and help contain the cost of the project.

### Project Leadership

Project leadership is another important issue executives need to resolve early on in the development process. Executives need to appoint someone who is widely respected in the organization and has sufficient knowledge, credibility, integrity, and technical experience to lead the project. As Krault and Streeter (1995) succinctly argued, large projects are more likely to succeed if they are led by individuals who have a clear understanding of the application-domains and have the requisite software knowledge to guide and coordinate the efforts of the project teams.

Although such individuals may be difficult to identify, their impact on projects cannot be underestimated. The diverse issues that a project leader may be required to address include, for example, "resolving conflicting requirements, negotiating with the customer, ensuring that the development staff shares a consistent understanding of the design, and providing communications between . . . contending groups" (Curtis, Krasner, and Iscoe 1988, 1284).

Thus a respected project team leader with the backing of senior management and the authority to make critical decisions is an important signal to the rest of the team about management's commitment to the success of the project. The project leader must be required to report on a regular basis to senior executives on the progress of the project; on specific problems encountered in the course of the project such as budget overruns, schedule delays, or changes in the scope of the problem; and on the credible steps being taken to resolve those problems in order to bring the project into compliance with the expected results. As noted, one of the responsibilities of the project leader is to maintain the right balance among the three elements—resources, features, and schedule— that constitute the project triangle. It is the responsibility of the project leader to ensure that requirements changes resulting in additional and/or revised systems functionalities are properly factored into the revised resource needs and schedule modifications. When the requirements changes are significant, the project leader must request additional resources and make revisions to the schedule to reflect the overall changes in the project development. The project leader must constantly work to control the requirements changes and whenever feasible, use flexible design architecture to minimize the extent of resource and schedule changes resulting from volatility in the requirements.

### Active Involvement of Executives

Executive involvement in the project should be perceived throughout the organization as active rather than passive. This will convince the team members of the commitment of top management to the project's success. Such an impression will in turn elicit an equally significant commitment to the project from the team, which recognizes that success on the project will reflect favorably on them and will probably advance their careers within the organization. Another beneficial side of the issue is that executives will become aware much sooner than usual if the project is experiencing any difficulties, which, if not resolved appropriately and quickly, can lead to problems later on. Such valuable project information obtained on a timely basis will enable executives to take the steps needed to resolve the problems, but failing that, to move quickly to extricate the organization from the project and minimize the organization's losses. It is especially important that executives guard against the problem of overcommitting organizational resources to failing projects. Specifically, active involvement of executives in the life of the project entails undertaking key steps with regard to project management and control.

### Project Management and Control

A number of related issues—for example, project reviews, project audits, technical experience, and form of executive involvement—fall into this category and thus will be discussed separately as follows.

**Project Reviews**    Project review meetings must be held frequently with the project leadership and must cover all aspects of the project, from technology-related issues to project economics (i.e., costs and completion schedule) and organizational issues. The evidence suggests that organizational politics and/or disagreements tend to dominate decisions on software project cancellation, and so it may be prudent for executives to pay particular attention to the organizational behavioral issues involved in the project selection or approval and development processes (Ewusi-Mensah and Przasnyski 1991, 1994). Behavioral processes, as Curtis, Krasner, and Iscoe (1988) point out, can also be at the root of problems preventing us from gaining greater understanding of the factors that influence project development success.

**Project Audits**    It is useful to distinguish between project reviews and audits. Projects must be reviewed regularly to determine if sufficient progress is being made toward their stated goals and objectives, and within the prescribed time frame. Project audits must be conducted by outsiders, either internal or external to the organization and to its project team, to verify the work of the project management with respect to the results of the project reviews. Unlike project reviews, audits can be infrequent and can be conducted whenever senior management feel they are warranted. Resistance to project audits may suggest hidden problems with the project that should immediately raise some concerns with senior management. The auditor(s) selected must be technically capable, credible, and unbiased toward either senior management or the development team; any questions about their integrity will rightly raise doubts or questions about their findings.

**Technical Experience**    The technical skills, knowledge, and experience, in conjunction with the relevant application-domain knowledge, and the general competence of the technical staff should be another concern requiring executive involvement. Executives need to be fully convinced of the capabilities of the in-house technical staff to tackle the project successfully. Whenever their assessment of the situation raises doubts, it is wise to seek outside assistance from technically competent companies that specialize in the kind of systems development effort being undertaken. In this regard, employing the services of outside consultants to supplement in-house expertise can be beneficial to the project team. However, the process by which consultants are chosen should be carefully scrutinized to ensure that the organization ends up with precisely the help it needs. Also, where the company's competitive position will not be compromised, it will be all right to seek advice from other colleagues in the industry as to how to undertake a project of that magnitude and significance.

**Form of Executive Involvement**    Executive involvement in the project should not only be restricted to the regularly scheduled review meetings with the project leader. From time to time executives should arrange to meet with as many of the project team members as possible, for the following purposes: to convince and reassure the team of the company's continued commitment to the project and of the value the executives place on the work the team is doing; to find out firsthand from the various members of the team what, if any, specific problems are being encountered and what the executives can do to help move the project along successfully; and to open up a dialogue with the team so that in the event that the project leader is less than forthcoming, the executives will have a chance to learn directly from the team members how the project is progressing.

Despite their possible lack of technical background, executives should resist the tendency to defer every major decision on the project to the project leader or the technical people. In fact, if necessary, consultants can be brought in to review the work of the project team and report their findings to management, as was done in the case of the Confirm project. The upshot of all this is to make executives well informed on the progress of the project and to enable them to stay on top of the "small" problems that might otherwise mushroom into the bigger issues which end up destroying projects.

### Technology Base/Infrastructure

Equally important to the success of the software project is the technology infrastructure in the organization prior to the start of the project. Having the necessary technology in-house indicates that the organization most likely has the in-house expertise and experience to use it appropriately in the project development. Of course, for some projects the existing in-house technology may not be adequate, making it necessary to acquire new or additional technology to fill the identified need. In such an instance, a careful assessment needs to be made to ensure that the in-house technical expertise and experience will be up to the challenge. In addition, sufficient time must be factored into the prospective project schedule to give the project team members time to learn and work with the technology prior to having to use it in the project. All these technology-related factors must be fully vetted by senior management in consultation with the project or IT leadership before a final decision is made to proceed with the development. Failure to consider all these technology-related factors may be laying the foundation for the eventual collapse of the project. In this respect Confirm, FoxMeyer's Delta, and DIA's BHS projects are classic examples.

### User Involvement

The project leadership and senior management should seek the active involvement of a diverse group of users as participants in the requirements definition and design stages of the development process. Whenever such participation is visibly absent, senior executives should act swiftly to determine the basis for this and take corrective action to restore the link. The level and frequency of interaction between the user groups and the technical personnel should be high, almost day-to-day, especially in the early, critical conceptual stages of analysis and design, in order to clarify the varied issues that are bound to crop up in the course of the project. The objective is to foster an environment in which cooperation, communication, learning, and an exchange of views on the technical capabilities of the system vis-à-vis the users' expectations and the information needs are a significant part.

On the other hand, the frequency of interaction and communication between the users and senior management involved in the project need not be as high as between the users and the technical personnel. This level of interaction must not be viewed as an end run to bypass the project leadership to obtain information, but rather as another independent source of information senior management can take advantage of to gain access to differing views, which may otherwise elude them, on the project development. Nonetheless, this interaction is critical to successful project development for conveying the level of senior management commitment to and interest in the successful outcome of the development process to both the users and technical groups. When the level of interaction and communication is judged satisfactory by all three stakeholder groups, the likelihood of project success may be significantly increased. User involvement in software development projects is a necessary but not a sufficient criterion for project development success. There is still a significant risk of project failure or abandonment if there is no active involvement from the technical personnel and from senior management, as was the case in CODIS.

### Cost of Project

Escalating project cost is often cited as one of the reasons for project cancellation. Executives, therefore, need to be fully apprised as to how the funds appropriated for the systems development are being spent. The development cost of a project tends to increase over time and reaches a peak at the coding and testing stage. Research has shown that the cost of corrective design errors tends to increase dramatically the later in the development process such errors are detected because so much rework and retesting are required. Thus to rein in the overall cost of the project development, executives need to take steps to ensure that work done in the critical early stages of analysis and design, in particular, fulfill all expectations and meet the highest standards. Executives should also do all they can to minimize the problem of "creeping, fluctuating or conflicting" requirements specifications, which can contribute substantially to escalating project development costs.

**Schedule Delays**

Executives should also resist the temptation to add more people to the project team if the project begins to experience schedule delays. Brooks's ([1975] 1995) admonition of "the mythical man-month" should be taken seriously here because the more people that are added to the project, especially in the later stages, the more likely the project is to fall further behind schedule, notwithstanding Abdel-Hamid and Madnick's (1990) contrary claim, because of the communication delays and the learning curve necessary to bring those new participants up to the current project staff's level of knowledge. It is, therefore, necessary that estimates of the technical staff required to do the job be carefully reviewed for accuracy, taking into consideration possible emergencies (like illness), the learning necessary among team members especially in the requirements phase, and other issues that if left out create a far rosier picture of the project's human resource requirements and completion schedule than is warranted. In addition, those involved should be the most capable in the company of tackling the project; when this is not possible, outside assistance should be sought to augment the in-house capability.

**Project Cancellations and Aftermath**

The incidence of project failures, runaways, and abandonment will be substantially minimized if the issues discussed in the preceding section are satisfactorily handled in the course of project development. Senior management should be concerned about how project cancellation decisions are made and the repercussions they have for the organizations and their projects teams.

### Project Termination Decision

The decision to cancel a software project should not be taken lightly, because it has far-reaching implications for employee morale, due to the often-bitter feelings it generates among some team members. Still, it is sound management practice not to delay the inevitable when every reasonable attempt made to rescue the project has failed. In essence, termination of the project should never be ruled out as one of the options available to executives in managing the project. Once the decision to terminate the project is made, how it is implemented becomes just as important. The cancellation decision can take place at any juncture in the project's systems life cycle based on failure to meet expected deliverables, including costs overruns and schedule delays, associated with each phase of the systems development effort.

### Postmortems of the Canceled Projects

The decision to cancel a project, once made, should be communicated sensitively to the entire project team, preferably by the executive directly in charge, and reasons for the cancellation should be provided at this time. In most cases the evidence suggests that even if the team is aware of the possibility, the need to communicate the termination decision directly to the project's participants, as opposed to allowing them to hear it from the office rumor mill, will have a significant impact in reassuring the team of management's good intentions and will help minimize the extent of the blame game that sometimes follows (Ewusi-Mensah 1998; Ewusi-Mensah and Przasnyski 1995; Glass 1998).

Whenever possible, the impact of the decision on individual careers should be minimized so as not to create an atmosphere where individuals would be unwilling to discuss with management what went wrong and why in the aftermath of the decision. Frequently, abandonment decisions are so badly handled by companies, culminating in the firing and/or demotion of some key technical personnel—as was the case in the

Confirm and CODIS examples—that even those unscathed feel intimidated and so refrain from voicing their opinions on what went wrong and why. This is often the basis for "the code of silence" that exists in the computer industry with respect to discussing project failures (Ewusi-Mensah and Przasnyski 1995). If we are to move beyond the current state of software practice, we have to come to grips with the need to examine failures and shortcomings in order to gain insights that will significantly improve the technology, and the art and practice, of software development projects in organizations. Executives can play an important and constructive role in this learning effort.

## Breaking the Code of Silence

Soon after the decision to cancel the project has been made, and even before it is communicated to the team, executives should begin the process of determining what went wrong. Someone of senior rank and of high repute in the company should be appointed to examine all aspects of the development effort with a mandate to uncover the underlying reasons for the failure. Assurances of nonrecrimination must be fully extended to all project participants. They should all be encouraged to speak with the person(s) in charge of the investigation for the sole purpose of helping the organization gain knowledge from the experience that may prove valuable in future systems development work. The intent is to help the organization recoup some of its investments in the abandoned project by learning from the experience. In this vein I suggest making the learning paradigm discussed in chapter 8 part of an organization's software development practice. This will build a knowledge base of development experiences and lessons that can provide insight into the factors that contribute to project failures in their development environment, and will provide lessons applicable to future systems development efforts. The complexity and conceptual nature of systems development projects contribute to our difficulty in understanding "all the possible states" of the system, which may in part contribute to "product flaws, cost overruns [and] schedule delays" (Brooks 1987, 11). Consequently, taking steps to identify the causes of the project failure will increase our insight into the systems development process and thus help minimize the recurrence of similar problems in the future.

**Conclusion**

Software development projects will always be characterized by risks and uncertainties, which are ultimately the sources of the projects' failures. As in any experimental process, the ability of the experimenter to control the sources of errors will largely determine the accuracy and validity of the experimental results. Unfortunately, the innovative nature of the software development process makes it extremely difficult for the project team and its leadership to control even the identifiable risk factors, making project failures unavoidable in some cases. Consequently, for the long-term benefit of the software industry, organizations should, as a matter of policy, institute formal mechanisms for uncovering the underlying reasons for failed or abandoned projects on a regular basis. Maintenance and enhancement of successfully implemented systems are routinely undertaken in organizations because it is considered standard practice that any new system will have to undergo some changes—either corrective or adaptive—in the course of its life, if it is to continue to be useful or beneficial to the organization. By the same token, the formal practice of learning from the experiences of past failed projects, through postmortems, will produce a wealth of ideas and information that can be viewed as returns on the organizational resources invested in those failed projects. If more organizations adopt the practices of the engineering professions in dealing with systems failures, as advocated by Petroski (1992), we may see a marked decline in the number of failed projects in the software industry. Even as each new project attempts to stretch the limits of the technology, we may have a better sense of what is possible as opposed to what is not feasible in systems development efforts. Still, more studies are needed to enable us to better understand the whole constellation of issues surrounding the failure of software development projects. This information will help organizations to better understand how to plan and manage new projects to minimize the chances of failure and improve organizational performance in the delivery of new systems.

# References

Abdel-Hamid, T. K., and Madnick, S. E. "The Elusive Silver Lining: How We Fail to Learn from Software Development Failures." *Sloan Management Review* 32, no. 1 (1990): 39–48.

Anthes, G. H. "IRS Project Failures Cost Taxpayers $50B Annually." *Computerworld*, October 14, 1996a, pp.1.

Anthes, G. H. "IRS: Tough to Get Any Respect." *Computerworld*, October 14, 1996b, pp. 28.

Applegate, L. M. *BAE Automated Systems: (A) and (B), Teaching Note.* Case study no. 5–399–099. Boston: Harvard Business School Press, 1999.

Barki, H., Rivard, S., and Talbot, J. "Towards an Assessment of Software Development Risk." *Journal of Management Information Systems* 10, no. 2 (1993): 203–225.

Barki, H., Rivard, S., and Talbot, J. "An Integrative Contingency Model of Software Project Risk Management." *Journal of Management Information Systems* 17, no. 4 (2001): 37–69.

Barwise, J. "Mathematical Proofs of Computer System Correctness." *Notices of the American Mathematical Society* 36, no. 9 (1989): 844–851.

Berghel, H. "The Y2K E-Commerce Tumble." *Communications of the ACM* 44, no. 8 (2001): 15–17.

Blum, B. I. "Improving Software Maintenance by Learning from the Past: A Case Study." *Proceedings of the IEEE* 77, no. 4 (1987): 596–606.

Blum, B. I. "A Taxonomy of Software Development Methods." *Communications of the ACM* 37, no. 11 (1994): 82–94.

Boddie, J. "The Project Post-Mortem." *Computerworld*, December 7, 1987, pp. 77–82.

Boehm, B. W. *Software Engineering Economics.* Englewood Cliffs, NJ: Prentice Hall, 1981.

Boehm, B. W. "Seven Basic Principles of Software Engineering." *Journal of Systems and Software* 3 (1983): 3–24.

Boehm, B. W. "Software Risk Management: Principles and Practices." *IEEE Software*, January 1991, pp. 32–41.

Boehm, B. W. "Project Termination Doesn't Equal Project Failure." *Computer*, September 2000, pp. 94–96.

Bronzite, M. *System Development: A Strategic Framework*. London: Springer-Verlag, 2000.

Brooks, F. P., Jr. "No Silver Bullet: Essence and Accidents of Software Engineering." *IEEE Computer*, April 1987, pp. 10–19.

Brooks, F. P., Jr. *The Mythical Man-Month: Essays on Software Engineering*. Anniversary edition. Reading, Mass.: Addison-Wesley, [1975] 1995.

Brooks, F. P., Jr. "The Computer Scientist as Toolsmith II." *Communications of the ACM* 39, no. 3 (1996): 61–68.

Bulkeley, W. M. "When Things Go Wrong." *Wall Street Journal*, November 18, 1996, p. R25.

Capers Jones, "Patterns of Large Software Systems: Failure and Success." *IEEE Computer*, March 1995, pp. 86–87.

Chikofsky, E. J. "Changing Your Endgame Strategy." *IEEE Software*, November 1990, p. 87.

Cohen, M. J., March, J. G., and Olsen, J. "A Garbage Can Model of Organizational Choice." *Administrative Science Quarterly* 7 (1972): 1–25.

Cole, A. "Runaway Projects—Cause and Effects." *Software World* (UK) 26, no. 3 (1995): 3–5.

Collett, S. "Hershey Earnings Drop as New Warehouse, Order Systems Falter." *Computerworld*, October 26, 1999.

Collier, B., DeMarco, T., and Fearey, P. "A Defined Process for Project Postmortem Review." *IEEE Software*, July 1996, pp. 65–71.

Collins, T., and Bicknell, D. *Crash: Learning from the World's Worst Computer Disasters*. London: Simon and Schuster, 1997.

Constantine, L. L. *On Peopleware*. Englewood Cliffs, NJ: Yourdon Press/Prentice Hall, 1993.

Corti, G. "Risk, Uncertainty and Cost Benefit: Some Notes on Practical Difficulties for Project Appraisals." In J. N. Wolfe, ed., *Cost Benefit and Cost Effectiveness*, 75–87. London: Allen & Unwin, 1973.

Curtis, B., Krasner, H., and Iscoe, N. "A Field Study of the Software Design Process for Large Systems." *Communications of the ACM* 31, no. 11 (1988): 1268–1287.

Dash, J. "Two Big Failures Cite Cap Gemini." *Computerworld*, December 13, 1999.

Davis, G. B., and Olson, M. H. *Management Information Systems: Conceptual Foundation, Structure, and Development*. New York: McGraw-Hill, 1985.

DeGrace, P., and Stahl, L. H. *Wicked Problems, Righteous Solutions: A Catalogue of Modern Software Engineering Paradigms.* Englewood Cliffs, NJ: Yourdon Press/Prentice Hall, 1990.

DeMarco, T., and Lister, T. *Peopleware: Productive Projects and Teams.* New York: Dorset House, 1987.

Denning, P., and Dargan, P. "Action-Centered Design." In T. Winograd, ed., *Bringing Design to Software,* 105–119. Reading, MA: Addison-Wesley, 1996.

Denzin, N. K. *The Research Act.* New York: McGraw-Hill, 1978.

De Young, L. "Organizational Support for Software Design." In T. Winograd, ed., *Bringing Design to Software,* 253–267. Reading, MA: Addison-Wesley, 1996.

Dijkstra, E. W. "The Structure of 'THE'-Multiprogramming System," *Communications of the ACM* 11 (1968): 341–346.

Edstrom, A. "User Influence and the Success of MIS Projects: A Contingency Approach." *Human Relations* 30, no. 7 (1977): 589–607.

Eischen, K. "Software Development: An Outsider's View." *Computer,* May 2002, pp. 36–44.

"ERP Stumbles." Comptroller's Report. *Computerworld,* May 2000.

Ewusi-Mensah, K. "Evaluating Information Systems Projects: A Perspective on Cost-Benefit Analysis." *Information Systems* 14, no. 3 (1989): 205–217.

Ewusi-Mensah, K. "The Abandonment of Information Systems Development Projects in Organizations." Proposal to the National Science Foundation, Loyola Marymount University, 1991.

Ewusi-Mensah, K. "Critical Issues in Abandoned Information Systems Development Projects." *Communications of the ACM* 40, no. 9 (1997): 74–80.

Ewusi-Mensah, K. Interview Notes of IS Group: The CODIS Project, 1992, p. 8. Available from the author.

Ewusi-Mensah, K. "Why IS Development Projects Are Abandoned: A Diagnosis from User Perspectives." Working paper, College of Business Administration, Loyola Marymount University, 1998.

Ewusi-Mensah, K., and Przasnyski, Z. H. "On Information Systems Project Abandonment: An Exploratory Study of Organizational Practices." *MIS Quarterly* 15 (March 1991): 67–85.

Ewusi-Mensah, K., and Przasnyski, Z. H. "Factors Contributing to the Abandonment of Information Systems Development Projects." *Journal of Information Technology* 9 (1994): 185–201.

Ewusi-Mensah, K., and Przasnyski, Z. H. "Learning from Abandoned Information Systems Development Projects." *Journal of Information Technology* 10 (1995): 3–14.

Fetzer, J. H. "Program Verification: The Very Idea." *Communications of the ACM* 31, no. 9 (1988): 1048–1063.

Fetzer, J. H. "Author's Response [to various letters about 1988 paper]." *Communications of the ACM* 32, no. 3 (1989): 377–381.

Fisher, G. H. *Cost Considerations in Systems Analysis*. New York: Elsevier, 1971.

Flowers, S. *Software Failures: Management Failure—Amazing Stories and Cautionary Tales*. London: Wiley, 1997.

GAO. *Tax Systems Modernization: Management and Technical Weaknesses Must Be Corrected If Modernization Is to Succeed*. Report to the Commissioner of the Internal Revenue Service. GAO/AIMD-95-156, July 1995. Washington, DC: GPO.

GAO. *Tax Systems Modernization: Actions Underway But IRS Has Not Yet Corrected Management and Technical Weaknesses*. Report to Congressional Requesters. GAO/AIMD-96-106, June 1996. Washington, DC: GPO.

GAO. *Medicare Transaction System: Success Depends upon Correcting Critical Managerial and Technical Weaknesses*. Report to Congressional Requesters. GAO/AIMD-97-78, May 1997. Washington, DC: GPO.

Gibbs, W. W. "Software's Chronic Crisis." *Scientific American*, September 1994, pp. 86–95.

Gladden, G. R. "Stop the Life-Cycle, I Want to Get Off." *Software Engineering Notes* 7, no. 2 (April 1982): 35–39.

Glaser, G. "Managing Projects in the Computer Industry." *Computer*, October 1984, pp. 45–53.

Glass, R. L. *Software Runaways: Lessons Learned from Massive Software Project Failures*. Englewood Cliffs, NJ: Prentice Hall, 1998.

Glass, R. L. "The Realities of Software Technology Payoffs." *Communications of the ACM* 42, no. 2 (1999): 74–79.

Halper, M. "IS Cover-Up Charged in System Kill." *Computerworld*, August 10, 1992a, p. 1.

Halper, M. "Outsourcer Confirms Demise of Reservation Coalition Plan." *Computerworld*, August 3, 1992b, p. 1.

Halper, M. "Marriott Suit Damns AMR Role in Confirm." *Computerworld*, October 12, 1992c, p. 8.

Halper, M. "Too Many Pilots." *Computerworld*, October 12, 1992c, p. 8.

Harel, D. "Biting the Silver Bullet." *Computer*, January, 1992, pp. 8–20.

Hedberg, B. "How Organizations Learn and Unlearn." In P. C. Nystrom and W. H. Starbuck, eds., *Handbook of Organizational Design*, 3–27. Oxford: Oxford University Press, 1981.

Heinrich, E. "Money to Burn." *Infosystems Executive*, October 1998, pp. 10–16.

Hoare, C. A. R. "Programming: Sorcery or Science?" *IEEE Software*, April 1984, pp. 5–6.

Howard, A. "Software Engineering Project Management." *Communications of the ACM* 44, no. 5 (2001): 23–24.

"IRS Admits Its Computers Are a Nightmare." *San Francisco Chronicle*, January 31, 1997, p. A1.

"IRS Computer Project Has 'Very Serious Problems,' Rubin Says." *Los Angeles Times,* March 29, 1996, p. D1.

"IRS Drops Internet Filing Plan." *San Francisco Chronicle*, November 11, 1996, p. A3.

"It Doesn't Compute." *San Francisco Chronicle*, February 2, 1997, editorial page.

Ives, B., Hamilton, S., and Davis, G. "A Framework for Research in Computer Based Management Information Systems." *Management Science* 26 (1980): 910–934.

Ives, B., and Olson, M. "User Involvement and MIS Success: A Review of Research." *Management Science* 30, no. 5 (1984): 586–603.

Jesitus, J. "Broken Promises? FoxMeyer's Project Was a Disaster. Was the Company Too Aggressive or Was It Misled?" *Industry Week*, November 3, 1997, pp. 31–37.

Johnson, J. "Chaos: The Dollar Drain of IT Project Failures." *Application Development Trends* 2, no. 1 (1995): 41–47.

Keider, S. P. "Why Systems Development Projects Fail." *Journal of Information Systems Management* 1, no. 3 (summer 1984): 33–38.

Keil, M., Cule, P. E., Lyytinen, K., and Schmidt, R. C. "A Framework for Identifying Software Project Risks." *Communications of the ACM* 41, no. 11 (1998): 76–83.

Keil, M., and Robey, D. "Blowing the Whistle on Troubled Software Projects." *Communications of the ACM* 44, no. 4 (2001): 87–93.

Klein, G., Jiang, J. J., and Tesch, D. B. "Wanted: Project Teams with a Blend of IS Professional Orientations." *Communications of the ACM* 45, no. 6 (2002): 81–87.

Krault, R. E., and Streeter, L. A. "Coordination in Software Development." *Communications of the ACM* 38, no. 3 (1995): 69–81.

Kumar, K. "Post Implementation Evaluation of Computer-Based Information Systems: Current Practices." *Communications of the ACM* 33, no. 2 (1990): 203–212.

Lehman, M. M. "Programs, Life Cycles, and Laws of Software Evolution." *Proceedings of the IEEE* 68, no. 9 (1980): 1060–1076.

Lehman, M. M. "Uncertainty in Computer Applications and Its Control through the Engineering of Software." *Software Maintenance: Research and Practice* 1 (1989): 3–27.

Leith, P. "Fundamental Errors in Legal Logic Programming." *Computer Journal* 29 (1986): 545–552.

LJX FILES. "The Complaint in Brown v. Andersen Consulting." 1988. Available at ⟨http://wwww.LJX .com/LJXFILES/bankruptcy/andersen.html⟩.

Lucas Jr., H. C. *Why Information Systems Fail.* New York: Columbia University Press, 1975.

Lyytinen, K. "Different Perspectives on Information Systems: Problems and Solutions." *ACM Computing Surveys* 19, no. 1 (March 1987): 5–46.

Lyytinen, K., and Hirschheim, R. "Information Systems Failures—A Survey and Classification of the Empirical Literature." *Oxford Surveys in Information Technology* 4 (1987): 257—309.

MacCormack, A. "Product Development Practices That Work: How Internet Companies Build Software." *MIT Sloan Management Review*, winter 2001, 75–84.

MacCormack, A., Verganti, R., and Iansiti, M. "Developing Products on 'Internet Time': The Anatomy of a Flexible Development Process." *Management Science* 47, no. 1 (2001): 133–150.

Maglitta, J. "Learning Lessons from IRS's Biggest Mistakes." *Computerworld*, October 14, 1996, p. 30.

March, J. G., and Olsen, J. P. *Ambiguity and Choice in Organizations.* Bergen: Universitetsforlaget, 1976.

Marciniak, J. J. ed. *Encyclopedia of Software Engineering.* Vol. 1. New York: Wiley, 1994.

Markus, M. L. "Power, Politics and MIS Implementation." *Communications of the ACM* 26, no. 6 (1983): 430–444.

McCarthy, J. *Dynamics of Software Development.* Redwood, WA: Microsoft Press, 1995.

McFarlan, F. W. "Portfolio Approach to Information Systems." *Harvard Business Review* 65 (March–April 1981): 68–74.

McPartlin, J. P. "The Collapse of Confirm." *Information Week*, October 19, 1992, pp. 12.

Mearian, L. "Highmark Sues KPMG over Failed IT Project." *Computerworld*, November 7, 2001a.

Mearian, L. "Insurer Sues, Claims KPMG Mismanaged Billing Project." *Computerworld*, November 12, 2001b.

Modha, J., Gwinnett A., and Bruce, M. "A Review of Information Systems Development Methodology ( ISDM ) Selection Techniques." *Omega* 18, no. 5 (1990): 473–490.

Montealegre, R., Knoop, C. I., Nelson, H. J., and Applegate, L. M. *BAE Automated Systems (A): Denver International Airport Baggage-Handling System."* Case study no. 9-396-311. Boston: Harvard Business School Press, 1996.

Neumann, P. G. "System Development Woes." *Communications of the ACM* 40, no. 12 (1997): 160.

Newman, M., and Noble, F. "User Involvement as an Interaction Process: A Case Study." *Information Systems Research* 1, no. 1 (March 1990): 89–113.

Nicholson, L. "Executive Says Administrative-Software Failures Are Part of Fine-Tuning." *Philadelphia Inquirer*, November 6, 1999.

OASIG. "Why Do IT Projects So Often Fail?" *OR Newsletter*, September 1996, pp. 12–16.

Olle, T. W., Hagelstein, J., Macdonald, I. G., Rolland, C., Sol, H. G., Van Assche, F. J. M., and Verrijn-Stuart, A. A. *Information Systems Methodologies—A Framework for Understanding*. 2d ed. Reading, MA: Addison-Wesley, 1991.

Osterland, Andrew. "Blaming ERP." *CFO: The Magazine for Senior Financial Executives* 16, no. 1 (2000): 89–93.

Oz, E. "When Professional Standards Are Lax: The CONFIRM Failure and Its Lessons." *Communications of the ACM* 37, no. 10 (October 1994): 29–36.

Parnas, D. L. "Software Aspects of Strategic Defense Systems." *Software Engineering Notes* 10, no. 5 (October 1985): 15–23.

Patton, M. Q. *How to Use Qualitative Methods in Evaluation.*, Newbury Park, CA: Sage, 1987.

Patton, M. Q. *Qualitative Research and Evaluation Methods*. 3rd ed. Thousand Oaks, CA: Sage, 2002.

Petroski, H. "History and Failure." *American Scientist* 80 (November–December 1992): 524–526.

"PG&E Dumps CIS Project." *PCWEEK* 14, no. 17 (April 28, 1997): 1.

Powers, R. F., and Dickson, G. W. "MIS Project Management: Myths, Opinions, and Reality." *California Management Review* 15, no. 3 (spring 1973): 147–156.

Pressman, R. S. *Software Engineering: A Practitioner's Approach*. New York: McGraw-Hill, 1992.

Ramamoorthy, C. V., Prakash, A., Wei-Tek, T., and Usuda, Y. "Software Engineering: Problems and Perspectives." *Computer*, October 1984, pp. 191–209.

Reyment, R., and Jöreskog, K. G. *Applied Factor Analysis in the Natural Sciences*. Cambridge: Cambridge University Press, 1993.

Rifkin, G. "What Really Happened at Denver's Airport?" *Forbes, SAP Supplement*, August 1994, pp. 111–114.

Rittel, H. W., and Webber, M. M. "Dilemmas in a General Theory of Planning." *Policy Sciences* 4 (1973): 155–169.

Robinson, H., Hall, P., Hovenden, F., and Rachel, J. "Postmodern Software Development." *Computer Journal* 41, no. 6 (1998): 363–375.

Ropponen, J., and Lyytinen, K. "Components of Software Development Risk: How to Address Them? A Project Manager Survey." *IEEE Transactions on Software Engineering* 26, no. 2 (2000): 98–111.

Saarinen, T. "System Development Methodology and Project Success." *Information & Management* 19 (1990): 183–193.

Sage, A. P., and Palmer, J. D. *Software Systems Engineering*. New York: Wiley, 1990.

Sauer, C. *Why Information Systems Fail: A Case Study Approach*. Henley-on-Thames, Oxfordshire: Alfred Waller, 1993.

Sillince, J. A. A., and Mouakket, S. "Varieties of Political Process during Systems Development." *Information Systems Research* 8, no. 4 (1997): 368–397.

Simon, H. A. *The Sciences of the Artificial*. 2nd ed. Cambridge, MA: MIT Press, 1984.

Sommerville, I. "Software Process Models." In A. B. Tucker, Jr., *The Computer Science and Engineering Handbook*, pp. 2259–2277. Boca Raton, FL: CRC Press, 1997.

Songini, M. "Halloween Less Haunting for Hershey This Year." *Computerworld*, November 2, 2000.

Standish Group. "Chaos." Sample research paper, May 1995. Available at <www.standishgroup.com>.

Standish Group. "Chaos." Sample research paper, May 1998. Available at <www.standishgroup.com>.

Stedman, C. "Update: Failed ERP Gamble Haunts Hershey." *Computerworld*, October 29, 1999.

Stedman, C. "IT Woes Contribute to Hershey Sales, Profits Decline." *Computerworld*, February 2, 2000.

Stockman, S. G. "The Recovery of Software Projects." In B. A. Kitchenham, ed., *Software Engineering for Large Systems*, 209–219. London: Elsevier Applied Science, 1990.

Szilagyi, J. G. "Bank of America's Masternet System: A Case Study in Risk Assessment." In R. L. Glass, ed., *Software Runaways: Lessons Learned from Massive Software Project Failures*. Englewood Cliffs, NJ: Prentice Hall, 1998.

Tait, P., and Vessey, I. "The Effect of User Involvement on System Success: A Contingency Approach." *MIS Quarterly* 12 (March 1988): 91–108.

Tellioglu, H., and Wagner, I. "Software Cultures." *Communications of the ACM* 42, no. 12 (1999): 71–77.

Walz, D. B., Elam, J. J., and Curtis, B. "Inside a Software Design Team: Knowledge Acquisition, Sharing and Integration." *Communications of the ACM* 36, no. 10 (October 1993): 63–77.

Wasserman, A. I. "Information System Design Methodology." *Journal of the American Society for Information Science* 31, no. 1 (1980): 25–44.

Wheatley, M. "ERP Disasters; Bet the Company; and Lose." *Financial Director*, March 1, 2000, pp. 35–39.

Whiting, R. "Development in Disarray." *Software Magazine* 18, no. 9 (1998): 20.

Winograd, T. "Introduction." In T. Winograd, ed., *Bringing Design to Software*, xiii–xxv Reading, MA: Addison-Wesley, 1996.

Wysocki, Jr., B. "Pulling the Plug: Some Firms, Let Down By Costly Computers, Opt to 'De-Engineer'." *The Wall Street Journal*, April 30, 1998, pp. 1–2.

Yourdon, E. *Death March: The Complete Software Developer's Guide to Surviving "Mission Impossible" Projects*. Englewood Cliffs, NJ: Prentice Hall, 1997.

Zellner, W. "Portrait of a Project as a Total Disaster." *Business Week*, January 17, 1994, p. 36.

# Index